Open the Door

How to Excite Young People About Poetry

EDITED BY

Dorothea Lasky, Dominic Luxford, and Jesse Nathan

HARRIET MONROE POETRY INSTITUTE
"POETS IN THE WORLD" SERIES EDITOR
Ilya Kaminsky

MᶜSWEENEY'S BOOKS
SAN FRANCISCO

Open the Door: How to Excite Young People About Poetry is a copublication
of The Poetry Foundation and McSweeney's Publishing.

For more information about McSweeney's, see www.mcsweeneys.net
For more information about The Poetry Foundation, see www.poetryfoundation.org

Hardcover ISBN: 978-1-938073-28-1
Paperback ISBN: 978-1-938073-29-8

First printing, 2013

Contents

Part 3: Lesson Plans

Editors' Note

The information in this book is provided as a resource and source of inspiration for poets to consider when thinking about creating community, excitement, joy, and learning around poetry for younger audiences. Ideas and knowledge about the topics in this book are ever changing, so we present this book in the spirit of an evolving conversation. The content derives from a broad spectrum of contributors who have an extensive range of viewpoints and experiences. Their discussions often describe the general issues at hand and include ideas about resources or poems; however, this information is not meant to be exhaustive or address any reader's specific situation, and inclusion is not an endorsement of specific content or of a particular course of action. Readers are invited to consider the materials and topics raised in the book, as well as other available resources, while they make thoughtful decisions based on their values, priorities, and circumstances. Readers should seek additional answers and resources that address their specific circumstances, wishes, and needs, as well as relevant laws.

The authors of the essays made great efforts to provide accurate, relevant information on a wide range of topics. However, many details are liable to change and, in many instances, are subject to interpretation. The publishers cannot accept responsibility for any consequences arising from the use of this book.

Acknowledgments

Thank you to the Harriet Monroe Institute and to Ilya Kaminsky, Beth Allen, Lauren Ricke, Daniel Moysaenko, Catherine Barnett, Kathleen White, Charlotte Crowe, Elizabeth Wachtler, Matthew Zapruder, Georgia Popoff, Jared Hawkley, Sarah Marie Shepherd, John Lusk Babbott, Flynn Hoxby, Ryann S. Wahl, Fred Courtright, Zachary Cupkovic, Susan Hogan, Gabriel Kalmuss-Katz, Jessica Kovler, Robin Reagler, Ethan Nosowsky, 826 National, the Berkeley Public Library, the San Francisco Public Library, the Cecil Green Library at Stanford, Teachers & Writers Collaborative, Jane Hirshfield, Kristin Hanson, and Irena Yamboliev, on whose dining room table in the Mission District of San Francisco the final files for this book were assembled.

Introduction: Opening the Door

INTERVIEWER: When did you first realize you wanted to become a poet?

WILLIAM STAFFORD: I've thought about that, and sort of reversed it. My question is, "When did other people give up the idea of being a poet?" You know when we are kids we make up things, we write, and for me the puzzle is not that some people are still writing, the real question is why did the other people stop?

One of the traditional aims of art has been to defamiliarize the familiar, but for children, the defamiliarization process isn't needed: Every phase of childhood is new. Every stage in the ongoing process of growth upends and rearranges the child's world. As a result of meeting each moment with fresh eyes, children are natural artists and, once old enough to speak, natural poets.

"Teaching really is not the right word for what takes place: it is more like permitting the children to discover something they already have," wrote poet and educator Kenneth Koch in *Wishes, Lies, and Dreams*, his influential 1970 chronicle of teaching poetry to elementary-school students. "Treating them like poets was not a case of humorous but effective diplomacy, as I had first thought; it was the right way to treat them because it corresponded to the truth." Too often, though, children stop acting like poets when they start learning about poetry—about the forms and rules, about the right and wrong ways to think about, and express their experiences of, life.

Though many excellent books have been written on teaching poetry to kids, most also assume a traditional academic setting. This book, by contrast, does not take for granted such a setting and often looks beyond that framework toward nonprofit, community-based organizations that aim to unite poetry and children. While there are certainly benefits to teaching in schools (funding, regularity of schedule, and required attendance, for example), there are also real, sometimes huge, advantages to teaching poetry beyond the walls of academia. A call to action for poets who want to teach poetry in their communities, *Open the Door* is also a practical guide for those interested in developing their pedagogical skills, or even in setting up community poetry programs of their own.

> Teaching poetry is one important way to help children become human beings who are fully awake to the world.
>
> —Megan McNamer

The book is organized into three sections. Part 1 consists of a mix of newly commissioned and influential past essays on the importance of teaching poetry to children. Part 2 is made up of a roundtable discussion, edited from surveys sent to sixteen model organizations throughout the United States, on practical ways to set up and maintain a thriving poetry organization or afterschool program. And Part 3 offers a more direct and practical how-to feature: sample lesson plans.

All in all, we hoped to create a lively, engaging book, a collection of writings that explores the many ways to encourage the youngest of today's poets in their discovery of what poetry can mean in their lives. But before jumping in, let's take a look back at some of the more recent developments in arts education from which this book grew.

Teachers & Writers Collaborative, Poets-in-the-Schools, and Kenneth Koch

Beginning in the mid-1960s, and inspired by the cultural revolution spreading across the country, a public-school reform movement began to gain momentum. For the writers and educators convened at a series of national conferences in 1965 to address ways to transform public educa-tion, "There seemed to be a shared conviction that the teaching of English was 'a disaster area.'" The minutes keeper at one conference at Columbia University put the overall feeling soberly: In the public-school system

> children do not learn to write as a means of telling the world about themselves or as a way of telling themselves about themselves. They learn that writing is limiting, that they must take on a "standard language" for writing, and [that] standard language bears little relation to the language they are speaking or using to communicate. And if writing is separated from the self, reading is divorced from life.

From within this climate, many education leaders became convinced that poetry, and the arts generally, might best be taught by instruc-tors from outside the traditional textbook-focused, assessment-driven educational climate. Two years after these conferences, some of the country's top writers—including Grace Paley, Muriel Rukeyser, Kenneth Koch, June Jordan, and Anne Sexton—founded Teachers & Writers Collaborative, a nonprofit organization whose mission was to bring writ-ers into schools to stimulate students' appreciation of literature and, generally, to reanimate the teaching of creative writing. Since its found-ing in 1967, Teachers & Writers has played an active role in the education of more than 760,000 children.

> The nuttier the assignment, often, the better the result.
> —Theodore Roethke

A few years after the founding of Teachers & Writers, the idea that practicing writers and artists might best be suited to teach those subjects went mainstream, and the National Endowment for the Arts began fund-ing poets-in-the-schools (PITS) programs around the country. Today there are dozens of poets-in-the-schools and writers-in-the-schools (WITS) programs in the United States, which collectively reach more than 100,000 students each year.

As suggested by the popularity of these programs, poetry may be presented most successfully when teachers are able to find creative alternatives to traditional pedagogical practices. An emphasis on teaching the formal elements of poetry, grades, and other number-based forms of evaluation too often result in students feeling alienated from poetry. Teachers who are able to resist some of these institutional pressures can enliven poetry for children—especially small children—by focusing instead on qualities such as freedom, spontaneity, affirmation, personal expression, and the encouragement of open, creative exploration.

This leads us back to poet and educator Kenneth Koch (1925–2002). No discussion of the history of teaching poetry to children would be complete without paying due reverence to Koch who, in 1968, sponsored by Teachers & Writers, began teaching poetry to students at P.S. 61, an elementary school in New York City. Compared to the "groans of disapproval and cries of anguish" that too often greet the introduction of poetry into classrooms, Koch's students would clap and cheer as he entered the room. Koch wrote two groundbreaking books from these experiences: *Wishes, Lies, and Dreams* (1970) and *Rose, Where Did You Get That Red?* (1973).

> The trouble with a child's not being "crazy" is that he will instead be conventional.
>
> —Kenneth Koch

In the "maelstrom of creation" that was frequently Koch's classes— "I let the children make a good deal of noise. Children do when they are excited, and writing poetry is exciting"—Koch met his students at their level, which was, with a little encouragement, astonishingly high. Koch reported that his pupils wrote poems that "would make me gasp," and after glancing through the many student poems included in each volume, it becomes clear why. That Koch was able to see, and help animate, the natural poet in each child is palpable on every page. Poet Jordan Davis writes in his essay "Fears, Truths, and Waking Life" that "The key to understanding Kenneth Koch's work with children and using it as a model for your own teaching is that you have to take children seriously— their feelings, their ideas of beauty, their ways of using the language." Koch's two books have served as inspirational models for countless teachers since their publication.

Onward: On Starting an Organization of Your Own

During the next several decades, moments of innovation and promising theoretical developments played tug-of-war with budget instability and the increasing pressure of standardized assessments. These same decades saw growth, however, not only in the number of nonprofits engaging young people with poetry, but also in the diversity of their programming. A glance though the organizations in Part 2, for instance, reveals offerings that include in-school and out-of-school classes, teacher-training programs, residencies, festivals, reading series and open mics, camps, research centers, spoken-word and hip-hop education and presentation, online and location-based audio and visual resources, websites with every conceivable material and tool, magazines and book publications, a literary garden, and a text-based art gallery. Yet amid this diversity, some themes stand out as especially noteworthy for those interested in starting a youth poetry organization of their own.

> Teaching in museums, parks, and gardens opens up opportunities that we don't have in the classroom for students to observe, discover, and respond to through writing.
>
> —Susan Grigsby

People

First and foremost are the people you are involved with—your employees and volunteers, the ultimate measure of any arts organization. Martin Farawell, poetry program director of the Geraldine R. Dodge Foundation, responded to our question about the best way to maintain a thriving poetry organization:

> The answer is deceptively simple: surround yourself with good poets and good teachers, and listen to them. No matter how brilliant, original, or exciting you may find your own ideas about teaching poetry to be, the impact of any program you create will depend on the quality of the people going out into the field and doing the work.

And the two qualities most commonly cited as responsible for a staff member's long-term success? Perseverance and passion.

Collaboration

Also of special importance, according to Part 2 respondents, is maintaining collaborative, conversational relationships with other organizations. Advice was generally this: As much as possible, and without losing your unique organizational identity, become part of a network of like-minded and sympathetic regional and national organizations. Make sure your organization is an active participant in the big picture. Partnership is not just for growth, but often for survival.

Keep Your Ear to the Ground

Another essential quality is cultural relevance. Just as an organization devoted to hip-hop performance may have made less sense a few decades ago, the glimmerings of an organization that makes perfect sense a decade from now may only be emerging. Youth art organizations exist to teach and inspire, but the specific modes for doing so most effectively continue to evolve in tandem with the culture in which the organization is located. "Remain relevant," writes Kevin Coval of Young Chicago Authors. "Poetry is contemporary art. Alive NOW. About the worlds we inhabit this moment. The work and words should reflect, refract, represent, and re-present these realities."

> Anyone who's ever visited a poetry group for teenagers held in any inner-city church basement or community center has seen firsthand how much poetry matters.
>
> —Martin Farawell

Fun

And finally: make it *fun*. According to one study, most people stop reading poetry because they find it "abstruse and lifeless." Should you decide to start an organization of your own, it will be up to you to change that. One way to do so is to unleash the creative energy that likely brought your students to you in the first place. "All the motivation is intrinsic instead of extrinsic," writes Jeff Kass of Neutral Zone. "Perhaps that is the biggest advantage of writing workshops outside of school: kids who engage in such workshops do so solely with the goal of improving as writers." Tap into that energy, and hang on.

What can be said of teaching poetry to children also holds true for poetry organizations in general. "Poetry will always be a wild animal,"

William Stafford writes in his essay "The Door." Though your organization will need to maintain some level of stability in order to survive, beware of being *too* stable. As Dave Eggers writes about starting 826 National, "We let it all unfold naturally, even chaotically, and that kept it vital and surprising."

> Imagine wildly.
> —Terry Blackhawk

There is, finally, only one real measure of this book: whether it encourages readers to help create opportunities for young people to become more engaged with poetry. There are a million ways of doing so. We hope *Open the Door* provides some inspiration and guidance along the way.

— *Dominic Luxford*

SOURCES CITED

Collom, Jack, and Sheryl Noethe. *Poetry Everywhere: Teaching Poetry Writing in School and in the Community*. New York: Teachers & Writers Collaborative, 2007.

Galt, Margot Fortunato. *The Circuit Writer: Writing with Schools and Communities*. New York: Teachers & Writers Collaborative, 2006.

Gioia, Dana. *Can Poetry Matter? Essays on Poetry and American Culture*. St. Paul: Graywolf Press, 1992.

Koch, Kenneth. *Rose, Where Did You Get That Red? Teaching Great Poetry to Children*. New York: Vintage, 1990.

——————. *Wishes, Lies, and Dreams: Teaching Children to Write Poetry*. New York: Harper Perennial, 1999.

Lopate, Phillip, ed. *Journal of a Living Experiment*. New York: Teachers & Writers Collaborative, 1979.

Parr, Michelann, and Terry Campbell. "Poets in Practice." *The Reading Teacher* 60, no. 1 (2006): 36–46.

Popoff, Georgia A., and Quraysh Ali Lansana. *Our Difficult Sunlight: A Guide to Poetry, Literacy, & Social Justice in Classroom & Community*. New York: Teachers & Writers Collaborative, 2011.

Reagler, Robin. Phone conversation with author. October 26, 2011.

Schwartz, Lisa K., Lisbeth Goble, Ned English, and Robert F. Bailey. *Poetry in America: Review of the Findings*. Chicago: Poetry Foundation, 2006. PDF available at www.poetryfoundation.org/foundation/initiative_poetryamerica.html.

Stafford, William. *Writing the Australian Crawl: Views on the Writer's Vocation*. Ann Arbor: University of Michigan Press, 1978.

Teachers & Writers Collaborative. 2012. www.twc.org.

Part 1
Essays

The Read-Aloud Handbook[1]

Jim Trelease

What's Right or Wrong with Poetry

If "lobster" were an important subject in the curriculum, we would have lobster classes for twelve straight years: where to find them, how they live, and, of course, how to catch, prepare, cook, and eat them. But if, after graduating from school, the end result was a lifelong loss of appetite for lobster, there would be a general reassessment of the lobster curriculum. And this is precisely what has happened to poetry in the United States—except no one is reassessing the poetry curriculum.

The contrast between how children respond to poetry and how adults do is seen most strikingly in two facts:

1. Until *The Road Less Traveled* surpassed it, Shel Silverstein's collection of children's poetry, *A Light in the Attic*, held *The New York Times* record for the longest time on its bestseller list (186 weeks).

---

1. First published in Trelease's *The Read-Aloud Handbook* (New York: Penguin, 1995).

2. The worst-selling department in bookstores is adult poetry; it sells so poorly, many stores no longer even stock it.[2]

Poetry dies for most people on graduation day. The thickest coat of dust in a public library can be found in its poetry section. Considering how much time is spent in secondary classrooms dissecting poetry, one would expect graduates to be ravenous poetry consumers. Wrong. Why is this so?

One of poetry's strengths is its brevity. A poem is not a novel or a short story, yet it can be very revealing in its smallness—like one of those see-through Easter eggs. A poem should add up to something, a slice of life. One expert put it this way: "Unless a poem says something to a child, tells him a story, titillates his ego, strikes up a happy recollection, bumps his funny bone—in other words, delights him—he will not be attracted to poetry regardless of the language it uses."[3]

Therefore the choice of poets and poems will have everything to do with how children react to poetry. But the American approach ignores those factors. It is more interested in "covering the core curriculum" than creating lifetime interest. The higher the grade level, the more obscure and symbolic and less humorous and understandable the poetry becomes. Because all the poetry is obscure, every poem must be dissected like some kind of frog in biology class, and we end up making poetry appear so unnecessarily complicated, people like children's author Jean Little decide not to stop the next time they come to the "woods on a snowy evening."[4]

This attitude of the secondary faculty may be a result of the Segal Syndrome (in honor of Erich Segal, the Yale classics professor and author

---

2. Nicholas Zill and Marianne Winglee, *Who Reads Literature?* (Cabin John, MD: Seven Locks Press, 1990).

3. Patrick J. Groff, "Where Are We Going with Poetry for Children?" *Horn Book Reflections* (Boston: The Horn Book, 1969), 181.

4. Jean Little, "After English Class" from *Hey World, Here I Am!* (New York: Harper, 1986).

of *Love Story*). Usually associated with college faculties, but often spilling down to high school English departments, the Segal Syndrome works like this: A professor's esteem on the faculty is in inverse proportion to his or her public popularity; that is, if a professor writes a book, the more copies it sells, the lower he sinks with his peers; the fewer it sells, the higher the peer rating. "After all, if the public understands and enjoys him," the faculty reasons, "how deep can the guy be?" Extended to poetry, if anyone can understand it—or, God forbid!, someone laughs over it—how deep can it be?

The Segal Syndrome affects even elementary grade poetry. Shel Silverstein, Judith Viorst, and Jack Prelutsky are three of the most popular children's poets of the last twenty-five years, yet none of them has collected any of the major poetry awards from the academicians. (How good can they be if the kids like them?) If teachers or parents are sincerely interested in turning children on to poetry, they need to look first at which books actually work with children and then at why they work.

To begin with, all three poets can be serious but, more often, they make young people laugh. And laughter is a dirty word with some educators. As Garrison Keillor once noted in an interview with Larry King, humor may be one of the things missing in the American poetry picture. King mentioned that Keillor was going to a poetry reading that evening at Georgetown University, a reading with Roland Flint, whom Keillor described as "the only very good poet in America who is really funny. In American poetry, there's an excess of symbol and a dearth of humor," Keillor noted.[5] Any high school student in America would have agreed with him.

In an effort to find the poetry pulse of middle-grade students, Karen Kutiper exposed 375 Texas seventh-, eight- and ninth-graders to 100 poems (10 a day for 10 days, from a variety of forms), and surveyed their preferences. In a listing of their top 25, there were tongue-twisters,

---

5. Garrison Keillor radio interview on *The Larry King Show*, February 23, 1993.

limericks, nonsense poems, and two poems each by Shel Silverstein and Jack Prelutsky. Nearly all their favorite poems were narrative (with an emphasis on humor), all but one rhymed, and only two could be considered serious. The ninth-graders, however, showed a slightly higher preference for serious poetry, a sign of maturity and perhaps a signal to teachers that serious poetry can be taught if you keep in mind that readers are first interested in story or narrative.[6]

If secondary schools included more narrative and more humor in the poetry curriculum, there might be more interest in complex poetry as adults. In any case, the old prescription hasn't worked, so why keep prescribing it?

Where the Sidewalk Ends, by Shel Silverstein, is so popular with children, librarians and teachers insist it is the book most frequently stolen from their schools and libraries. Over the last eight years I've asked eighty thousand teachers if they know *Where the Sidewalk Ends* (two million copies in print), and three-quarters of the teachers raise their hands. "Wonderful!" I say. "Now, who has enough copies of this book for every child in your room?" Nobody raises a hand. In eight years, only eighteen teachers out of eighty thousand had enough copies in their rooms for every child.

I continue, "Do each of you know the books in your classroom no child would ever consider stealing?" They nod in recognition. "Do you have enough copies of *those* books for every child in the room?" Reluctantly, they nod agreement. Here we've got a book kids love to read so much they'll steal it right and left and we haven't got enough copies; but every year we've got twenty-eight copies of a book they hate.

If we wish children to believe poetry is important, the *worst* way to

---

6. Karen S. Kutiper, "A Survey of the Adolescent Poetry Preferences of Seventh-, Eighth-, and Ninth-Graders" (doctoral dissertation, University of Houston, 1985). See also: "Using Junior High Readers' Poetry Preferences in the Classroom" by Karen S. Kutiper and Richard F. Abrahamson, in *Literature and Life: Making Connections—Classroom Practices in the Teaching of English,* P. Phelan, ed. (Urbana, IL: National Council of Teachers of English, 1990).

teach it is to develop a two-week poetry block, teach it, and then forget it—because that's what children will do with it. The *best* way is to incorporate meaningful poetry throughout the day. . . .

Horse in Egg by Matthea Harvey

Poetry Is an Egg With a Horse Inside

Matthea Harvey

Our concerns as adults and as children are not so different. We want to be surprised, transformed, challenged, delighted, understood. For me, since an early age, poetry has been a place for all these things. Poetry is a rangy, uncontainable genre—it is a place for silliness and sadness, delight and despair, invention and ideas (and also, apparently, alliteration). Giving children poems that address the whole range of the world, not just the watered-down, "child appropriate" issues, makes them feel less alone. Corny as it sounds, if children find poems that express things they have themselves thought and poems that push them beyond what they have themselves imagined, they'll have a friend for life. This is the story of how I found that friend.

In the first poetry workshop I ever took (my junior year in college), my professor, Henri Cole, handed out a page of quotations about poetry from luminaries such as Yeats, Eliot, and Stevens. One of them read:

> "Poetry is an egg with a horse inside."
>
> —Third grader

I have no idea who or what that third grader grew up to be (I'm guessing a poet, miniature-pony breeder, astronaut, or molecular gastronomist), but I still remember the thrill I felt seeing that quote included. I don't remember the quotes by those beloved poetry stars, but decades later, I include that third grader's quote in my handouts, and it seems to surprise and delight my students as much as it did and does me. Lucie Brock-Broido knows the quote too (maybe they were in a class together?), and once when I was in her office after visiting her class, she showed me her scrumptious collection of eggs with little horses inside.

This spurred me to do a photo-illustration of my own because for the last six years, I've been taking photographs to title or illustrate my poems. I sorted through my collection of small horses (yes, I have such a collection; in fact I have drawers and drawers of miniature things) and finally found one horse that almost perfectly matched the brown eggs I had in the fridge. I cracked one open with a spoon, let all the egg white and yolk run out, and carefully inserted the horse, tail first. Voilà! He looked as though he was just making his way out—tottering on his spindly front legs, wondering if he would ever get the back two out and what on earth might be ahead of him. On a day when I'm truly open to the world (the pigeons pecking their shadows on the roof next door, the snow on the still-green trees), that's what life feels like to me—a bit terrifying but pretty beautiful. When I'm on a plane and I hear the man three rows back saying, "I am a salmon geneticist," I want to add "who was recently kissed in the mist" to make his statement even more Dr. Seuss–ish. When I hear tennis player Rafael Nadal say in an interview, "Hopefully the book will like to the people," I immediately imagine, if this weren't an accident of his somewhat limited English, what it would be like if authors truly felt this way and went peering into living rooms to see if their books looked contented. There are days when image and language and story positively buzz in the air.

Children feel this—they're learning language, and they want to play with it. It's why when my friends tell their children I'm a poet, the kids inevitably want to play rhyming games with me. And I am happy to play! Confession: I was a child rhymer. I drove my two older sisters crazy by rhyming all the time, and I mean *all the time*. Partly it was to annoy them (I was the youngest sister, after all), but mostly I just loved rhyme. I still do. My father liked to make up songs. One favorite was created during a trip to Denmark where we stayed in a cabin infested with earwigs. One of the verses was "*Eine Earwig, der ist Klein, schläft immer am Matthea's Bein*" (which, translated, means, "One earwig is little and likes to sleep on Matthea's leg," though the rhyme doesn't come through in English).

Yukiko Kido's wonderful book *Snake Cake* introduces kids to families of rhyme. (There are others in this series—notably *Pig Wig*, *Wet Pet*, and *Quack Shack*, written by Harriet Ziefert and illustrated by Kido.) In *Snake Cake*, it's the *-ake*, *-oat*, and *-ant* word families, so the child learns the word *snake*, then *bake*, then mixes them together, coming up with such delightful combinations as "snake bake," which is accompanied by a picture of a snake baking in the sunshine, for example. I gave *Snake Cake* to my friend Frances's little son, Sebastian, really because he loved snakes, not because of the rhyme, but it was amazing how quickly he took to it. In the middle of lunch, he looked up at me with great delight and exclaimed, "Matthea quesadilla!" I'm not sure I've ever felt quite so proud (and understood). Children's interest in rhyme is innate, and I think it should be celebrated—I've seen children wilt a little after being told that "real" poems don't rhyme.

The first poem I remember giving me a sense of what poetry could possibly do was "Bed in Summer," by Robert Louis Stevenson, from *A Child's Garden of Verses*. Its rhyming was part of the appeal.

> In winter I get up at night
> And dress by yellow candle-light.
> In summer, quite the other way,
> I have to go to bed by day.

I have to go to bed and see
The birds still hopping on the tree,
Or hear the grown-up people's feet
Still going past me in the street.

And does it not seem hard to you,
When all the sky is clear and blue,
And I should like so much to play,
To have to go to bed by day.

Like children throughout time, I'd had this exact experience (minus the candlelight) and been mystified by it. Here was a poem that articulated those summer hours after 8:00 p.m., when it was clearly too light to go to sleep, and the winter mornings with the shrill alarm clock waking me when clearly I was supposed to be asleep. I deeply admired the way my bewilderment was put in a neat rhyming parcel, with Stevenson saying it much more succinctly than I ever could.

My older sister was a fan of Ogden Nash, Edward Lear, and Edward Gorey (whose macabre humor tickled my particular black velvet heart as well), so soon I was reveling in the wordplay of their poems for children. This one by Ogden Nash was and is a particular favorite.

The Shrimp

A shrimp who sought his lady shrimp
Could catch no glimpse,
Not even a glimp.
At times, translucence
Is rather a nuisance.

Is there anything more delightful than the idea that a partial glimpse would be a "glimp"?

As an adult, I discovered the marvelous children's book *Scranimals*, illustrated by Peter Sis and written by Jack Prelutsky, whom the Poetry Foundation chose as the first children's poet laureate in 2006. *Scranimals* is about hybrid animals (usually combined with flowers or food) such as the pandaffodil and the antelopetunia. Ask your young students to create hybrids of their own and watch them go to town writing poems about bearhubarb and puddingfish.

Fourth grade, though, may have been where I really caught the poetry bug. My teacher, Mr. Zuege, a man famous for spitting on the first row when he got excited, introduced us to May Swenson's unforgettable "Southbound on the Freeway."

> A tourist came in from Orbitville,
> parked in the air, and said:
>
> The creatures of this star
> are made of metal and glass.
>
> Through the transparent parts
> you can see their guts.
>
> Their feet are round and roll
> on diagrams or long
>
> measuring tapes, dark
> with white lines.
>
> They have four eyes.
> The two in the back are red.
>
> Sometimes you can see a five-eyed
> one, with a red eye turning

on the top of his head.
He must be special—

the others respect him
and go slow

when he passes, winding
among them from behind.

They all hiss as they glide,
like inches, down the marked

tapes. Those soft shapes,
shadowy inside

the hard bodies—are they
their guts or their brains?

I've never forgotten being given this alien view of a freeway, pondering how the creatures would look at the cars and think that they were the only inhabitants of the planet. And what did it mean about what the aliens looked like if they mistook people for their cars? Have your students imagine aliens landing in another place—a sports arena, a McDonald's, a poetry reading, a birthday party. What might the aliens conclude about the world from that particular locale—that humans worship boxes tied up with ribbon, for example? What form do the aliens take, and how does that affect their perception? For that matter, how does physical appearance affect the way humans see the world?

Our concerns as adults and as children are not so different. We want to be surprised, transformed, delighted, understood.

But no one said it was a happy horse emerging from that egg. There is another, sadder poem that I carry around in my wallet. It was given to me by a poet who teaches poetry to children.

Sadness Is

Sadness is a sky blue
mountain
in the house.

—Jillian Bell (age eight)

I'm not sure I've ever read a poem that so precisely conveys the hugeness and strangeness of the way sadness can take over—the way that when you're sad, sometimes you don't fit into your surroundings; the sun is shining and you're blue. Or your sadness transforms the world—the wet dog looks sad, not funny or sweet, and the garbage even sadder. Poetry helps both adults and children traverse complex emotional terrain. It can present a beautiful picture of bewilderment (a subject about which Fanny Howe has a wonderful essay), or it can make something legible that was blurred before. It helps people see into one another's heads, helps them understand one another. How can that not be incredibly important? I think we should expose children not only to the silly, funny, and imaginative poems but also to angry, sad, and difficult poems, as well as poems that may make them snicker, as in this eighteenth-century Japanese haiku by Kobayashi Issa: "The straight hole / I make by pissing / in the snow by my door".

In your classrooms (however defined), pick poems that will speak to kids' lives—give them a poem about characters or situations they know already (Little Red Riding Hood, Derek Jeter, the Wonder Pets), but also give them poems that can crack open their understanding of the world, such as this mind-blowing haiku from Bashō—"year after year, on the monkey's face, a monkey's face"—or this one from Richard Wright: "With indignation / A little girl spanks her doll— / The sound of spring rain." Give them poems that invent other worlds. One exercise I've done with

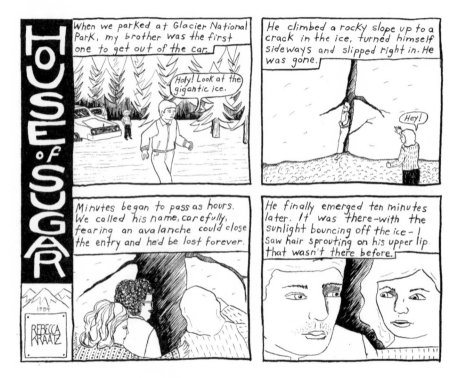

Courtesy of Rebecca Kraatz

both adults and children is to give them an entry from *A Dictionary of Imaginary Places*, by Alberto Manguel and Gianni Guadalupi, and then ask them to write a poem from the perspective of an inhabitant of that world.

Don't underestimate what your students can understand or how comfortable they may be with not understanding. Make a small anthology of contemporary poems for them, and let them pick one they would like to memorize. Give them "Dream Song 28: Snow Line," by John Berryman,

Courtesy of Paul Tunis and Kameron Quinlan

and talk about how he makes the voice sheep-like, how it alternates between "I" and "we" because of the way sheep often move in a group, how the sheep says of the sheepdog, "The barker nips me but somehow I feel / he too is on my side." Ask them to choose an animal and think about how it might sound if it could speak English. Might the cat sound snooty? Would an excitable dog use lots of exclamation marks? Would the hedgehog use mostly consonants because of his prickly exterior?

Show children poetry that works with other genres, such as poetry comics. There are many examples of "The Poem as Comic Strip" on the Poetry Foundation website; there's *Poetry Comics: An Animated Anthology*, by Dave Morice; Kenneth Koch's *The Art of the Possible: Comics Mainly Without Pictures*; and Rebecca Kraatz's *House of Sugar*, which she doesn't classify as poetry but which couldn't be more poetic. Have kids make comics out of poems they love. Have them illustrate one another's poems, or bring in adult artists who will take the children's work seriously and make it into something new. (One example I love of this kind of collaboration is a piece that writer and comics artist Paul Tunis did with student Kameron Quinlan). Have children make collages, then switch with a classmate and write a poem about the other child's image. Make them into little poetry guerillas—have them write poems on a foggy window and then take photographs as the poems fade away or print their poems on colored paper and hide them in interesting places where people will find them (in a deposit envelope at a bank, tucked into a takeout menu). Ask them to imagine the craziest ways they could get poetry out into the world—a haiku about headaches etched into a Tylenol, a security system that uses Emily Dickinson lines as laser tripwires, notes of perfume translated into letters of the alphabet so that when someone asks you what scent you're wearing, the answer is a poem.

I've worked with Community-Word Project (CWP) in New York City, an organization that brings poetry into underserved schools. CWP has children write group poems, starting with "My world is …" or "My heart …," which ended up with this memorable line: "My heart reads red science books." Creating a poem that encompasses all their voices, which they can read aloud as a group, can give them a simultaneous sense of individuality and community. Or have them collaborate, as in Joshua Beckman and Matthew Rohrer's book *Nice Hat. Thanks.*, having two students alternate saying words (with a third transcribing) until they've written a poem as a pair. Another thing I love about CWP's teaching strategy is that classes end with "*Viva la palabra! Somos poetas!*" or "Long live

Renovated Mushroom (Tip-Top Tire Rubber Patch Kit) by Nina Katchadourian.
Courtesy of the Artist and Catharine Clark Gallery, San Francisco.

the word! We are poets!" I know so many adult poets who are shy of the word—what would happen if everyone had this experience of being self-identified as a poet early on?

Both "Sadness Is" and "Poetry Is an Egg With a Horse Inside" are definitions of poetry. And maybe that's the way into all of this: teach children early about the transformative swing door of simile, the rabbit hole of metaphor, and how poetry can be or do anything they want it to. Let them feel that poetry is full of exuberant possibility by playing a game of "Poetry Is": Poetry is a burning cabin watched by foxes. Poetry is a mushroom with bicycle tire patches. (This one was inspired by Nina Katchadourian's *Renovated Mushroom* artwork, in which she did exactly that.)

Poetry is a peacock in a pea coat. Poetry is a UFO made of marshmallows. Poetry is a bowlful of dead bees (a tip of the hat to Robert Hass's

"A Story About the Body"). As Stephanie Strickland writes, "Poems are words that take you through three kinds of doors: closed doors, secret doors, and doors you don't know are there." And Charles Simic: "Poetry: three mismatched shoes at the entrance of a dark alley." If poetry is all these things, what *can't* it do?

The Process of Opening Gifts: How Permission Catalyzes Writing

Jack Collom

Imagine you're a student in a school of walking. You go to class one day and some graceful person enters, saying, "Let's dance!" Exciting! Frivolous! Possibly even frightening. You might not feel able to dance. You might not want to be seen dancing. If you're reluctant, however, the invitation to dance might well be extended first in the form of an invitation to walk—initially, just pickin' 'em up and layin' 'em down. The dance person might say, "Think about the soles of your feet, swing those hips, get a rhythm going, try something funny, see how efficiently you can just glide along." Step by step the walk becomes dance, is seen to be dance because dance is "magic walk." In this scenario, the invitation moves the spirit; the actual steps and the steps behind the steps are the substance. Together they lead from the known to the half-known and onward. Let's term this invitation *permission*.

Permission in Practice

I want to make clear here what I mean by *permission* and, I hope, forestall any quick dismissals that might arise from confusing the word with *permissiveness*. *Permission* is particular; *permissiveness* is general, unfocused. Permission says, "You can write 'the darkness swept my feet with fear,' though nobody has ever written it before—*especially* because nobody has."

Ultimately, the self gives permission, but the process can be encouraged by examples, atmosphere, and even exhortations (poetry teacher as 5 percent football coach).

For one thing, I always, with myself, with students, with anybody, "go for the poem."

Art—in any language and/or in any medium—teaches people to pay attention. That's the secret, right there. When people pay attention, they become aware of process and the exact moments they are in. They also become in touch with larger moments, as in all of living. Paying attention is being alive.

In class, in real life, of course, the process isn't perfect. Hurray! Perfection is not the aim. Some kids will resist writing or will resist writing with candor and the kind of *exploratory focus* that turns exploratory focus from an oxymoron into the vitality of living in more than two dimensions. When a child balks or slacks off or can't get it, you can consult, warmly, with him or her, but your primary allegiance is to the group as a whole. You can also patiently permit the group energy to catch that child up.

The place of permission in writing is far more than creative word games and pats on the back for beginners. Even the works of Shakespeare were an important phenomenon of permission. I think much of what keeps the vast majority of writers from achieving a Shakespearean level— what most people would perhaps call lack of talent and let the matter rest unelaborated—is a certain (or uncertain) fear about exceeding the safe bounds of tradition. Shakespeare gave himself permission. This is not to say that Shakespeare was a pure experimenter—obviously not. He utilized tradition and innovation in incredibly intense blends. His transitive verbs alone amount to a stormy continuum of motion in all things, large and small, and new and untrammeled energy has everything to do with permission to try unexpected words. Perhaps Shakespeare gave himself permission to exercise what was later known as the Napoleonic mind: the ability to focus on many things at once. One of his key lines is "There are more things in heaven and earth, Horatio, than are dreamt of in your philosophy."

Permission is obviously the life force that animates an artist like Jackson Pollock, but it acts just as instrumentally in the more delicately radical advances within the poems of, say, T.S. Eliot. But as important—as essential—as permission is, the exercises in giving and taking permission are not meant to replace traditional instruction in poetry composition or in literature. I strongly believe in multiple approaches to the teaching of writing and consider the close study of writers and how they achieve their effects essential. I've regularly used writings by Bashō, William Blake, Federico García Lorca, Langston Hughes, Thomas Jefferson and friends, Denise Levertov, Carl Sandburg, Charles Simic, Gertrude Stein, Wallace Stevens, Walt Whitman, and William Carlos Williams, to name a few, in elementary, middle, and high schools. These texts should accompany, and intertwine with, hands-on explorations such as those that follow and much more.

From these exercises, I hope you'll see that poetry is magic talk and that teaching and learning are, in part, opening gifts.

Writing Permission

Imagine you're a student in a talking and writing school. You go to talking class one day and some writing person says to you, "We're going to write!" This could be an exciting, frivolous, or frightening prospect. Or boring. But there's no time to dwell on all that because the writing person (henceforth WP) is already laying out the details of the activity. You're asked to write some of your own memories, say. The WP reads aloud examples written by students like you and asks, "How many can remember something like that?" The writings are funny. You're supposed to begin your entries with the words I remember. The invitation is there, and the permission—invitation aflow—is buzzing in the air. You listen to "I remember" poems by other kids, and you can hear, and see, that when a particular third-grade girl wrote, "I remember when I smelled a rose, the whole thing broke," it was a moment of energy caught by words of energy: engaging, humorous, and heartbreaking. Nice sounds too. The WP repeats, "I remember when I smelled a rose" and repeats it again— "That's musical! Humming *m*'s, liquid *r*'s and *l*'s, pleasant rhythm. But then the tone changes! 'The whole thing'—that's a weird way to talk about a flower! And broke has a harsh *k* at the end. This third grader made a line of excellent poetry in the middle of talking on paper. I don't think she thought to herself, 'Let's see, I'll make the sound and sense work together: first part smooth to reflect the rose's beauty, second part odd and crackly to express that I stuck my nose in too far and busted the flower.' She probably didn't calculate it, but even small children are language experts in small ways. They've been using language for thousands of hours and have precise feels for its humors and emotions. That's what we can build on to begin to realize poetry."

Back to narrator-as-student: And, wow! Somebody wants to hear or read the details of your days expressed in the words and rhythms you actually think and talk in! And it doesn't have to be roses and noses; it could be baseballs, scrambled eggs, yells of pain, specks of dust, snot, whatever you have.

Warm Up the Group

Now, let's say you're the WP, and you're warming up the class to write. You facilitate excitement through examples, spark originality through the variety of examples, exercise light guidance through comments on examples, stir up positive feeling through and in the examples' details. Always talk up details. Advise students to go way beyond saying "I remember going to the movies." Encourage them to relate whom they went with, what they wore, that they walked on sunshiny Walnut Street, that the Bijou Theatre looked like a big pink castle, that they accidentally spilled Coca-Cola all over Betty's lap but that they both laughed because the movie was about dogs dressed up in Buster Brown clothes with blue ribbons. Kids are good at details but often neglect them.

All these are "palpable hits." Permission is more than ushering people into generalizations. That would be like feeding someone the word food. My thesis is that poetry in the introductory stage—and in some very important sense or senses, the introductory stage lasts for a poet's entire lifetime—is largely a matter of tangible permissions given and taken. These permissions tend to brush away clichéd thinking in favor of original images. "Weirdness" is a good permission, especially when it becomes somewhat specific: "knowledge graveling," "boxing with the clouds," et cetera.

Here's another way to think of it: most art forms—music, architecture, painting, et cetera—depend much more heavily than poetry does on a body of expert techniques peculiar to the art. Though people do sing in the shower and do make sketches, there's no massive continual preparation in daily life for music and painting. But poetry arises from speech, common speech. Kids are conversant, in practice, with complex aspects of the psychology and music of language. Although poetry as a developed art does have its own formidable, beautiful, technical side, such as the subtle shaping of a sonnet's thought (or Dada's delicacies), the word artist profits by remembering that much of poetry's very complexity resides in the immensely detailed, framed semi-mastery of language that almost everybody gets in the course of daily living. And much of poetry's technical work exists in turning this already-extant speech complexity into outgrowths of its own forms, on paper or in the air. In a way, you teach your students to go beyond the teachings that already pervade the culture regarding what a poem is "supposed to be." That is, you teach kids to pull poetry primarily out of themselves. Thereafter, learning exterior systems of poetry will not be a mechanical task but an extension of the familiar.

All this is not to claim that turning a second grader "loose" must result in Shelleyesque productions—but, measured in flashes, poems by the very young can come closer than one might expect. The "childlike" is what nearly all committed poets seek to preserve or revive. It is the freshness, the animating spark in the collisions of the syllables, the original movement of language that happens easily in childhood. The world is as complex as a patch of mixed wildflowers in a field. Children see their world, in their brightest moments, as an interesting arrangement of things; they see what adults tend to lose in the flurry of labels and expectations.

Case by Case

Recently I spent a few days in Casey Middle School. Master teacher Val Wheeler's motto is Poetry All Year. She likes to use poetry as a lead-in to a variety of subjects, as if the poetic sense were the lubricant to all learning.

I'll try here to present a typical workshop and will provide some specific examples from Casey Middle School eighth-grade students and other sources.

"I remember" poems, which are prosy as well, make a fine beginning. The rules couldn't be simpler: begin each line (or paragraph) with I remember. The main suggestion: use detail. I give students many examples from other kids, which helps bring about what I call the "necessity of poetry," the active realization that there are infinite options at any point.

To help students relax, I say such things as, "Many memories were disastrous at the time but become funnier as time passes."

A sixth-grade girl thought of this line: "I remember when a bike ran over me and it felt good 'cause I just felt the wheels and I wanted him to run over me again." This example shows the jazzy (variable) rhythms of speech. I read it again and suggested that we could dance to it.

I tell the students that the memories don't have to be important life events. Another sixth-grade girl wrote, "I remember when I flopped down in a chair and closed my eyes." This speaks as profoundly of life as an account of graduation day.

I exhort students to keep unusual language, as shown in this example, written by a sixth-grade boy: "I remember when I locked myself in the bathroom in the dark. The darkness came over me like a monster and swept my feet with fear." The words swept my feet with fear show poetry doing its job of keeping the language alive.

I mention similes and metaphors as ways to look at more than one thing at once. Example: "I remember first getting a fever and feeling like someone was ironing me," wrote a sixth-grade boy. I point out how fresh his comparison was and offer a few more examples of "I remember." Then the students write, and most of them read aloud. I praise specific phrases, rhythms, innovations, strange connections—and urge the other class members to comment as well.

From this experience, everyone realizes that poetry, or creative writing, can take place using the details of life expressed as vernacular speech rhythms. These are basic and lovely validations.

The Acrostic Poem

Teachers often use acrostics as a species of wordplay, usually a ladder of adjectives with which students can describe themselves, usually as self-esteem exercises. But if the students see various example poems in which the lines run out to indefinite lengths before folding back into acrostic shape, they may create more intricate, suggestive portrayals.

I typically begin with a poem by a first-grade Brooklyn girl, by way of demonstration.

> B lue is a color, a
> L ovely color that is
> U nder the sun
> E verywhere, even in thunder

She started with a repeat of the spine word; she didn't have to. I point out that the lines flow into each other and are not discrete units. I ask students (whatever age) if this is a rhyming poem. They say no. I ask them if they can find rhymes *within* the lines. Someone notices *under* / *thunder*, and I say, "This counts as word music." The repetitions of *color, a, is,* the *un* / *sun* rhyme, and the three *v*'s placed fairly close together are all moments of word music, rhyminess. I ask students about *thunder*, a sound: How can this be *blue*, a color, and we all accept the kinesthetic association. ("Thunder's blue when it's there, in blueness," someone said once.)

Next I give students this compact gem, written by a seventh-grade boy, to show how swiftly one can capture the great and small duties of attention.

> O pen your mind to the
> U niverse, and
> R un back home to get your lunch.

Students can pick a spine word from anywhere, perhaps the classroom wall, as the fourth-grade girl who wrote this did.

N othing is more beautiful than a
U niverse.
M ama, Mama give me a
B all.
E ast is the way.
R ounding is the sound.
S ound is my number.

I later used *Sound Is My Number* as the title of a course book on poetry.

There are many more acrostic aspects and possibilities to show. I end with this abecedarian (written in fifteen minutes by a fourth-grade girl), which I "explain" as a fairyland that is, ultimately, whisked away.

A magnificent rainbow
Bellowed the sky with rays of color
Cast the beautiful fairies
Dawned the twilight's mist
Even turned the world to rubies
Fascinating
Gorgeous
Heaps of gold and silver are here
I never heard the music the gold played
Jungle of white ivy—I
Know the world is all turned around
Lovely the perfect place to be by the
Murmuring brooks of crystal blue
Nothing ever would turn the world back—
Open the golden doors
Past the mountains of ice

Quiet place
Running past the silver trees—the
Sun is made of white diamonds
Turning the twilight to dawn
Unicorns made of white rubies
Violets of shimmery purple
White beautiful bushes
eXtraordinary
You will find the magic there
Zap—it's gone forever.

One day, at the Aurora Quest Academy in Aurora, Colorado, I showed the first graders the basic principle of acrostic poems. Six-year-old Graciela, who had come from Mexico and begun to learn English only fifteen months earlier, created the following poem (word for word, letter for letter).

P oems is poetry and don't know if it is even or
O dd is it a rainbow with different colors that is not
E nough for me is it a beautiful butterfly in the sky is it a
T ree in the tropical forest that the leaves are green and
R ed or is it a yo-yo I know it is a red light
Y o-yo. It jumps and

P rances is it a big big huge puzzle like and
O flying in the sky like the different rainbow
E nough it is a bunch of things that it booms out of your
M ind. Poetry fills your mind of words and I can't think of
   anything.

Chant—Repeating and Changing

Another very basic writing idea is the chant poem. Poetry has existed as long as talk, in one reckoning at least. Certainly its beginnings were oral, as shown by the great collections of song and recital from preliterate peoples. Poetry may have begun ceremonially, around a fire, accompanying dance.

Primeval nonsense-syllable works resemble avant-garde abstractions. Repetition is rife and rhythmic in modern art. Contemporary poets have revived the energy and musicality of such initiations.

A good way to get chant poetry going in the classroom is through repetition and change. Here are a few pieces by schoolchildren that can be vividly performed.

The first is untitled, from a fourth-grade girl. Asking the kids to try to explain this poem's chant structure can inspire them: it's not only letting go, though it's partly letting go. Here the formal trick is repeated breakdown, each one followed by add-on steps.

Cats go crazy

         Cats go crazy like

Cats go crazy like me

         Cats like

Cats like to

         Cats like to go

Cats like to go crazy

         Cats like to go

Cats like to go downtown

         Cats like to

Cats like to drive

         Cats like to drive cars

Cats like to drive a car but bang boom crash

         Cats like to

Cats like to wreck
             Cats like to wreck into
Cats like to wreck into you
             Cats like people
Cats like people to
             Cats like people to scratch
Cats like kids
             Cats like kids to
Cats like kids to play
             Cats like kids to play with
Cats are dead because they got in so many wrecks—

This next piece, written by a middle-school girl, resembles those dances that dash from freeform to ballet and back.

Satin Slippers

Satin slippers
Satin slippers dance on the marble floor
Satin slippers
Satin slippers dance
Dancing gracefully sliding on the floor
On the floor
On the marble floor
On the marble floor satin slippers dance
Dance satin slippers
Dance
Under the spotlight
Dance
Satin slippers
Dance

This poem by a sixth-grade girl has a tiny but classic twist.

> I
> I have
> I have a
> I have a great
> I have a great life.
> Great, I have a life.

In a truly wild exchange between languages, between emotions, between different kinds of surprise, a high-school girl extends the chant in the following poem.

> Person 1 Person 2
>
> Ha, Ha, Ha, Ha.
> Ha, Ha, Ha, Ha
> Laugh ha, ha, ha
> 2—Smile big.
> 1—I love you.
> 2—Smile bigger.
> 2—*Tus Palabras*
> 2—*Me llenan de emoción.*
> 1—*Me gusta todo de ti.*
> 1—*Pienso en ti*
> 2—*Piensas en que?* Laughs
> 1—*En eso.*
> 2—*Lleva sus dedos y los corre por su cabello.*
> 1—*En eso.*
> 2—She bites her lower lip.
> 1—*En eso.*
> 2—*Se pone roja.*

1—*En eso.*
2—*Le dice "Te amo."*
1—*En eso!*
2—*YO TE ADORO*
1—*En eso. También en eso!*

In a final example, a young writer gives an antic rendition of the possible self-possessed stream of consciousness that cats seem to deal in:

Chant le Chat

What's that?
The cat.
The cat is lying flat
on the rug. I want
the cat to lie on my lap.
But the cat
doesn't want that. The cat,
that cat, knows where it's at.
Where it's at is where she is,
is where she lies.
I don't mean she,
the cat, lies. She never lies.
That's clear. She's a cat. Cats know
what's what,
and that's that.
She's never been drug
from the fireplace rug
by any two-legged lug
all aflap
to somebody's lap,
because she has claws

sharp
as a note from a harp.
Where she sat
that's where she'll sit
and that's that.

All these chants are intensely rhythmic, and spirited performances should be encouraged. Perhaps a bit of dancing or costuming might be appropriate: a cat mask, a classmate performing rhythmic accompaniment, or the like.

The Question Is the Answer

Years ago, I made up what I call "questions without answers." I was thinking of how the huge, deep questions—"What is life?" "Who am I?"—have no conclusive answers or solutions; one is inclined to throw enough small answers at them to fill a bookcase, which is of great value.

In fact, a good, suggestive definition of poetry is "questions without answers"; poetry seeks flashes and stretches of infinite variability and doesn't oversimplify.

I read/perform for the students several striking, differing example pieces.

How come I can't think of a word?
What is a word?
Wait, I do know,
Oh, I know, but what is a word?
Wait, I do know but
What is a word? Do I know?
Wait, I don't know, what is a word?
Do I know?

The first-grade boy who wrote this poem pretended he didn't know what a word was—but he wound up using lots of them. He also demonstrated the zigzag tentativeness of the moment-to-moment mind (as against the pretend dignity of the speechifying mind).

Written by a tenth-grade girl, the following poem about the mind both contrasts with and resembles the previous poem.

What Is in the Mind?

In the midst of the hollow
something scratches as though it were the wind,
beating the door, tearing the soul.

Like a sealed box:
nothing may enter;
nothing may leave.

Like an empty skull
it pulls the sea.

The following example, written by a seventh-grade boy in a Migrant Program, shows the beauty and lyricism of the inquiring mind.

Where does the wind go?
I don't know, where does the
wind go? O I know where the wind
goes, in a cave. No no,
I can't know where the
wind goes. O I know where the
wind goes, in a hole.
No no, I don't know where it goes.
O I think the wind goes

around the world. No no, the
wind goes around you.

After a few more examples, I ask the kids to choose questions they would like to explore. And they do. It's one of my very best lead-in ideas: it encourages, structurally, the search for multiple truths at any given point.

Getting Used to Time

"I used to, but now" has long been a popular exercise. Although it is very simple, it implies complex changes. Advise students not to write the obvious—"I used to be a kitten, but now I'm a cat"—and tell them that each metamorphosis needs a twist that opens up into newness for readers or listeners. To show students what you mean, read this example, written by a first-grade girl in less than fifteen minutes.

> I used to be a can but now I'm recycled!
> I used to be an egg but now I'm cracked.
> I used to be the sun but now I'm the moon.
> I used to be a horse but now I'm dogfood!
> I used to be paint but now I'm a painting.

The following couplet is by a first-grade boy.

> I used to be a thought but now I'm poetry.
> I used to be dead but now I'm alive.

This example by a second-grade girl takes the exercise into tricky identity realms.

> I used to be Mom but now I'm Dad.

I used to be a baby but now I'm a pacifier.
I used to be a puppy and I still am.

Encourage students to add commentary to the ground statement, as in this example by a fifth-grade girl.

I used to be an apple but now I'm a staple.
Ow! That person is pressing really
Hard like the teeth everybody was using to bite me when I
    was an apple.
I used to be number 6 but now I'm number 7. I wish I
    could be 8—I miss being an
even number.

Another variation on this exercise—"I used to be afraid of, but now"—has the added virtue of demystifying fear. A third-grade girl wrote this piece.

I used to be afraid of clumsiness, people with long
    fingernails.
Now I'm afraid of my Mom falling in love and leaving me....
I used to be afraid of my sister.
Now I'm afraid of things like surgery, drugs—and my Mom
    getting remarried.
I used to be afraid of Frankenstein.

And from another third-grade girl.

I used to be afraid of the toilet.
The blowdryer.
I used to be afraid of taking a shower.
I used to be afraid of being home by myself.
I used to be afraid of our dog Shadow when he tried to bite

me while I was getting on the monkey bars.
I used to be afraid of the bus driver in first grade.
I used to be afraid of boys with long hair that would ride
the bus.
Now I'm afraid of the bad dream lady who lives under
the bed.

One could complete an autobiography using this form. Other emotions can, of course, also be brought into play, with rich results: I used to like, love, eat, see, et cetera. This exercise used to be considered especially appropriate for very young children because of its apparent simplicity, but now it's seen to be good for all ages because of its inner complexity. As an eighty-year-old, I find it as useful as light.

Saving the Planet

One April 22 many years ago, I was driving to an elementary school wondering how to urge the kids to honor and participate in Earth Day. A lifelong nature lover, I decided to ask them to write list poems of "things to save." Some points have developed over time.

1. Emphasize detail. Tell the students not to save just "trees" but to save "that gnarled old apple tree behind Grandma's house that I've climbed every summer gobbling cool red/ white fruit and that I once fell out of and broke my collar-bone, but I love it as much as I love the blue sky."

2. Talk about the need to care for, not destroy, nature— just a little. Avoid preachiness. Ask the class, "Is there any nature in this room?" Some child will say, "Us!" Yes! People try to pull themselves out of nature, but we're all part of it, whichever way we turn. The wood and paper

come from trees, the glass is made of sand, the plastic and metals are dug out of the ground, et cetera.

3. Point out to students that colorful language, rhythm, and variety in their poems will help bring the poems to life and have an effect, perhaps even an effect on the world.

4. I advise the students that, keeping in mind that nature is threaded and lit and vapored all through their lives, they might include in their "things to save" poems items that are not obviously "nature." You'll find many in these examples, as in this poem by a fifth-grade boy.

Things to Save

The darkness of shadow-like wolves
Darting across the night like
Black bullets, and the moon
Shimmering like a sphere of glowing mass.
Let us save lush grass, green
As green can be, but, best of all,
Imagination glowing with joy aha,
Images it is composed of, it is this
That is making the Earth grow
With flavor and destination.

A fifth-grade boy uses his powers of description to illuminate the treasure the world is.

Please Save

All the little birds chirping like tiny gold chimes
The cats romping in my daydreams during class
Giraffes stretching necks to reach leaves as green as the

hat on a leprechaun's head
The little fish the size of a fingernail and the whale as big
    as two buses
Sunlight shining off of the turquoise lake looking like tiny
    pieces of gold being
sprinkled out of the sky...

In the following poem, a fifth-grade girl mixes her own daily plea-sures with the natural world that spreads out all around her. She brings out the quality of "all-oneness."

Things to Save

I'd like to save the sweet chocolaty candy bars that melt in
    your mouth,
The warm cozy pillow that you can't wait to sleep on.
I'd like to save green meadows that you run barefoot
    across running and running
until you collapse on the wet soft grass,
The hot days when you try to eat ice cream but it melts
    and plops on your foot,
I'd like to save the amusement parks where you go on a
    twisty ride and throw up
all over yourself but that's just what you thought would
    happen,
I'd like to save the little green bug my big brother
    viciously killed six months ago,
I'd like to save the world all green and blue and beautiful,
I'd like to save the little things that everyone enjoys.

This is a writing idea that I pursue during any and every part of the year because every day is Earth Day.

Examples and Variety

I use sixty to eighty different writing prompts in schools. This does not count the endless collaborations, which are a story in themselves. When writing bits or single lines of a poem (or sentences of prose) in a pass-around style, children can't help but see (and generally enjoy) that there's a huge possible diversity of places to go, wherever a person is. Certainly there is keen value to the opposite sense: that of seeking the essential thought or vision in a thing or situation or motion. I think that education—and art is a part of the heart of education—must lead into both at once: rigor and vigor, the comprehension of a blue sky and the specialty of a bird, the dimension that contradiction offers.

One could say the opening-up sense leads to the world; the closing-down sense leads to a diamond, which can be a world in itself. Poetry is, among many other things, defined by its climbing or riding up and down the fractals.

Another of my very favorite staples is a writing activity I call "poems on poems on poems." It's a good final exercise in a series but can also fit anywhere (as can poetry itself). I say, "We're going to write about poetry but not abstractly. Please don't simply write, 'I like poetry because it helps me express myself' or, contrariwise, 'I dislike poetry because it's boring.' Turn it into images: 'When I write poetry, at first my brain feels like an old rusted piece of junk in the field. Maybe the mice build nests in it. But then I get going, and my brain is like a racecar zooming through the Salt Flats at 300 mph, spitting out cinders.'"

This can prompt so many possibilities! You can mention categories: comparisons (simile, metaphor), stories, fantasy, acrostics, warnings, bright sound bites, analyses (colorful), and many others, including students' own inventions.

A sixth-grade boy in New York City wrote this lovely comparison.

A poem is like a
Slow
Flash of light
Because it
Comes to you piece
By piece.

World by word—marvelous! *A Slow Flash of Light* became the title of a book of children's writings on poetry that I put together. One of the many approaches to this exercise is telling a story in which poetry is personified. A person hears a knock on the door and opens it—and there's Poetry! What does it look like? An avalanche of ice? A little bug trying to get into the brain? A ten-foot-tall goddess wearing purple robes? The person invites Poetry in for tea and cookies. What does Poetry do? Tell secrets of life in a deep, sable voice? Run around the table and try to eat the person up?

I often use a poem by Billy Collins, a former US poet laureate, to help illustrate the story mode of writing about poetry. Here's the poem, which dramatizes the crucial implication that the "real meaning" of a poem is much more than a "confession" of "meaning."

Introduction to Poetry

I ask them to take a poem
and hold it up to the light
like a color slide

or press an ear against its hive.

I say drop a mouse into a poem
and watch him probe his way out,

or walk inside the poem's room
and feel the walls for a light switch.

I want them to waterski
across the surface of a poem
waving at the author's name on the shore.

But all they want to do
is tie the poem to a chair with rope
and torture a confession out of it.

They begin by beating it with a hose
to find out what it really means.

What better way to show that poetry is not just words but a living creature!
     Following are a few of the most inspiring "poems on poems" I've collected over the years. This one was written by a high-school boy.

Poetry is a rabid butterfly
     clawing at your eyes.
Poetry is spackle
     filling the holes in your emotions.
Poetry is a large Newt
     eating the crickets of reality.
Poetry is a twister
     ripping you away from your small farm in Kansas.
Poetry is a hermit's left shoe
     full of holes but still in use.
Poetry is simply Poetry.

Some might not term this work inspirational, but it can definitely help liberate the imagination.

Here's another, by a fifth-grade ranch boy in Idaho; it rises directly from his life.

> Poetry is like wind blowing you away
> and rain hitting you on the head, and riding
> horses in the rain and snow.
> Roping cattle in the mud
> and throwing hay in the thunder
> and lightning.

A sixth-grade girl in New York City wrote this.

> Poetry is like
> having a snake
> in your room
> and you don't know what to do.

This piece shows that poetry isn't just life's frosting but can be intimately scary and mysterious.

A one-liner by a fourth-grade girl is full of originality and implied energy.

> Poetry is like the alphabet talking all at once.

A second-grade girl wrote lines that remind me of a shamanic vision of descent into and return from the nether regions.

> Poetry is like a lake full of glares of the stars.
> The texture makes me like a beautiful woman.
> I like that when I dream.
> I always dream of the lake I see before my eyes.
> Oh-oh oh-oh, I love lakes like that.

Maybe it'll be a magic lake, or stars.
When you think of lakes or rivers or swimming pools or
    oceans—
be careful of the ocean if you dream of there.
I can't stand when I drowned in the lake.

The lake said, "Oh, did she have to die?"

I can't stand people who die.

The lake spits me out and I come back to life.

Oh I am beautiful when I get out of the lake.
He dresses me up beautiful.
How can I repay?

A Word About Collaborations

Collaborative poems, wherein (mostly) the papers are passed during composition between two or more students, can certainly introduce new kinds of thinking, though these new ways are built out of previous knowledge. Pass-around poems can be done fruitfully in an endless variety of ways: switch papers after an acrostic line, after a set number of words, after a sentence, after a fragment, after a covered-up line (Exquisite Corpse), after an equal sign. There are many more variations. Also collaborative are mistranslations, insertions of announced words, collage techniques, placing words out of order in a grid, writing what fits in one exhalation of breath or what a person sees upon opening his or her eyes, et cetera. This variety in itself encourages students to think of their poetry as a vast range of potentialities.

    Collaborating with other people—or with the world and the words it gives off—can result in wonderful works of art. Such collaborations can strengthen students' ability to write wonderful works on their own and can lead them into discovering the surreal within their real. These new connections, many of which arise from chance or spontaneity, are often recognized, in time, as being real and important.

Permission to Wrap It Up

After introducing all these exercises at Casey Middle School, I asked Val Wheeler for her teacherly insights. She said that I had offered the kids a structured permission, which was good because total freedom wouldn't "fly" with them. She also said that she had learned in the sessions the power of a routine: each day, the same basic shape (introduction, description, examples, writing time, comments) with variations. This permission could be productively combined with different stuff tumbling through, as in a mountain stream. In nature, the predictable can, with its secret complexity, set up the unpredictable, give it ground to spring from. Distinct sprays and ripples, open atmosphere.

Val showed me her favorite pedagogical book, *The Having of Wonderful Ideas*, by her former teacher Eleanor Duckworth, who maintains, "The having of wonderful ideas is what I consider to be the essence of intellectual development." This, clearly, can happen only in an atmosphere of open exploration. Duckworth also says that "knowing the right answer" is the most passive of the virtues. In perfect correctness, there's no risk; it's automatic, thoughtless, and overrated.

Expansion

Permission, by its nature, opens up process. Speaking on the basis of scientific experiments, Duckworth writes, "Surprise, puzzlement, excitement, struggle, anticipation, and dawning certainty—these are the matter of intelligent thought." And, I add, they're the energy that matters in poems.

I interviewed some of Val's eighth-graders. A circle of eight, the students were a nice mix of Anglos and Latinos(as), boys and girls, extroverts and introverts. I asked what they thought about the poetry sessions we'd had. One boy said, "It was morning. I was so tired, I was random," which made me feel there is, after all, a virtue in exhaustion. A girl said she'd used "engaging prompts that kicked up a whole new thought process." They all liked the pass-arounds. "In 'I Am,' other people's thoughts melded with my ideas," explained another student. "You could hear what everyone thought." Others said that hearing classmates' lines gave them new rhythms and that they felt a sense of spontaneity and sudden insight. "Nothing triggers it," said the first boy. "It's really sudden."

We investigated further by doing a collaboration based on "The poetry was like..." We traded lines and sat in a circle. Here's an excerpt.

> The poetry was like the index of the world.
> Wrestling with a cloud.
> Inside-out-ness.
> Poetry is like Mike Jones saying, "I need a dime."
> Like grass painted purple.
> The poetry was like getting slapped by reality.
> The poetry was like eating and never getting full.
> The poetry was like a paper written tradeoff by the
>   opposite of God and the opposite of the Devil.
> Like playing checkers in a hurricane.
> Flying when your feet are glued to the ground.
>
> Like stepping on grapes.
> Swimming in teacups.
> The poetry was like a chair becoming alive.

The poetry was like Mike Jones singing, "I need a dime."

The poetry was like munching on knowledge.

Like animals all running through a forest.

A green sun.

A funny voice.

The poetry was like black stripes on a tiger.

It was like a black, stray line.

Inviting the Personal

It takes an invitation to activate the personal. Children and other people are made to realize that personal expression is generally not wanted. Other children cry, "Who cares!" Adults and near-adults gravitate to generalizations, thinking generalizations are larger than perceptions, whereas they're simply easier. This assumption leads to clichés, personal language that has lost personality through excessive repetition. Sometimes people use clichés because they are afraid to do anything other than join what seems to be the good sense of the majority. Other powerful inhibitions to personal expression may include the shyness caused by being in a cultural minority. Of course, the personal can easily be overindulged. The best writing is a balancing act between the subjective and the objective.

A girl at Casey said, "I never knew how to come up with something to write a poem about. After the lessons and demonstrations, I realized that a poem is about anything you want it to be. I'll never forget that."

At Casey, the students and I did a class-wide collaboration that speaks very much to this spirit of permission. Here are a few lines from that poem.

Permission

The feeling you get in the bottom of your stomach when
    you are on a rollercoaster.
Permission is the blank white page in front of you.
Permission is a sail for your boat.
Permission is the black squares on a checkerboard.
Permission is everything around you.
Permission is a red dot in a river of black.
Permission is non-refundable.
Permission is a mission.

Poetry is magic talk. Teaching and learning are, in part, opening gifts.

Life as Primary Text

James Kass

Or

How to start a nonprofit and sustain it for fifteen years during the height of the dot-com boom and bust (and re-boom and re-bust) when you're twenty-six. With no money. And the nonprofit is about brown kids, mostly, and poetry, mostly. Which everyone assures you there is no support for. And wait, they ask, what is it that you do exactly? You do that full-time? Really?

Right now, all across the United States, young people are picking up pens, filling blank pages, grabbing microphones, and stepping proudly onto stages to declare themselves poets.

These young writers come from all over the nation: from big cities and border towns, from Native American reservations and suburbs, from the Northeast, the Deep South, the mountains, the plains, the desert—the entire panorama. This is (quite literally) the voice of twenty-first-century America. It's a voice spoken with a passion and intelligence that transcends race, class, ethnicity, gender orientation, language, geography, politics, and history. It's a voice that speaks to the possible.

Sixteen years ago I started a poetry organization. Or, more accurately, I set up a few opportunities for young people to take free poetry-writing workshops in San Francisco. At that point, I wasn't really thinking "organization"; I figured it would be a part-time thing while I finished up my master's in fine arts in writing at San Francisco State, and worked as a teacher and a low-level PR person at the local PBS affiliate. In other words, something that would keep me busy before I moved on to my real career.

Little did I know that sixteen years later it would be an organization, and a $2-million-a-year one at that, serving tens of thousands of young writers across the country annually. And it would most certainly be a career.

This organization—Youth Speaks—has become a landing place for hungry young poets. Youth Speaks has been featured in media across the country, including two PBS documentaries and two seasons of original programming on HBO. Our poets have performed at the White House, the Sundance Film Festival, and pretty much every city in the country and every continent on the globe. The organization has created countless opportunities for teenagers to share poetry with many of our national literary, entertainment, political, and educational luminaries—from Robert Redford and Arne Duncan to Dave Eggers, James Earl Jones, Nancy Pelosi, Al Gore, Amiri Baraka, Bill Clinton, Nikki Giovanni, and seventy mayors from cities large and small. The young people proclaim that it has helped inspire a new generation to embrace and redefine poetry as a written and performative activity that speaks to them and through them. Some talk about the ways in which Youth Speaks has made visible the voices of thousands of youth who had previously been invisible.

Regardless, young writers today are helping shape contemporary poetry. Audiences are swelling. The art form is helping to create structure around provocative discussions and via innovations of form. Spoken-word events unveil deeper levels of civic and cultural engagement among young people while increasing literacy and providing incredibly dynamic evenings that celebrate the creativity and passion of young people.

But before all this, it was 1996, and I was in grad school pursuing my MFA.

I loved teaching, although I found the frustrations of the bureaucracy of classroom teaching uninspiring. But I learned in the classroom that if you're going to work with kids, you have to be present in every moment. Kids listen to everything you say, whether it seems like it or not. So I knew that if I was going to start working with young writers, I had to take it seriously.

It started with a name: "Youth Speaks," I wrote down. "Because the next generation can speak for itself." From the beginning, the organization was about creating free and public spaces for young people to find, develop, and present themselves. I found some donated community spaces, wrote down my ideas, gathered up a few of my peers, and talked some public high schools into letting me visit their campuses with some poet friends. We performed poems to recruit kids to our first series of free afterschool writing workshops at the San Francisco Public Library and at two community-based nonprofit art centers.

Previously I'd worked in an afterschool arts center. I'd done a little behind-the-scenes jazz production work, a little concert promotion in college, some low-level public relations at the local PBS/NPR station in the education department, a little classroom teaching, and I was interning at a literary magazine. So I knew enough about how to write a press release, put together a cheap brochure, and even scour the city for donated computers that we planned to give out to the first twenty kids who took at least twenty hours of writing workshops.

I'd always liked the idea of an afterschool arts program for teenagers, though I had no idea what the day-to-day management of such a program would look like. I really wanted to make sure that the workshops were free and open to kids who didn't have exposure to arts in their schools and weren't attendees of private arts classes. That meant, essentially, that my friends and I would have to do the work, and get all the spaces and materials donated, to keep it all free. And we vowed to keep it fun, too.

Yes, I went to graduate school. Yes, my writing was crucial to my sense of who I was. Like Joan Didion said, "Writing has taught me practically everything I know."

But the thing was, my graduate writing program, like so many across the country, lacked real diversity.

I was seeing—at least through the narrow prism of my MFA program—just who was being groomed to have a voice in this world. Those of us in graduate-level workshops were all trying to be professional writers, in one manifestation or the other. But our programs were not representative of the demographics of the late-twentieth-century Bay Area. So part of launching Youth Speaks was about creating a free and safe space where young people outside the sphere of other writing and arts programs could have the opportunities to be nurtured and supported in the development of their artistic voices.

Around that same time, I went to my first poetry slam. I already knew how much I loved to hear poetry out loud, but I had grown increasingly frustrated by just how poorly some poets read their work. I had been to dozens upon dozens of boring poetry readings (San Francisco is a terrific place to hear poetry read, boring and otherwise), and they were driving me crazy. I loved the work, but some of these poets were so insular in their sharing of their poems that I preferred reading them on my own, rather than hearing them ruin it for me.

But at the poetry slam, I saw something different. Not all the work was fantastic, but it was certainly the most diverse group of poets sharing a stage I'd ever seen. And it was not boring. The poets were youngish, very engaging, passionate about their work, and unafraid to share themselves with the crowd, to open themselves up to both positive and negative critique.

The poetry slam was the first place I saw an unadulterated celebration of language and writing and poetry that was raucous and fun and diverse. I'd been to plenty of book festivals and writing workshops, but this was different. This was alive.

One of the things I should mention is that when I started Youth Speaks, I figured that maybe over the years fifty or so young teenagers would participate, and when I got my degree, it would be a way for me to remain connected to arts and to education. I figured that it would give me some good experience for the many other things I wanted to do. I figured I could keep doing this Youth Speaks thing part time. But as it turned out, fifty young people showed up in the first two months. So I changed my thinking. I started reading books about fund-raising. I took free courses on how to run a nonprofit organization.

The population of young people coming out to the workshops continued to grow. I began talking to the people who ran the small theater hosting the adult poetry slam, and we began moving on the idea of holding a poetry slam for teenagers during National Poetry Month in 1997.

The poetry slams I was attending were exciting, and I began to see that the slam made fun of the idea of competitive poetry and at the same time challenged the writers to reach new heights in their writing and performance. Meanwhile, the young writers in the workshops were all responding positively to the videos and tapes I brought in of poets reading their work, so why not give them an opportunity to be celebrated in public in a fun, competitive way?

Again, I thought it would be great if ten kids came, but for that inaugural Youth Speaks Teen Poetry Slam, more than one hundred poets participated, drawing close to six hundred audience members over three weeks, selling out the small Mission District theater and getting a front-page article in the arts section of the *San Francisco Chronicle*. And, it turned out, this was the first teen poetry slam in the country.

So then we had more events, and more kids started showing up. And they kept showing up, saying incredibly provocative, thoughtful, and creative things in the workshops and from the stages. These young poets were writing poems about the environment, about education, about love, life, death. They were writing poems about abuse and power and lack of power—it was really an amazing array of voices. Then schools started calling me—instead of me calling them—because teachers were beginning to see their students grab on to the possibilities of poetry. Other theaters wanted young poets on their stages, and the San Francisco Bay Area Book Festival wanted the poets to read with Lawrence Ferlinghetti. Then people wanted to publish the poems, and to hear them again. Some foundations and companies even wanted to start giving us money.

Soon after, I set up a nonprofit, 501 (c)(3) organization whose mission includes working with young people to write poetry, to read poetry, and to share poetry. To expand poetry. To be active in the world while doing so.

And while the successes have been tremendous, I often measure them by looking back at the very first public Youth Speaks program. In October 1996, I took three poets with me to George Washington High School in San Francisco, a large public school with a diverse population.

One of the teachers had set us up in a one-hundred-seat auditorium. I had invited a few poets I knew to come perform a few poems, do a quick writing workshop, and let the kids know about the opportunities Youth Speaks was offering. I introduced my friends—we were a diverse group in our mid-twenties—and said we were poets. I asked if anyone in the room wrote poetry. Two hands crept up slowly. Everyone else in the room stared at us. After our performance and workshop, which went well and recruited three or four kids to the workshops, the teachers wanted to talk to us about how they hated teaching poetry because they didn't really know how to teach it. Kids, they said, had no interest at all. They were glad to see the spark we'd ignited in the room and hoped we could keep it up.

Recently, I went back to Washington High to observe how the school-visit program was doing. This was fifteen years after the first one. The one-hundred-seat auditorium was the same, but this time, when the Poet Mentor asked how many of the students wrote poetry, about half the kids in the room raised their hands. The teacher had been trying to get us to their school for months, but we had been all booked up, because now poetry is a hot thing on high-school campuses.

I'm not going to say that poetry's increased popularity is only because of Youth Speaks, but I will certainly say that Youth Speaks has helped inspire young people and teachers to think about poetry in a whole new way. Over the years, our numbers have continued to grow. We are now in more than fifty public middle and high schools each year in the Bay Area alone. Thousands of teenagers come out to our writing workshops, our monthly open mics, and our poetry slams. We have audiences in the thousands for our bigger events, and the work has spread nationwide.

In 1999, two people we'd worked with in the Bay Area moved to New York and Ann Arbor, respectively. Both opened up programs based on the model in the Bay, and both programs are still thriving.

In July 2012, Youth Speaks will hold its sixteenth annual Brave New Voices International Youth Poetry Slam Festival, an event that takes place in a different city each year. Each year so far, more than six hundred young writers from close to sixty cities have deeply engaged with the power of poetry. These six hundred young poets are selected through local events featuring tens of thousands of poets who want to go, all of whom are part of a generation hungry for the experience that spoken word can offer.

This is what I take away every year when I'm witnessing new writers come out to workshops, storm the stages at open mics, and take part in this amazing Brave New Voices Festival: the poetry of young people is helping to define the new American voice. These young writers are talking about critical issues in their lives, and they are doing so from every corner of the country. They are writing in the styles and sounds that make sense to them. They are tapping into the continuum of poetry but do not feel bound by it. Poetry has become a liberating force in their lives, and it allows them to put their identities, voices, power, and imaginations center stage.

I've heard more cheers and support for the new young poets who are reading something really important to them for the first time, the pages shaking, their voices cracking, than I've heard for the super-polished poet who is technically proficient but isn't really saying anything.

The way young people approach the word is a thing of real consequence to them, and this is what inspires me and, I imagine, the thousands of adults who keep coming out to support these emerging writers. The teens who are putting pen to paper and stepping onto stages take the opportunity to be heard seriously. They are telling real stories, sharing real joy, exposing real pain. To them, poetry is not a luxury. It's a necessity.

A couple of years into the life of Youth Speaks, we'd done a number of collaborations with City Lights. Lawrence Ferlinghetti—famously a curmudgeon—came up to me and said, "James, what I love about Youth Speaks is that these kids are doing what [the Beats] used to talk about. We believed that anyone could be a poet, that poets can write about anything they want to write about. It didn't need to belong to the universities or to the upper echelons. Poetry is for everyone. This is beautiful."

I'll never forget that.

I'm a product of creative writing programs. I have undergraduate and graduate degrees in writing and have been a student in dozens of writing workshops at two major universities. Through the years, I developed my own thoughts on how workshops should happen, who should be in them, and what they should be for. But it wasn't until the Youth Speaks workshops started filling up that I really began to see the poem-building space as sacred.

Where else can young people define themselves, using the simplest of technologies: pen, paper, and ink?

Young people tell me time and again that it was in these poetry workshops and performances that, for the first time, they got to write and speak about themselves. Not in reaction to anything, just in a space where they could say who they are. What matters to them. How they'd like to live their lives. How they think they are living their lives. What they love and what they want to change. It's a space that simply asks them to write— not to write well or write poorly, just to write. And to take it seriously.

Our approach to this is pretty simple: We offer a lot of programs. Teenagers just need to show up, and they do. And they keep showing up. It is now typical for us to sell out three-thousand-seat venues for poetry readings by teenagers on a Saturday night in downtown San Francisco. This kind of thing is happening all across the country.

Come hear them. They're pretty incredible.

Teaching Children to Write Poetry[1]

Kenneth Koch

Last winter and the spring before that I taught poetry writing to children at P.S. 61 on East 12th Street between Avenue B and Avenue C in Manhattan. ... I was curious to see what could be done for children's poetry. I knew some things about teaching adults to write, for I had taught writing classes for a number of years at Columbia and the New School. But I didn't know about children. Adult writers had read a lot, wanted to be writers, and were driven by all the usual forces writers are driven by. I knew how to talk to them, how to inspire them, how to criticize their work. What to say to an eight-year-old with no commitment to literature?

One thing that encouraged me was how playful and inventive children's talk sometimes was. They said true things in fresh and surprising ways. Another was how much they enjoyed making works of art—drawings, paintings, and collages. I was aware of the breakthrough in teaching children art some forty years ago. I had seen how my daughter and other

---

1. Kenneth Koch, excerpts from *Wishes, Lies, and Dreams: Teaching Children to Write Poetry* (New York: Chelsea House, 1970 and HarperCollins, 1999).

children profited from the new ways of helping them discover and use their natural talents. That hadn't happened yet in poetry. Some children's poetry was marvelous, but most seemed uncomfortably imitative of adult poetry or else childishly cute. It seemed restricted somehow, and it obviously lacked the happy, creative energy of children's art. I wanted to find, if I could, a way for children to get as much from poetry as they did from painting.

I: Ideas for Poems

My adult writing courses had relied on what I somewhat humorously (for its grade-school sound) called "assignments." Every week I asked the writers in the workshop to imitate a particular poet, write on a certain theme, use certain forms and techniques: imitations of Pound's *Cantos*, poems based on dreams, prose poems, sestinas, translations. The object was to give them experiences which would teach them something new and indicate new possibilities for their writing. Usually I found these adult writers had too narrow a conception of poetry; these "assignments" could broaden it. This system also made for good class discussions of student work: everyone had faced the same problem (translating, for example) and was interested in the solutions.

I thought this would also work with children, though because of their age, lack of writing experience, and different motivation, I would have to find other assignments. I would also have to go easy on the word "assignment," which wasn't funny in grade school. ... Another new problem was how to get the grade-school students excited about poetry. My adult students already were; but these children didn't think of themselves as writers, and poetry to most of them seemed something difficult and remote. Finding the right ideas for poems would help, as would working out the best way to proceed in class. I also needed poems to read to them that would give them ideas, inspire them, make them want to write.

I know all this now, but I sensed it only vaguely the first time I found myself facing a class. It was a mixed group of fifth and sixth graders. I was afraid that nothing would happen. I felt the main thing I had to do was to get them started writing, writing anything, in a way that would be pleasant and exciting for them. Once that happened, I thought, other good things might follow.

I asked the class to write a poem together, everybody contributing one line. The way I conceived of the poem, it was easy to write, had rules like a game, and included the pleasures without the anxieties of competitiveness. No one had to worry about failing to write a good poem because everyone was only writing one line; and I specifically asked the children not to put their names on their line. Everyone was to write the line on a sheet of paper and turn it in; then I would read them all as a poem. I suggested we make some rules about what should be in every line; this would help give the final poem unity, and it would help the children find something to say. I gave an example, putting a color in every line, then asked them for others. We ended up with the regulations that every line should contain a color, a comic-strip character, and a city or country; also the line should begin with the words "I wish."

I collected the lines, shuffled them, and read them aloud as one poem. Some lines obeyed the rules and some didn't; but enough were funny and imaginative to make the whole experience a good one—

> I wish I was Dick Tracy in a black suit in England
> I wish that I were a Supergirl with a red cape; the city of
> Mexico will be where I live.
> I wish that I were Veronica in South America. I wish that
> I could see the blue sky...

The children were enormously excited by writing the lines and even more by hearing them read as a poem. They were talking, waving, blushing, laughing, and bouncing up and down. "Feelings at P.S. 61," the title they chose, was not a great poem, but it made them feel like poets and it made them want to write more.

I had trouble finding my next good assignment. I had found out how to get the children started but didn't yet know how to provide them with anything substantial in the way of themes or techniques. I didn't know what they needed. I tried a few ideas that worked well with adults, such as writing in the style of other poets, but they were too difficult and in other ways inappropriate. Fortunately for me, Mrs. Wiener, the fourth grade teacher, asked me to suggest some poetry ideas for her to give her class. (I wasn't seeing them regularly at that time—only the sixth graders.) ... I suggested she try a poem in which every line began with "I wish." It had worked well for class poems and maybe it would work too for individual poems, without the other requirements. I asked her to tell the children that their wishes could be real or crazy, and not to use rhyme.

A few days later she brought me their poems, and I was very happy. The poems were beautiful, imaginative, lyrical, funny, touching. They brought in feelings I hadn't seen in the children's poetry before. They reminded me of my own childhood and of how much I had forgotten about it. They were all innocence, elation, and intelligence. They were unified poems: it made sense where they started and where they stopped. And they had a lovely music—

> I wish I had a pony with a tail like hair
> I wish I had a boyfriend with blue eyes and black hair
>   I would be so glad...
> —Milagros Diaz, 4[2]

> Sometimes I wish I had my own kitten
> Sometimes I wish I owned a puppy

---

2. Here, as elsewhere in this introduction, the number following the child's name indicates the grade he or she was in when the poem was written.

Sometimes I wish we had a color T.V.
Sometimes I wish for a room of my own.
And I wish all my sisters would disappear.
And I wish we didn't have to go to school.
And I wish my little sister would find her nightgown.
And I wish even if she didn't she wouldn't wear mine.

—Erin Harold, 4

It seemed I had stumbled onto a marvelous idea for children's poems. I realized its qualities as I read over their work. I don't mean to say the idea wrote the poems: the children did. The idea helped them to find that they could do it, by giving them a form that would give their poem unity and that was easy and natural for them to use: beginning every line with "I wish." With such a form, they could relax after every line and always be starting up afresh. They could also play variations on it, as Erin Harold does in her change from "Sometimes" to "And." Just as important, it gave them something to write about which really interested them: the private world of their wishes. One of the main problems children have as writers is not knowing what to write about. Once they have a subject they like, but may have temporarily forgotten about, like wishing, they find a great deal to say. The subject was good, too, because it encouraged them to be imaginative and free. There are no limits to what one can wish: to fly, to be smothered in diamonds, to burn down the school. And wishes, moreover, are a part of what poetry is always about.

...

Once I understood why the Wish Poem worked so well, I had a much clearer idea of what to look for. A poetry idea should be easy to understand, it should be immediately interesting, and it should bring something new into the children's poems. This could be new subject matter, new sense awareness, new experience of language or poetic form. I looked for other techniques or themes that were, like wishes, a natural and customary part of poetry. I thought of comparisons and then of sounds, and I had the children write a poem about each. As in the Wish Poems, I suggested a repetitive form to help give their poems unity: putting a comparison or a sound in every line. Devoting whole poems to comparisons and sounds gave the children a chance to try out all kinds, and to be as free and as extravagant as they liked. There was no theme or argument with which the sounds or comparisons had to be in accord: they could be experimented with for the pleasures they gave in themselves. In teaching painting an equivalent might be having children paint pictures which were only contrasting stripes or gobs of color.

In presenting these poetry ideas to the children I encouraged them to take chances. I said people were aware of many resemblances which were beautiful and interesting but which they didn't talk about because they seemed too far-fetched and too silly. But I asked them specifically to look for strange comparisons—if the grass seemed to them like an Easter egg they should say so. I suggested they compare something big to something small, something in school to something out of school, something unreal to something real, something human to something not human. I wanted to rouse them out of the timidity I felt they had about being "crazy" or "silly" in front of an adult in school. There is no danger of children writing merely nonsensical poems if one does this; the truth they find in freely associating is a greater pleasure to them—

> A breeze is like the sky is coming to you...
>
> —Iris Torres, 4

> The sea is like a blue velvet coat...
>
> —Argentina Wilkinson, 4

> The flag is as red, white, and blue as the sun's reflection...
>
> —Marion Mackles, 3

Children often need help in starting to feel free and imaginative about a particular theme. Examples can give them courage. I asked my fourth graders to look at the sky (it was overcast) and to tell me what thing in the schoolroom it most resembled. Someone's dress, the geography book—but best of all was the blackboard which, covered with erased chalk smear, did look very much like it. Such question games make for an excited atmosphere and start the children thinking like poets. For the Noise Poem I used another kind of classroom example. I made some noises and asked the children what they sounded like. I crumpled up a piece of paper. "It sounds like paper." "Rain on the roof." "Somebody typing." I hit the chair with a ruler and asked what word that was like. Someone said "hit." What else? "Tap." I said close your eyes and listen again and tell me which of those two words it sounds more like, hit or tap. "It sounds more like tap." I asked them to close their eyes again and listen for words it sounded like that had nothing to do with tap. "Hat, snap, trap, glad, badger." With the primary graders[3] I asked, How does a bee go? "Buzz." What sounds like a bee but doesn't mean anything like buzz? "Fuzz, does, buzzard, cousin." The children were quick to get these answers and quick to be swept up into associating words and sounds—

> A clink is like a drink of pink water...
> —Alan Constant, 5

> A yoyo sounds like a bearing rubbing in a machine...
> —Roberto Marcilla, 6

Before they had experimented with the medium of poetry in this way, what the children wrote tended to be a little narrow and limited in its means—but not afterwards. Their writing quickly became richer and more colorful.

...

---

3. At P.S. 61 some first and second grade classes are combined in one primary grade.

Another strategy I'd used more or less instinctively, encouraging the children to be free and even "crazy" in what they wrote, also had especially good results. They wrote freely and crazily and they liked what they were doing because they were writing beautiful and vivid things. The trouble with a child's not being "crazy" is that he will instead be conventional; and it is a truth of poetry that a conventional image, for example, is not, as far as its effect is concerned, an image at all. When I read "red as a rose," I don't see either red or a rose; actually such a comparison should make me see both vividly and make me see something else as well, some magical conjunction of red and rose. It's another story when I read "orange as a rose" or even "yellow as a rose"—I see the flower and the color and something beyond. It is the same when one writes as when one reads: creating in himself the yellow and the rose and the yellow rose naturally gives a child more pleasure and experience than repeating a few words he has already heard used together. As I hope I've made clear, the best way to help children write freely is by encouragement, by examples, and by various other inspiring means. It can't be done by fiat, that is, by merely telling them to be "imaginative and free."

...

II: Teaching Children to Write Poetry

Some things about teaching children to write poetry I knew in advance, instinctively or from having taught adults, and others I found out in the classroom. Most important, I believe, is taking children seriously as poets. Children have a natural talent for writing poetry and anyone who teaches them should know that. Teaching really is not the right word for what takes place: it is more like permitting the children to discover something they already have. I helped them to do this by removing obstacles, such as the need to rhyme, and by encouraging them in various ways to get tuned in to their own strong feelings, to their spontaneity, their sensitivity, and their carefree inventiveness. At first I was amazed at how well the children wrote, because there was obviously not enough in what I had told them even to begin to account for it. I remember that after I had seen the fourth-grade Wish Poems, I invited their teacher, Mrs. Wiener, to lunch in order to discover her "secret." I thought she must have told her students certain special things to make them write such good poems. But she had done no more than what I had suggested she do: tell the children to begin every line with "I wish," not to use rhyme, and to make the wishes real or crazy. There was one other thing: she had been happy and excited about their doing it and she had expected them to enjoy it too.

I was, as I said, amazed, because I hadn't expected any grade-school children, much less fourth graders, to write so well so soon. I thought I might have some success with sixth graders, but even there I felt it would be best to begin with a small group who volunteered for a poetry workshop. After the fourth-grade Wish Poems, however, and after the Wish and Comparison Poems from the other grades, I realized my mistake. The children in all the grades, primary through sixth, wrote poems which they enjoyed and I enjoyed. Treating them like poets was not a case of humorous but effective diplomacy, as I had first thought; it was the right way to treat them because it corresponded to the truth. A little humor, of course, I left in. Poetry was serious, but we joked and laughed a good deal; it was serious because it was such a pleasure to write. Treating them as poets enabled me to encourage them and egg them on in a non-teacherish way—as an admirer and a fellow worker rather than as a boss. It shouldn't be difficult for a teacher to share this attitude once it is plain how happily and naturally the students take to writing.

There are other barriers besides rhyme and meter that can keep children from writing freely and enjoying it. One is feeling they have to spell everything correctly. Stopping to worry about spelling a word can cut off a fine flow of ideas. So can having to avoid words one can't spell. Punctuation can also be an interference, as can neatness. Good poetic ideas often come as fast as one can write; in the rush to get them down there may be no time for commas or for respecting a margin. All these matters can be attended to after the poem is written.

Another barrier is a child's believing that poetry is difficult and remote. Poetry should be talked about in as simple a way as possible and certainly without such bewildering rhetorical terms as *alliteration*, *simile*, and *onomatopoeia*. There are easy, colloquial ways to say all these: words beginning with the same sound, comparisons using *like* or *as*, words that sound like what they mean. Poetry is a mystery, but it is a mystery children can participate in and master, and they shouldn't be kept away from it by hard words.

Again on the subject of language, the various poetry ideas should be presented in words children actually use. I don't think the Wish Poems would have been so successful if I had asked my students to start every line with "I desire." Nor would "My seeming self" and "My true self" have worked well in place of "I Seem To Be / But Really I Am." One should be on the lookout, too, for words and phrases which tell the child what to say and take him away from important parts of his experience: I think "make-believe" and "imaginary" are such words. When I told a teacher at another school about the "I wish" assignment, she said she had done almost the same thing but it hadn't turned out as well. She had had her students write poems in which every line began with "Love is." I've never heard a child say "love is" in my life, so I wasn't surprised that they hadn't responded wholeheartedly.

One bar to free feeling and writing is the fear of writing a bad poem and of being criticized or ridiculed for it. There is also the oppression of being known as not one of the "best." I didn't single out any poems as being best or worst. When I read poems aloud I didn't say whose they were, and I made sure that everyone's work was read every so often. If I praised a line or an image I put the stress on the kind of line or image it was and how exciting it might be for others to try something like that too. That way, I felt, the talent in the room was being used for the benefit of everyone.

The teacher shouldn't correct a child's poems either. If a word or line is unclear, it is fine to ask the child what he meant, but not to change it in order to make it meet one's own standards. The child's poem should be all his own. And of course one shouldn't use a child's poetry to analyze his personal problems. Aside from the scientific folly of so doing, it is sure to make children inhibited about what they write.

...

As in groups of good readers and writers, some children with writing problems are more inclined toward poetry than others; and some who can hardly write are more imaginative poets than many who write without mistakes. What seemed most important was that, of the children I taught, every one had the capacity to write poetry well enough to enjoy it himself and usually well enough to give pleasure to others, whether it was entire poems or surprising and beautiful images, lines, or combinations of words.

The educational advantages of a creative intellectual and emotional activity which children enjoy are clear. Writing poetry makes children feel happy, capable, and creative. It makes them feel more open to understanding and appreciating what others have written (literature). It even makes them want to know how to spell and say things correctly (grammar). Once Mrs. Magnani's students were excited about words, they were dying to know how to spell them. Learning becomes part of an activity they enjoy—when my fifth graders were writing their Poems Using Spanish Words they were eager to know more words than I had written on the board; one girl left the room to borrow a dictionary. Of all these advantages, the main one is how writing poetry makes children feel: creative; original; responsive, yet in command.

IV: Poetry in the Schools

Since children like writing poetry, and since it's such a good thing for them in so many ways, what can be done in the schools to help them write it? One thing is for a poet from outside to come and teach in the schools as I did. Another is for teachers already there to try teaching poetry. At P.S. 61 there was a great change. A lot of children there are writing poetry now who would not have been otherwise, and their feelings about it are different too. They may have had a distant respect for poetry before, but now it belongs to them. They really like it. Some have written twenty or thirty poems and are still raring to go. It is not our mysterious charm for which Ron Padgett and I are wildly applauded when we go into the fifth grade classroom and for which shrieks of joy have greeted us in other classrooms too. It is the subject we bring, and along with that, our enthusiasm for what the students do with it. It occurred to me some time ago that I was as popular and beloved a figure at P.S. 61 as certain art and music teachers had been at my grade school in Cincinnati. And that I was doing more or less what they had done, though in a form of art that, for all its prestige, has been relatively ignored in the schools.

The change in the children is the most evident, but the teachers have changed too. Once they saw what the children were doing, they became interested themselves. They have given their own poetry writing assignments, they put children's poems on bulletin boards along with their artwork, and they have the children read their poems in class and in school assembly. Before, I think, poetry was kind of a dead subject at the school (dormant, anyway). For all their good will, the teachers didn't see a way to connect it with the noisy, small, and apparently prosy creatures they faced in the classroom. But now they have seen the connection, which is that children have a great talent for writing poetry and love to do it.

New York City
January 1970

The Care and Feeding of a Child's Imagination[1]

Ron Padgett

I started teaching poetry writing at P.S. 61, an elementary school in New York City, at the invitation of Kenneth Koch, the poet whose work there has been presented in his book Wishes, Lies, and Dreams. *The program was sponsored by Teachers & Writers Collaborative, a nonprofit group that sends writers into schools to develop new ways of teaching writing. As a hand-to-mouth poet who had never taught, I thought the job sounded challenging but would give me time to write poetry and live my private life. However, as I worked with many different children, I became impressed with the beneficial effects poetry writing was having on their private*

---

1. "The Care and Feeding of a Child's Imagination" was written at the invitation of Phyllis Rosser, an editor at *Ms.* magazine, where it appeared, in the May 1976 issue. Although the piece is a hymn to the pleasures of imaginative writing, it takes a negative turn at the very end, an unfortunate attempt on my part to make the piece acceptable to what I imagined to be the *Ms.* audience.

Editor's note: Ron Padgett, "The Care and Feeding of a Child's Imagination" from *The Straight Line: Writings on Poetry and Poets* (Ann Arbor: The University of Michigan Press, 2000).

*and social selves. I felt I was being given a rare opportunity
for a poet in the twentieth century—to be directly useful to
society without compromising myself.*

I still find it hard to recognize myself when the teacher introduces me
formally to the class as "Mr. Padgett, the poet who is visiting us today...."
I feel dazed as I walk to the blackboard, draw an oval shape on it, and say,
to a group of seventh graders, "This is you." They giggle. "I mean, this is a
blob...." More giggles. "Let this blob represent the you that is your imagi-
nation, your personality, your mind, your Self, whatever there would be
left if your body disappeared." I write the number 24 above it to represent
one day and draw a line through the blob to mark off 8 hours for sleep.
Pointing to the 16 hour part, I say, "This represents your mental self in the
awake state, the you that is here right now. Most people think this part is
the whole story. But when you lie down and go to sleep at night, your
mind keeps on working, just differently, and sometimes very odd things
happen in it." (By now the kids see me zeroing in on the dream-mind.)
"This other part of the mind interests me a lot. When I was little I hated
to go to sleep, but now I love it, because I'm curious to see what's hap-
pening over in that mysterious part of my mind. Last night, for instance,
I dreamed..." and I go on to recount last night's sleep extravaganza. By
the time I'm finished, hands are up, kids anxious to tell me about their
favorite dreams or nightmares, dreams that are repeated or continued
the next night, funny dreams, romantic dreams, or how you can be in a
dream and outside it at the same time. Then I ask, "Were you ever in a
car, or a room, or outdoors, and suddenly you have this creepy feeling,
that this has all happened exactly the same, sometime before?" Some
gasp. Fifteen minutes ago we were total strangers. Now they are really
excited about their own personal mysterious, imaginative experiences.

I ask everyone to write down either a dream or a déjà vu experience,
being as specific as they can in their descriptions. Not "a monster chased
me," but "a green man with fiery pink hair all over his body walked toward

me." No, they needn't sign their papers, and, no, don't worry about spelling or grammar. This is not a test. A few kids complain, "I never remember my dreams." I whisper, "Make up something that sounds like a dream." Often they will go on to write about an actual dream they were hesitant to acknowledge. Others respond to "Remember a scary dream you had when you were little."

I read their dream writings aloud, including my own and the regular teacher's. Suddenly the room is filled with a sampling of the classroom unconscious. The anonymity adds to the fascination.

Dream Poem

I dreamed I was in a gigantic room. Everything was made of tiles, the walls, floors, everything. The only piece of furniture was a gold throne. I thought to myself, "What am I doing here? Oh well, I'll sit down." Then all of a sudden the left and right corners of the room opened. I could see beams of light coming in the corners. Very strong light and I could hear cheering. I stood up and a big dinosaur ran through the corner of light. I screamed and ran out the opposite beam of light and fell on a cloud that had sand particles on it. Then I dreamed I fell asleep. I've had this dream 4 times.

(Christine Riblett)

I suggest they keep a diary of their dream lives that they can use as a basis for short stories, fantasy tales, or science fiction. (I've found it helps to replay details from my dreams before I open my eyes in the morning and then write them down immediately.)

Because my basic interest is in creative writing, I encourage kids to say whatever they want, no matter how wacky, weird, or unconventional, and to forgo, if they wish, rules of spelling, grammar, rhyme, and meter.

They also have the freedom to write anonymously (until they feel confident enough to sign their work). Kids who have a terrible time spelling simple words naturally dislike writing but are often good storytellers. I take dictation from them, either individually or as a group. I don't want poetry writing to be confused with "schoolwork."

I am not, however, an "anything goes" type. I discourage personal viciousness and constant use of obscenity in writing. Doubtless therapeutic for some, they disconnect most children from their larger, more interesting selves.

I also discourage the kind of competitiveness that makes most kids feel anxious, unloved, and defeated, or vainly victorious: I do not single out the "best" works. Creativity should not be turned into a contest. I let kids talk while they work, move around the room, share ideas, copy from each other (if they feel they must), in short, behave in any way that isn't damaging to the group or to themselves. I encourage them to pay attention to their ideas, to take themselves seriously, even if what they're writing is funny, so that they know the content of their fantasies is not only acceptable, it is welcome.

A crucial moment for emphasizing this comes when I read the poems aloud. I pause to comment on things I like, as much with my tone of voice as with outright remarks. In fact I praise the poems like mad. Praise makes the kids feel good about what they've done; they've gone out on a limb in their writing, and by damn it worked, somebody liked it! Gradually they gain the self-confidence to write as well as they always could have, with greater ease, pleasure, and satisfaction. They come to appreciate their imaginations, and from there the imaginative lives of others.

By "imaginative lives" I don't mean just the world of the unconscious. One poetry idea called variously Here and Now, Right Now, or Poem of the Senses has the kids focus their attention on the immediate present. In order to present the Right Now idea I secretly study the walls, ceiling, desks, view outside, details of clothes, and gestures that stand out a little, while the teacher introduces me. "This room is very interesting,"

I begin. "Look at that crack on the wall: it looks like a bolt of lightning. The reflection on the clock face forms a bent shiny rectangle. A yellow pencil is lying on the floor pointing to a red tennis shoe that goes up and down. Do you hear that humming? I feel a little cool breeze on my face as I walk back and forth, and I feel my heart beating in my chest. Do you feel yours? I feel my throat vibrating as I talk. I don't smell anything." Laughter.

"Right now this room is a way it never was before and never will be again because tiny details are constantly shifting." I hold up a piece of chalk and let it drop onto the floor, where it leaves a small bite of chalk. "That chalk falling is now three seconds into the past. Now... it's six seconds into the past.... What I'd like you all to do is to blot out the past and future. Make yourself one big receiver of impressions: notice what you see, hear, feel (touch), smell, and sense right now. This can be outside your body and mind, like the light powder on the chalkboard; or inside, such as feeling your lungs fill with air or sensing an idea happening in your mind. Make a list—in sentences—of things you never noticed before or things you think no one else will notice. Not boring stuff like 'I see a wall,' but clear details, such as 'There are thousands of little holes in the green cinder blocks, each casting a shadow.' Or say what it reminds you of: 'The Vietnamese landscape is pitted with shell holes.'"

To make things easier I write on the board:

I see	I feel	I believe
I hear	I think	I imagine
I taste	I sense	I wonder
I smell	I know	etc.

The kids start craning their necks. Consciously focusing on details in the room is peculiar for them but exhilarating.

I see the dark mouth of a cave.

I hear the shouts of millions.
I feel high.
I think I am getting drunk off this class.
I smell a blue sea.
I imagine I am flying.
I know I am mad.

(Todd Robeson)

This type of poem also shows how repetition is a good substitute for rhyme and meter in teaching poetry to children because it creates a poetic structure without inhibiting their freedom of expression.

Actual events become dreamlike when they sink into the past. "Wouldn't it be great if you could get in a time machine and go back into the past?" I ask one class. "To see George Washington remove his false teeth or Christ right up there on the Cross, a prehistoric man learning how to make fire, the real live Cleopatra, the Titanic sinking.... Or into the future. What would we look like? Would we live in plastic bubbles? Hmm. As far as I know, we can't get into the future, but we can travel back into the past by using our own personal time machines, our memories."

I talk about how odd it is to have something on the tip of one's tongue, how wonderful it is to remember something beautiful and valuable that happened to you, how dim and dreamy to remember back to the age of three, or two.... If only we could remember how it was before we were born! Finally I say that today I want everyone to get into their own time machines and travel back to something they remember from long ago. It doesn't have to be an earthshaking story, but it should be as specific as possible, recalling colors and details. I tell them to start each story with "I remember...."

I remember when my sister was two, it was her birthday
and we went shopping to get a cake at Pathmark. We had
to wait on line for about 2 hours and when we got home my

mother found out that my sister had been sitting on the cake the whole time.

(Carl Johnson)

I remember when I was three or four my father was very mad at a '59 Ford and so mad he threw the keys at it and busted the ring and the keys went flying in the air and he came inside and mowed over everything and anything including me and he blamed me for it. It took us three hours to find 20 keys and we still didn't find one key, the key to the car.

(Tom P.)

Dream Poems, Here and Now Poems, I Remember—these depend directly on the personal experiences of the writers. There are other poetry ideas that are more mechanical but no less fun, such as acrostics.

I ask the kids to volunteer a word or a name, the first one that comes to mind. One kid calls out "Jackass."

"OK, I'm going to write this word in the traditional Chinese fashion, up and down."

J
a
c
k
a
s
s

"Someone give me a word, any word, that starts with *J*."

"Jackknife," one kid says.

"Yes, that's good. Any others?"

"Jupiter."

"Japan!"

"Jellybean!"

"Those are all terrific. Let's take jellybean." Which I do. "OK, now what word begins with *A*?"

"Ambulance?"

"Great! Now let's put *jellybean* and *ambulance* together by adding some things before and after *jellybean*."

By now the kids are either cracking up or staring in amazement at this peculiar teacher or racing ahead in their minds. In any case they are learning how to do an acrostic.

We finish the example at the board, and I read it aloud:

> The Jellybean drove an
>> Ambulance to South
>> Carolina because he was a
>> Kook who
>> Always
>> Started
>> Speeding wildly

Everyone's laughing.

"Pick a word of your own," I tell them—"and do an acrostic, just as we did at the board, putting in anything that pops into your mind, no matter how silly."

> *Onions*

> July smells like
> Onions when it is
> Hot and
> Niagara Falls

Runs dry because
Onions clog the
Immense
Merging of the
Entire
Roto Rooter Company

(John Roimer)

Another writing method kids enjoy is collaborating as a class, dictating lines to someone at the board. This is also a good way to start with a class that hates writing, like one fourth grade group I taught. Here is their class collaboration:

God and His White Underwear

Angels are workers of God
Angels are the shoeshiners of God
Does God wear shoes?
No, he's a spirit
He might wear spiritual shoes
He puts on his underwear
It's pink and white
He goes to New Jersey
There he visits his family
In his family are George Washington, Babe Ruth, Mister
          McGoo and Mister Boogie
They dance
Then God takes an elevator
Like Jack and the beanstalk
And he's a rocket
Going to the moon, to the sky, to outer space

In a more advanced fourth-grade class the kids chose partners and wrote alternating lines. These fourth-graders had a lot of experience writing poetry, which can be seen in this sample that still makes me dizzy with envy:

What's Inside the Moon?

What's inside the moon?
    There's hot water inside.
What's the sky made of?
    It was made out of white snow.
If you cut the sun open what would you see?
    Terrible looking enemies.
When you write you look at your words have you thought
    of cutting open a letter to see what's inside?
    No. But if a person was crazy the answer would be yes.
What's inside colors?
    There's pink stars.
Where is the end of the universe?
    In back of the swimming pool.
How old is adventure?
    It is 60,00 years old.
Which color is older, black or white?
    Black because you can outline me.

(Vivien Tuft and Fontessa Moore, P.S. 61, New York City)

Sometimes with younger kids I sit down at the class typewriter and wait for them to come over and start dictating to me. One second-grade class didn't need much encouragement. They rushed over to dictate:

Sneezes of Hair

In the middle of the night
A hand comes out and says, "Hiya, honey,"
And kisses her in the lips
And she makes him baldheaded and he says, "I'm bald!
    I'm bald!"
And he puts pepper on his head
And it sneezes up

It became so exciting, one kid climbed up on top of my head, searching for sneezes of hair, I guess.

At first, kindergartners were hard to teach because of their inability to write words or to concentrate very long, but I found them so much fun to be with that I usually let them look in my pockets, pull my beard, put toys on my shoes, etc. Then one day I enlisted the aid of five sixth-graders, good poets who had been writing for several years. I gave them some ideas for poems the kindergartners might like: "You know how your mother or father always says the same things. What do they say at your house? If your dog or cat or fish could talk English, what would they say? If a tree or a leaf or a mountain could talk, what would they say? A table? Imagine a talking table! A talking shoe? The moon talking! A glass of milk!" We broke into flying wedges, each sixth-grader in charge of three or four little kids. They worked much better with the sixth-graders than they had with me. Here are two poems dictated that day.

Poem

When a leaf drops it goes
    tic, thoup, roasp,
wee wee weeee, ahhhhh

My Daddy Says

My Daddy says walk the dog
My Daddy says clean the cat
My Daddy says keep the tiger in the cage
My Daddy says brush your teeth
My Daddy says meow
My Daddy says wa wa wa Indian
My Daddy says eat the dog and leave the cat
My Daddy says ruf, ruf, ruf
My Daddy says feed the monkey bananas
My Daddy says I drive him bananas
My Daddy says don't get dirty
My Daddy says play it cool

I encourage kids to use my ideas in any way they like, even to the point of replacing them with their own ideas. One boy, San Lum Wong, newly arrived from China and just beginning to learn English, wrote the following poem when I asked his class to write Love Poems:

The Funny World

The world is funny. The earth is funny. The people is
funny. Somebody in funny life. Somebody given a life
change the funny. The magic is funny. The funny is
magic. Oh, boy a funny funny money happy.

I defy you to write something in Chinese half as beautiful about love after three months of studying that language.

Sometimes a student will hand me a manuscript, something written at home in private. Such a poem was that of Liz Wolf, a seventh-grader.

I Kiss No Ass

I follow no footsteps because the ones I start to make
    I end
And I don't need your sun
'Cause I am my own sun, I can make light for myself,
    so I can see the light
I don't need your gentle fingertips because I have my own
    two hands
And I have no room for hassles
No time, I don't have any need for it and it doesn't have
    any need for me
You can use your army and shield to knock me down
But my feet are planted to the ground
You tell me to "kiss ass"
I want to say, "Don't they know I have a mind too,
I'm not stupid!"
But what I say is "I kiss *no* ass."

Once kids come to appreciate their own writing, they have an improved, in fact a corrected, opinion of themselves, because one's language is as integral a part of one's self as an arm or leg. By getting in touch with their creative imaginations—which is sometimes a scary business, not a cutesy-pie world of daffodils and little hills—they see more clearly into themselves, and this clarity gives them a sense of personal value. Creativity is not something to be tacked on to the curriculum, it's essential to growing and learning.

Educational administrators and classroom teachers are beginning to see that imaginative writing is not just a "cultural enrichment" to which they "expose" their kids. By having kids indulge themselves in the wild and wacky world of the imagination, presto: schoolwork improves, school becomes a bit more fun, and the printed word loses some of its tyranny.

When kids can look at books and articles and say, confidently, "I write too," they are much less likely to acquiesce to the printed word without question, less likely to become mindless victims of mindless power.

First Class[1]

Theodore Roethke

Stick out your can, here comes a lesson-plan.

*

Flat words from a fat boy. What pearls are there to cast to colleagues?

*

To teach by suggestion or "intuitively" takes more time than teaching by precept or lecturing. For you carry the students in your mind and in reading think, "There's a swell example to show Flossie..." To teach very fast, by associational jumps—to teach a class as a *poem*—is dangerous but very exciting. It is possible to build up a "charge" with a group and blast away in a kind of mass diagnosis.

*

I used to teach like killing snakes: a constant pressuring.

*

To teach too intensively is to get so involved in particular psyches that there can be an actual loss of identity; destructive both to student and teacher. I remember a student saying, "You carry us farther than we

---

1. Theodore Roethke, "First Class" from *Straw for the Fire: From the Notebooks of Theodore Roethke 1943–1963*, selected and arranged by David Wagoner (Port Townsend, WA: Copper Canyon Press, 2006). Selected notebook entries (1950-53), first published in *The Antioch Review* (1969), then in *Straw for the Fire*.

could ever go alone. Then when you're gone, it's too much to face." Let's face it: much of this kind of teaching may perform the function of psychiatry, but it is absolutely fatal to proceed from such a premise or become self-conscious about what you're up to.

*

My teaching is a variety of coaching, really: both athletic and musical.

*

Most good teachers attempt the Socratic assumption of ignorance, but are often handicapped by their very real and sometimes vast knowledge: I have the advantage over such fellows in that I really don't know anything and can function purely: the students *have* to teach themselves.

*

If you teach by suggestion, there must be plenty to suggest from—a bale of examples. Anthologies are often inert.

*

You're referee, and sometimes the job is as hazardous as in ice hockey. Sure, it's possible, with a tweed jacket and a pipe and a choice collection of polysyllables to hold certain of the young at bay, to cow them. But they won't be the best ones.

*

We expect the hot flash and we get the cold stale inert lumpish inanities, the heavy archness, the smirking self-satisfaction.

*

Are there dangers? Of course. There are dangers every time I open my mouth, hence at times when I keep it shut, I try to teach by grunts, sighs, shrugs.

*

To the extent that I talk, I am a failure as a teacher.

*

You can't go out to all of them: all the way. That way lies madness and death. As it is, you work harder than most psychiatrists—and get much further faster, more humanly, painlessly.

*

I ask you: I beg you: bring to this task all the sweetness of spirit you possess. Leave your neuroses at home, and while there, make them work for you, or exorcise them from your best being.

*

A too excessive concern over students can mean: (1) death of the teacher; (2) distortion of the student: a sense of weakness or reliance.

*

The essential thing: that they not be loused up, warped, unduly twisted, played upon, brought to the wrong ends, led to the stony pasture.

*

I'd rather just sit around and dribble little bits of teaching wisdom... one of the more valiantly disorganized minds of our time.

*

In teaching, gruffness may be the true *cortesía*.

*

In writing you must go ahead; in teaching, so much of the time, you must go back.

*

I take it I'm to stand up for Poesy, but not say anything to make anyone nervous. For you know: one of the problems of the lyric poet is what to do with his spare time; and sometimes it becomes the community's problem too. It worries people. I know when I came out to Seattle, the head of my department said, "Ted, we don't know quite what to do with you: you're the only serious practicing poet within 1500 miles." I sort of was given to understand I had a status between—if it were Oklahoma—between a bank-robber and a Congressman.

*

Teaching: one of the few professions that permit love.

*

Look, I'm the greatest dumb teacher alive.

*

You think and I'll say.

*

Look how "wicked" we are: we have a poet who's a full professor.

*

A hot shot of the hard word—is that what you want? I feel strangely diffident. I'm a sport, an anachronism: nobody ever told me where to go.

*

I've had a most savage attack of humility of late; the notion that seems to horrify some of you is that you're not only expected to do some work, but actually supposed to teach the teacher. I assure you that is astonishingly easy to do.

*

How wonderful the struggle with language is.

*

The recording apparatus must be mature: complete and steady enough to rely on itself. There can't be any brash barkings into the bass drum or simpers off into the wings or cozy thigh-crossings: everybody hates the unformed. You're a speaking fœtus, get it? A soft-boiled egg wobbling on one leg, looking for the edge of a cup or saucer... You roar, not from a true disquietude of the heart, but from growing-pains...spiritual teething. This fledgling's cheep would disgrace a magpie.

*

When you roar, make sure it's from a true disquietude of the heart, not a mere temporal pinch... In the end, if you aspire to the visionary's toughness, you not only have to chew your own marrow, but then must spit it in your neighbor's eye.

*

In this first assignment just care about words. Dwell on them lovingly.

*

For Christ's sake, awake and sing! You're as conditioned as old sheep.

*

It's the damned almost-language that's hardest to break away from: the skilled words of the literary poet.

*

The artist (not the would-be): you may have deep insights—but you also need the sense of form. Sometimes the possession of the first without the second may be tragic.

*

Good poets wait for the muse, the unconscious to spring something loose, to temper and test the promptings of the intuition with the pressures of craftsmanship: they can think while they sing.

*

If only this rare rich ripe deviousness could be put to some useful work.

*

I'll deliver you, dear doves, out of the rational, into the realm of pure song.

*

It's true many of the lessons are the same; in fact, almost reduce themselves to one lesson: cutting. But the applications, the variations are infinite.

*

To be too explicit destroys the pleasure. This the Irish know, to whom the half-said's dearest.

*

I have to be concrete. Everything else scares the hell out of me.

*

Immobility is fatal in the arts.

*

To bring you out of that purposelessness—surely that is a great thing, even if you move but an inch from yourselves...

*

The artist doesn't want to be articulate about something until he is finally articulate. One can talk away certain themes, spoil them.

*

That intense profound sharp longing to make a true poem.

*

One form of the death wish is the embracing of mediocrity: a deliberate reading and rereading of newspapers...

*

Today there's no time for the mistakes of a long and slow development: dazzle or die. Would Yeats's career be possible in this country today?

*

The "other" poems in Yeats...had to set the stage for his best work. If he had not written at such length, he might not have been heard.

*

What would you rather be—happy or Hölderlin?

*

Much of poetry is an anguished waiting.

*

One of the virtues of good poetry is the fact that it irritates the mediocre.

*

I can't understand the condescension many "professional" poets have for the young. Usually it seems defensive, a form of fear or even a kind of jealousy.

*

Uncle Easy,
You mustn't be queasy:
I haven't forgotten
Cousin Rotten.

*

Behold the heavy-footed bard
With rhythms from the lumberyard.

*

In him all the oafs, dolts, bumpkins, and clods, living and dead, connect and contend.

*

A bewildered bardling: no real feeling except a thin intense hatred of his contemporary superiors.

*

The gutsy, self-appreciating tone
Is something only he can make his own:
The true provincial wit, he never reads
Except the thing his little spirit needs:
I find it comic that he speaks of *voice*
Who never made a rhythm without noise.

*

A great one for hurrahing early work; but as soon as the subject departs from the rude thumps and lubberly staves of the lisping idiotic boy, he has "abandoned his muse" or is depending on mere cleverness. What a burden he bears, carrying the weight of criticism for us all. How fiercely he guards his few nuggets of wisdom. In the perpetual hunt for merit, he is content to scavenge.

*

The critics: they have taught poets much about what not to do—for one thing, to avoid pleasing them.

*

The critic's attitude: this poem exists for me to verbalize about it.

*

A culture in which it is easier to publish a book about poetry than a book of poems.

*

These shabby detractors; these cheap cavilers, gurgling with their jargon: they're fatter in the head than the worst priests of disillusion.

*

The pip-squeak peripheral dippers: they could come to a full circle in the middle of a plugged nickel: it's no good declaring them frauds: they retain their dubious virtues. It's true in the tiny areas they leak and squeak in: sand-fleas of the soul on the immense beaches of desolation.

Meanwhile the wind's where it is: the sun plays in the dark leaves of the acanthus. Locality is alive...

*

How do I know what I said? Half the time I wasn't listening.

*

I was committed to the future: and in a sense only the future existed.

*

I don't think anybody ever yearned more for a public than I did.

*

What have I done, dear God, to deserve this perpetual feeling that I'm almost ready to begin something really new?

*

A profound dissatisfaction with these tin-cans, frigidaires, barbered prose, milk and water fantasies.

*

If poetry can kill you, I'm likely to die.

*

The exactly right goose to a tired psyche: the Socratic method is exhausting with uneven material; worse with limited. To hell, I say, with the conference. It's enough for me to listen, and cut away, and suggest, quickly. Come up before or after class. None of this breast-feeding.

*

Well, well, have I become no more a dug? Let's have an end to this shameless breast-feeding from one who doesn't pretend to know anyway: you don't cut the mustard always with silver: Any old stick, pie-tin, or pencil's material to beat out the meter of happy bones.

*

We may not be going far: but even beyond the door is a great way in this journey. "I've lost it," he said: the gift for the creative reverie. I no longer listen and wait, but hear only the snapping clichés, our whole life driving toward coarse abstractions.

*

A honey-seeker numb as a bee in November.

To recover the fine extravagance, the bravado, the true bravura...

To find my own labyrinth and wind there,

A placid worm...

You two trees, don't think you're a wood...

My feet leap with the dancing dead...

What to do when the fresh metaphors flash forth—that is a facer...

For who would tinker when the muses say?

I call the light out of someone else.

Sing up, sing all, a Socrates of fury.

Children's Poetry

Eileen Myles

One of the really good gigs for a poet in the seventies was teaching poetry to kids. There seemed to be a lot of public funding for poetry in the schools back then and there were two organizations in New York City alone, Poets & Writers and Teachers & Writers Collaborative, that supplied poets for that function. Lots of known and upcoming poets became part of this practice and you'd always hear about it. In a reading the poets would get up and read their students' poems. It was a little soft-edged for me. I'd roll my eyes because now (yawn) we were having to hear what the sainted children wrote. I was still aiming to be a kid and a poet, and I didn't have so much room for these silly pet tricks.

Yet there are lines some kid wrote that are still a part of my head: "When I grow up I want to live in my house," for instance. I mean generally being the poet teaching kids in a school sounded like a good gig and yet like most administrative things I just couldn't figure it out. How to get in on it. I assumed that "those people"—the ones who hired poets in the schools—wouldn't like me. Would know I was bad. I made a few vague passes—mailing those applications in—and nothing ever came back. Word was that the woman who ran it mostly liked to hire men. Most of the people I knew reading kids' poems aloud were guys. Children needed male role models in the classroom and it was an opportunity for guy poets to make dough. Good for them. Groan. I sort of assumed that it was because I was so clearly a lesbian in my work and that wasn't what people wanted to send into our schools. I had a secret longing to teach queer kids at Harvey Milk High School, which is New York's LGBTQ high school, but I never lifted a finger. So it never happened. I suppose if I think about it honestly, kids scare me. The little bit of substitute teaching I did right out of college was largely a painful and humiliating experience that dissuaded me from wanting to teach for a long while. Cause kids just look at you with those big eyes—and I instantly feel like a fraud. Like, what's she hiding. I couldn't imagine a way in.

As a child I had instinctively recognized that poetry disseminated values. It was rolled out in school right next to prayers and the Pledge of Allegiance as part of the larger tapestry of things we supposedly belonged to—but I knew also that those poems were corny. "Blessings on thee, little man, / Barefoot boy, with cheek of tan!" What was that about? The pleasure of these early poetry experiences was not the dull one of moving my mouth to make these treacly lines with fifty other sets of lips in grade school after lunch, standing with our bellies stuck out, heads swarming with other things. No. What I liked was being home in the afternoon after dinner with my family and seeing how quickly I could memorize the poem. Poetry proved my mind was strong. Not only could I remember everything on the list of things my mother sent me to the store to buy, jingling the list in my mind as I walked, but also I could commit a page of poetry to memory in half an hour. Next came the allure of funny poetry I could spout for my friends outside of school. Mostly it was that stupid poetry from Mad Magazine: "I think that I shall never hear / a poem as lovely as a beer...." And then finding *bad* poetry in an anthology in college. Gregory Corso's "Marriage," throwing weird names into the world: "Radio belly!" "Cat shovel!"

Poetry became the exemplar of private vindictiveness and funniness and personal mourning—flipping *that* space into the world. I knew it, I grew it, it was there.

So despite the fact that I was female, that I couldn't play dad and wouldn't be an appropriate choice to teach poetry to children in the classroom, and despite the fact that kids scared me and I knew I would be bad at it— where to begin—my own poetry teaching experience nonetheless began to form in response to the poetry workshops I took as a young adult. I began to understand that teaching poetry was a kind of collective word game, and how you learned it in the easygoing intensity of the workshop (as highly individualized as dating) was also how you developed the teaching practice in yourself, witnessing and practicing and meeting one another in the workshop's playful intimacy.

And sadly, those free programs—the ones I went to at the Poetry Project in the seventies now cost money—and the ones in public schools have been largely cut out of budgets, and when they do exist the tales of censorship are legion. Yes we want poetry in the schools and yes it would be lovely if the children would produce their own publication but no we certainly will not fund the publication of poems that include such words as "pee-pee," "caca," and "butt." And what about "fag"? So even when the money was a little bit there, it could easily be cut, silencing poetry. All of this was just part of the cultural wars of the eighties and nineties. Which only further demonstrated to my mind that poetry is powerful. The need is radiantly there. Today when I meet young art students and I'm out of things to say I ask them what they're reading. Do you like poetry. And surprise, the young artist tells me she's a huge fan of Lucille Clifton, Ron Silliman, John Wieners, Arthur Rimbaud. How do you know about them I ask assuming they're probably family. Or French. Well there were always poets in my school when I was a kid. And let's just have a little moment of silence there.

Because for every person like me who ferreted poetry out of bookstores in states of depression, and found common cause for their warped natures in that literature anthology we never cracked in high school, there is an entire generation who learned from those poets in schools, who had actual poetry teachers, who took poetry class just like art class—and I think it's why today's art world is flooded by words. We put it there, all those jerky poet guys reading their kids' poems, and that one heterosexual woman, she did that too. Not just reciting poetry, but writing it—this was taught in school! That's a revolutionary act.

I will tell you why. It is the most cherished gift of a lifetime, language, especially the idle use of it that's all furry, snippy, lazy, concatenous, and tough. Language in the hands of poets is a squalling baby and an old man. It's a creaky, sentimental, surprisingly weird woman. Of course it's totally trans. It's queer. And presupposing that you learned it somewhere (illiteracy is a related but entirely other subject), the point is that language is free and it is the medium that gives us the knowledge that other people think too, and it offers us a way to transmit our thoughts. Language is the ultimate human tool. Portable, invisible, and it zips around the world at no cost. And poetry is language's first use and its last. While so many languages are dying right now, people continue chanting its poetry. Each and every one of them.

I do have one story specifically about teaching the children. Actually they weren't children. They were charming thugs, high-school students, at-risk kids in an at-risk town, Provincetown, Mass. Provincetown is at risk cause everything's for the real estate and the summer folk, nothing for the schools, the local kids. Really, are there schools here? the condo owner asks on his deck. I lived there in the winter to absorb the sounds of the New England working class, my own native tongue, and to be surrounded by the ocean and a wild and duney landscape, and to write a book. My friend Kathe Izzo was single-handedly doing the cool thing: she had created for the troubled teens in her town something she called the Shadow Writing Project, funded by the Mass. Cultural Council. She found kids in the streets, she went into classrooms at Provincetown High, she went to gigs where kids with guitars played out. Kathe had managed to persuade these "bad" kids to take part in an afterschool program. Some liked poetry, reading, a few already wrote songs because they were in bands and imagined that writing poetry would stoke the output of their songwriting. However she did it Kathe had corralled twelve awkward radiant teens to meet in the public library one evening a week to write. It went on for three or four years. One February night in the winter I was Shadow's guest. So bringing poetry to the kids for me was not a gig. It was a favor. I liked Kathe, I liked her work. I thought it was cool she was doing her Shadow thing. And she had created a job for herself.

What should I do? I asked her. Read, just read your work, she smiled. I explained to them that really I was a poet, that I grew up in Massachusetts. Though I happened to live in New York. I knew one kid in school who was a poet and we would pass notes in class and our notes were poems. We actually got in trouble for these notes so my first work was incendiary, I explained. They didn't laugh. I don't even know if that kid still writes poetry. I was thinking out loud. And weirdly (I was digging a really big hole for myself), the next poet I met, a guy in college, Brian Rattigan, lived in P-town in the summer. He was from Watertown. They nodded. He came down here to work in restaurants and write poems. He worked at Sal's. He drowned at Cape Cod Light. But it's not like all poets die. I'm alive. I think. I looked around nervously. Finally they laughed. OK I'm going to read some of my poems. It's very hard to read at a table with people sitting with you. The poetry reading generally as we understand it today is constructed around a little bit of distance, or even a whole lot. The whole thing, the sipping water, the remarks between poems, all of it is artificial. The poems come quietly into the world, often after a lot of activity, intense feeling or thought, and usually I share the poem with one person then—my girlfriend, or for years I would call someone on the phone and read it, but you know cell phones don't work so well. I think it's because you're not home. I think I probably told them this because to sit at the same table sharing my work made me feel both very connected to them and full of shame too—for having a body, for being alive, for wanting them to like my work, for making something invisible visible, and then for being the evidence of that bleeding, by being there. That whole trashy dancing cave scene in my head...stepping out. The place where art and poetry begins. Is it okay? Each time after a poem I looked up, usually saying nothing followed by I'll read another. Do you want to talk at all? I asked. One kid said did you write those all at the same time. No, this one, I said, shaking a page, I wrote last week, and some of these are really old. Like fifteen years. I like to show what I'm thinking and where I am. I think of a poem as something that does what nothing else can. Not a movie, I guess a song can do this too, but a song has to make it simple. A poem can be a really quiet show, but very complex. It goes inside and out. It reflects the pattern. They were listening.

Usually at this point, said Kathe, smiling, we do some writing. They all pulled out their notebooks. They may have liked me but this is what they were waiting for.

So what would you like us to do, she asked. It was like she was flirting. But that's Kathe's style. And I wanted to be helpful. They were so young. Seventeen at most, I think. I wonder what they think about their lives right now. I thought of one of my favorite poems, which is almost nothing at all. By the eighth-century Chinese poet Tu Fu. Supposedly it was his first poem. I love the idea that you write a poem your whole life. You preserve *that* culture.

Now I am six
I feel very strong
And open my mouth
With a Phoenix Song!

Six was my favorite birthday too. I don't want to make their poem be about being children though. Some of them were in bands. People think these kids are no good. They say "at risk" but they mean already lost. This is like a little jail. Poetry is, too. One of the things I like to do is always to think of the thing, the worst thing, and make it good. Flip it. Even just in my head walking down the street. If it's really hot like in the 90s in New York in the summer, "It will always be this way" I think. I don't know why but that makes it cooler. OK I've got it:

Write a poem from any age in your life—doesn't have to be your age now, or an age you've been. And go down the drain with it. Go down the drain one kid laughed. Yes totally. What does that mean asked the smart girl. I don't know. I haven't written it yet. Just make it up. You can't do it wrong. I guarantee. Just go, just fall. Everyone.

I felt so happy. I loved being six. I had a great party, it was the first time I had friends.

I was six, I had lost my snake...

I mean, I think that meant a plumber. Right. A plumber uses a snake. But that's not what anyone would think. Everyone was writing. It was quiet in the library. You could hear cars on the street, the librarians were picking up their papers and putting books on the shelves. Reserve. It's a little cold in here. People look up when they write. They are look-ing into an abstract space. A new one, all mind yet all these same wavy distractions come in. Maybe. You can't trust that anyone is having the same experience, ever. That's the anarchy of poetry, seeing what anyone has gathered, giving a shape to it...

Years later, I met Kathe again, in San Francisco. It was amazing to bump into her. Where are those kids today, I asked. When I go to Provincetown I always see Shadow kids in the street, she said. That was the best time in my life, they say. They say to Kathe you saved my life. Mostly they say let's go write. That's exactly what they say. One girl who still lives there keeps saying I should start a Shadow group. Shawn Kelley, do you remember her, she was on that artist boat that went down the Mississippi. You know, Swoon. Shawn's doing great. She looks great. And Carmine is in a band. But no they really mean it. They would walk into a café. They would do it right now. Let's write. That's it. That's Shadow. That's the gift, Kathe said. Just to want it.

The Change Agents[1]

Phillip Lopate

The Era of the Consultant

It was inevitable from 1967 onward, with the schools throughout the country troubled about their sense of purpose and the students bored and rebellious, that administrators would turn to experts in entertainment for inspiration. Poets, theater directors, multimedia artists, jugglers, dancers, philosophers were suddenly asked to bring new life to the routine of the classroom. What would result from this chemistry no one was willing to guess. How sincere the invitation was differed from school to school. In some schools the expectation may have been nothing more than a day's entertainment, the way one hires a magician to keep the children occupied at a birthday party; in other cases, the hopes may have gone much deeper. Artists are often sought out, when they are not being ignored, to effect a spiritual regeneration in people's lives which is really beyond their powers.

The almost religious hopes which creativity excites (religious in spirit as well as in approaching the Infinite) may stem from the fact that

---

1. Phillip Lopate, "The Change Agents" from *Being with Children* (New York: Doubleday, 1975 and Poseidon Press, 1989).

art is one of the last vocations left with a degree of autonomy and self-sufficiency. A teacher who is not much impressed with the manner of a poet visiting his or her classroom may still feel that the children have gained something merely by being exposed to a person who lives by his self-expression.

I am talking now of a desperate situation. Only desperate people would throw open their school doors and welcome shaggy poets to mingle with their young. Americans traditionally distrust poetry and think it the most frivolous of arts. But the poet has certain practical advantages. He is portable, he is inexpensive, and in some mysterious way he may excite children into writing, which may awaken a taste for reading, which may lead to higher reading scores and happier school boards. Nevertheless, it was understood by schools requesting visiting writers that the poet should not be pressured or consciously programmed toward that end but should be allowed to steer his or her own course. The very innocence of artists about educational matters was considered a potential asset, in that they might be less inclined to duplicate the standard curriculum.

Naturally, misunderstandings resulted; and they resulted quite logically from the initial paradox of wanting strangers to visit a classroom and stir things up and, on the other hand, resenting the turbulence which the passing experts left behind. The errors surrounding these programs were analyzed with rare honesty by Martin Kushner, an arts administrator, who confessed:

> Artists have been dropped into the school like paratroopers onto a strange terrain. Few instructions were given. They had to scout teachers, seek allies, and do the best they could without a great deal of experience. We had many meetings early in the year with the teachers, but these talks were perfunctory. Each artist was simply present in the school to turn kids on, to do his thing, to involve teachers. Indeed, we had selected artists who fancied

themselves aesthetic paratroopers and so made their jumps enthusiastically. But how much more we could have achieved with more knowledge of school life and adequately prepared welcome mats manned by school and community people who knew a lot more about what was dropping out of the sky into their laps! We had objectives but they were abstractions. Since no artist can ever really be adequately prepared for a school situation unless he is directly from the community, we know we must be more thoughtful, "up front," and honest about ourselves early with all school personnel. We must state clearly what we are attempting to do—what we believe in. If the administration's point of view differs greatly from ours, then we must either determine whether the difference should exist in the schools and be important tools for learning, or, we have to find another school more willing to experiment.[2]

These misunderstandings are like the ones faced by the WPA–sponsored Writers Project in the 1930s. Nevertheless, the writer-in-the-schools program has suggested at least an embryonic hope of a model for writers to regain a useful role in the daily productive world without relinquishing their identity as artists. Even with the risks attached to such collaborations, no more fruitful experiment could be imagined, since writers need, in addition to a steady income, the emotional nourishment of a workplace, while schools need more poetry, in the largest sense of the term.

The importation of writers into the schools may be seen as part of a larger pattern—the era of the consultant, in which the disinterested expert, who is not engaged in the political intrigues and promotional ladder within the institution, enters the institution, presumably free to

---

2. Quoted in *Artists in the Classroom* (Connecticut Commission on the Arts: 1973).

put forward a fresh viewpoint. It was a high-ranking official in the Ford Foundation who first coined the term "change agent" to describe a kind of roving catalyst who could go into an ailing institution, size up the problem, and set people moving in a productive direction.

Necessary to the identity of the change agent was that at a certain point he leave. For how else could he maintain his objectivity and his *specialness*? It would dissolve in the bath of the institution; he would be sucked into the petty murk and become just another grumpy, backbiting employee. Even if he kept up his "transformational" ability, this line of thinking went, his continued presence would engender a passivity and dependence on the part of his colleagues. No, the change agent had to leave.

The change-agent concept seems to me the most odiously impersonal and presumptuous imaginable. Yet it sums up the dilemma in which many writers working in the schools are placed. They have been assigned a role of eternally Different, and they can either exploit that, resist it, evade it, submit to it, or subvert it, depending on the particular circumstances and temperament of the writer. In any case, it remains a frame for their actions that they can never ignore.

At the forefront of the movement to bring writers and artists into the schools was Teachers & Writers Collaborative, started by Herbert Kohl in 1966. I joined the Collaborative in 1968, a year that marked the height of discontent with American educational institutions. The school-reform movement had been gathering steam; the first wave of muckraking books by Holt, Kozol, Kohl, Herndon, Dennison, and Conroy had appeared or was soon to appear; and many people seemed to be coming to the conclusion that the American school system was on the point of collapse.

I considered myself part of a second line of reformers, who had inherited the new atmosphere brought about by the impact of the first group on the schools, profiting from the wedge they had made, at the same time as walking into the confusion and mistrust which that initial wave of attack had left behind. The schools had been put on the defensive—which did not necessarily mean that they would transform themselves, only that we were in for a period of much more self-conscious, ambiguous behavior.

The exposé literature had helped to generate an accusatory atmosphere in which many classroom teachers felt vaguely guilty in advance, afraid of "killing the children," afraid to assert a strong point of view because it might be suppressing different opinions. Teachers distrusted themselves, checked their intuitions, became tentative, easily manipulated by children, and, finally, irritated at having to live up to an impossible standard. They had tried; they had bought all the books and taken notes and gone in to transform their classrooms, and their classrooms had stayed essentially the same. And when they went to apply the message of Caring, it didn't seem to be enough. In fact, they had always cared: that was nothing new. Most teachers do care about their children and want good lives for them. A perplexed mood began to develop among certain teachers, which rose to anger at these freedom experts: *the anger of the 70s at the 60s*, for a promised liberation that never came.

Of course it wasn't the fault of the writers for arousing hope. Arousers of hope should not be expected to deliver as well, or no one would take on that function. On the other hand, the critical map of the schools which they had handed down was incomplete. If it showed very truthfully how some children were being squashed by their teachers, it failed to show enough the other instances, the normal everyday resourcefulness with which many classroom teachers meet challenge after challenge and which has to be seen to be believed—a selflessness that is accepted by them as part of their job, like firemen entering a burning building.

But when I began as a writer in the schools, I understood little of the complexity of the classroom teacher's job. I was appalled by the monotony and chained expression that I saw everywhere, and impatient to change all that as rapidly as possible. Naturally I kept getting into trouble. First I was asked to leave a commercial high school for encouraging the students to put out their own (not faculty-censored) literary magazine. Then I encountered censorship problems in a small private school in California, where I also walked into a power struggle between the teachers and the headmistress. I allied myself with the striking teachers and was fired as their "ringleader" (a compliment I always felt was exaggerated). For a while I worked as a roving poet, sent by state arts councils from town to hamlet to make brief teaching appearances in local schools. After that I worked in a high school dropout rehabilitation center in East Harlem, where again I found myself in disagreement with the agency's educational philosophy. The scenario was wearing a little thin. Even I was getting bored with this idealistic young man who enters a school and wins the love of students and gets bounced out because conservative meanies won't understand. Perhaps I was following the reform literature too closely. I knew how to pursue a righteous course which would lead inexorably to a confrontation and my dismissal; I knew how to lose nobly, but did I know how to succeed? There had to be a way to do creative work with students and survive in an institution. I wasn't prepared yet to accept idealistic masochism as the only option.

By now I understood a little more about the power structure of schools: the importance of having parents on your side, the ethnic politics of communities, the district pressures—all those things they never tell writers when they send them on the road to "open up" classrooms. And I was becoming more sensitive to the factor of timing in introducing changes; that is, the humane rate at which people could take in new ideas without losing their personal balance or their loyalty to past beliefs. I had become convinced that it was equally important to develop a base of support for creative projects and to do them in full view of the community, with its approval, as it was to hit upon this or that "miracle" teaching idea.

When I came to Public School 90, I had skills but no community. I was twenty-seven years old. I was tired of being a wandering catalyst; I was homesick for someplace that would receive me and the contribution I had to make. I was very lucky. To find a proper set of circumstances for working today is like looking on the ground for traces of a lost civilization. In my case, I was sent into a public school to do something as vague as "help people be creative." I was responsible for training a whole team of writers to do the same, and for devising a collective mode of operation for which I could locate no precedent. We embarked without a map, without plans, without instructions, with nothing to go on but the good will of the natives....

Recitation, Imitation, Stillness

Jesse Nathan

One afternoon a couple summers ago, I taught poetry writing to a group of high school students at 826 Valencia, a writing-tutoring center for young people in San Francisco. I had never taught poetry to high school students. Right after I agreed to teach the workshop, I got nervous. Scared. My thoughts veered toward the frantic. Will they care? Will I look like an excitable fool while they stare at me blankly? What do I even say? I shouldn't have agreed to this.

So I called my older sister. She teaches high school students. She teaches Spanish, but she loves poetry, and she uses it in her classroom to teach language. Her students, she's told me before, are especially engaged by lessons that involve poetry. How do you do it? I asked. Break the class into small groups, she said. Have each group take a poem. Have them take a few minutes to discuss it among themselves. Ask them to figure out, as a group, how they'd read it out loud. Then have them recite it, as a group, to the whole class. You will see.

And what I saw unfold when I followed this plan is, I think, an argument for teaching young people about poetry, and an argument for the importance of that teaching in and out of schools. What I saw and experienced was an inspiration—I glowed for weeks afterward every time I thought back over the workshop. And out of that thinking came, eventually, a philosophy of sorts for teaching writing poetry. It has three parts: recitation, imitation, and stillness.

RECITATION

1.

Named after its street address in the Mission District of San Francisco, 826 Valencia was founded in 2002 by educator Nínive Calegari and author Dave Eggers.

2.

Calegari and Eggers were looking for a way to support overburdened teachers and connect working adults with the students who could use their help the most. Because the space was zoned for retail, they needed a storefront. They decided on a pirate supply store. Behind the pirate store they built a writing lab, designed to be a place where kids would want to spend time, with a cozy reading tent, big worktables, lots of books. Word spread quickly, and soon every chair was filled with students working on their writing, and their homework generally, with trained tutors. Thanks to a corps of some 1,700 volunteers, 826 Valencia currently serves over 6,000 students a year. Inspired by the success of 826 Valencia, seven more 826 chapters opened in cities across the country: New York, Chicago, Ann Arbor, Seattle, Los Angeles, Boston, and Washington, D.C.—all of them running on shoestring budgets and powered by legions of volunteers, like me.

3.

So when someone at 826 Valencia asked me to teach high-schoolers something about writing poems, I agreed, got nervous, and called my dear sister. Revived by her suggestions, I picked out a handful of poems I would have my students recite in groups: "The Little Mute Boy" by Federico García Lorca, "April Rain Song" by Langston Hughes, "I'm Nobody—Who Are You?" by Emily Dickinson, "To Julia de Burgos" by Julia de Burgos, and a snippet of "Song of Myself" by Walt Whitman. I made copies of the poems to distribute. A little after 2 o'clock on the appointed day, I watched the students take their seats at the big wooden tables in a room featuring massive bookcases and portholes, a room with floors like the decks of a wooden ship, left from its former life as a weight room. The kids were quiet and intense, and I got nervous all over again. I explained my plan. I couldn't tell if it sounded like a good one to them or not.

4.

I want to say, by the way, that I remember getting up in front of the entire sixth-grade class and reciting a poem by Robert Frost, concentrating and breathing the words clearly, expressing them in a tone that felt right. It was an experience I hope every student has. I won't forget it.

5.

I think this is because the pleasures of poetry come to us early on—long before we learn to write. Poetry begins with our voices—speaking the form, creating the rhythm, shaping and tasting the words. Yet as we progress through school our encounters with poems are more and more often through print—words on a page that we read or write in silence.

6.

Somehow in many English classrooms it has become easy to overlook the deeply sonic quality of poetry. In our obsession with parsing what the author intended we end up pushing the poem away from young people, rather than working from a sense of the poem as a living, speaking thing, a thing that we can take into our lives and shape and own. This focus on the rather narrow question of author intention (though surely it has its place) is a special temptation to the scholar, to those committed to "high culture," to those whose preconceptions tend to direct attention toward written literature as the only location of poetry.

7.

Poetry's vocal roots hover ghost-like even as we read words silently. Writing remains a search for voices. Voice—a sound produced by vocal organs. After many multimillion-dollar studies, I've found that a common image in poems is the mouth. All of this raises questions.

8.

Why, for instance, are the most enduring bits of language so often nursery rhymes? These seemingly trivial verses live while newer and more ambitious compositions become dated and forgotten. Why?

9.

And what does the enormous growth nationwide of slam poetry events, particularly among young people, mean?

10.

For starters, to read a poem aloud is to feel it as a physical presence. And it feels good. Nursery rhymes are best spoken aloud. They are sing-songy because they were written to be sung. Their rhythms stick in the mind and keep the poems alive—passed from generation to generation. Young people especially seem to recognize this, and it might be why so many have striven recently to bring orality back to contemporary poetry. (Hence, for instance, the popularity of slam events.)

11.

Oral poetry, it should be said, is not an odd or aberrant phenomenon in human culture, nor a fossilized survival from the far past, destined to wither away with increasing modernization. In fact, it is a common occurrence in human society, literate as well as non-literate. It is found all over the world, past and present, from the meditative personal poetry of recent Eskimo or Maori poets, to medieval European and Chinese ballads, to the orally composed epics of pre-classical Greek in the first millennium B.C.E.

12.

Homer was an individual singer. He presumably acquired a repertory of songs from other singers and reproduced them in his own manner.

13.

Performing a poem written by someone else can offer a sense of meaning impossible to get from silent study alone. An oral reading can enact, say, how a given rhyme contributes to the devastating argument of a poem. Or it can reveal in other poems how this or that speaker owns the action of this or that stanza. It can dramatize point of view. It can highlight certain images. It can put the wonderfully disjointed music of, say, Emily Dickinson on a pedestal, emphasizing rhythm as perception. It can show a poem to be one person talking to another, or one person talking to herself (as in "To Julia de Burgos"), or someone talking to God, or all of these things, or none.

14.

I went on about these things to my students. They blinked politely. I divided them into five groups, gave each one a different poem. They were unspeaking and attentive, ready to dig in. One thing to remember is that kids flock to 826 Valencia. I think part of this is because they sense they will drive the process. There aren't very many rules foisted on them—no one pushes an aesthetic ideology down their throats. They come, they write, they think and read, they are tutored. They hang out. They learn to work, and they become better readers, and they do it all with grown-ups they think are pretty cool. They take the whole thing very seriously.

15.

So when I asked them to work with a poem in their small groups and figure out how to "read" it aloud, they got very serious and very excited. Hushed tones, huddled intensity, lots of notes scribbled and strategies hashed. They wanted more time than the fifteen minutes I'd allotted them. OK! I said.

16.

Reciting a poem out loud, I think, is compelling to young people in part because it's a less intellectualized way of getting at meaning, one not so bogged down by trying to explain the poet's intention. The performance itself makes an argument about what the poem means. To recite poetry aloud is fun, and it's also physical, a bodily activity.

17.

And a body is where a poem begins: A poem is a thought moving through a brainpan, but not only that. It is full of words, and in the reaches of the human psyche lies an awareness that words were spoken before they were written, were first delivered into the world via the machinery of tongues and airways and teeth.

18.

The learning that happens in this kind of choral reading thus comes from the act of mind required of the students. They have to plan how to read the poem, and this causes them to examine the poem's structure so that they can enhance its effect.

19.

One group had a poem with four stanzas, and someone in the group said, "Hey, there are four of us." So they each took one stanza and planned how to perform it.

20.

Participation in this case means being able to speak in one's own voice, and thereby simultaneously to construct and express an identity through idiom and style.

21.

Perhaps we can hear things we cannot see.

22.

The movement of air, the breath of meaning.

23.

My students seemed to know immediately that a poem spoken aloud feels different from the written version. The language itself acquires a special and quite original poetic quality. The poem, read aloud, becomes infused with the animating force of the speaker. We who hear the poem feel it with all its nonverbal aspects dialed up. We are subject to facial expressions, gestures, changes in inflection, pace, or tone, things undetectable on the page. We feel the reciter's idiosyncrasies channeled through the vehicle of the poem: a machine made, say, by William Wordsworth but fed through the singular and augmenting machinery of another—a different human being in a different time and place.

24.

This is not to suggest that experiencing poetry via performance should take priority over reading it on a page. Not at all. For me the primacy of the page remains. Rather, I view performance as one invaluable way to the page, a way to open a discussion on how a given poem can mean.

This is what happened at 826. The group that read the Dickinson poem read it playfully, coyly. The group that read the Whitman shouted it, emphasizing the exclamation points. What did these different reading choices mean? The hands went up around the room. One student thought Dickinson wanted to make people like her. One thought she was making fun of people. Someone thought Whitman was probably insane.

25.

For literature to help us live, we take it into our lives personally. We might go so far as to say we ought to take it into our bodies, literally. Scholarly detachment is irrelevant to high school students. It makes no sense to them. Why wouldn't you be deeply, messily involved with what you're reading?

26.

For, if we become involved with a text, we tend to invent a voice to hear it in. We invent what we assume is an appropriate tone of voice, the robust voice, say, of Whitman…

27.

Too, we should not overlook the possibility of applying *incongruous* voices to good writing. When the poetry of Wallace Stevens starts to sound a bit too solemn, I sometimes "hear" it in the voice of a Southern redneck. T.S. Eliot's poetry is particularly delightful when heard in an old-time hillbilly accent ("A-prul e-is thuh croo-list munth"). I like to imagine how William Carlos Williams's poems—so American—would sound in an Italian accent. Such unusual pairings result in what amounts to burlesque, but frequently in the burlesque you see clearly an aspect of the writer's work that was previously too familiar to be noticed. The forest and the trees are separated.

28.

And the same poem on the same occasion can play vastly different roles for different parts of the audience.

29.

Multiplicity is inherent in all the best poems anyway. The first condition of knowledge is mystery. Great poems are prisms, fracturing and throwing one beam of light everywhere. The doubleness and tripleness of meaning rattles in every line. A poem interpreted by students aloud—and often one group's interpretative recitation is different from anything you or anyone else would have thought of—teaches that nothing is ever one thing. A cigar is not just a cigar, even when it is.

30.

Part of poetry's perceived obscurity, part of the reason it's taught far less frequently these days in schools than, say, fiction, is that the methods employed by some teachers—I definitely recall certain bleak stretches of English class—drive all the personality out of a poem, as well as the feeling it can spring inside us. This sort of schoolteacher too often beats poetry into the ground with weighty, abstract words like *trochee* and *anapest*.

31.

Saying a poem out loud, I should add, is not a less challenging way of getting at meaning than picking it apart with terminology or questions about what the author intended. Rather, for many young people, it is truly an enormous stretch to stand up in front of the class to read a poem. But it's a challenge, I observed at 826 Valencia, that engages and empowers and helps kids to open the poem. Freed to experiment with pacing, inflection, gestures, differing voices, and other performative elements, the students unpack the poem's workings to discover both more about how it works and what it might mean.

32.

The basic point, then, is the simultaneity of "oral" and "written" literature. There is no deep gulf between the two: they shade into each other.

33.

And maybe it can't be overstated: it just feels good to say a poem out loud. I hiked alone to the top of a wooded hill in central Pennsylvania once to shout "Howl" at the top of my lungs. The birds became very silent. This was new.

IMITATION

34.

After they'd recited the poems as groups, I asked the students in my workshop each to pick one poem from the five they'd just heard delivered by their classmates. Then they had a chunk of time to rewrite it. To ape it. The more explicit the imitation and appropriation, I said, the better. At the same time, though I urged them to copy anything about it they wanted, I also asked them to be open to redoing anything about it that they wanted to. Find a word the author repeats, for instance, and change it in all occurrences to a new word-to-be-repeated. Or keep the verbs, but change the nouns. Or change the line length, but keep the adjectives. Introduce another speaker. Introduce lines that contradict the original lines.

35.

"We can just copy it?" someone asked. "Yes!" I smiled and shrugged. They were mildly suspicious. A second goal of this essay, then, is to dispel the idea that imitation is somehow cheap or cheating. Many young people seem to have this reaction, given all the gloomy stuff they hear about plagiarism and originality.

36.

But imitation, conscious imitation, is one of the great methods, perhaps the method of learning to write.

37.

The notion that the best way to teach young people to write poems is to give them a blank canvas and say go—I say that's not a very effective way. Constraints are good, and to assign the imitation of great poems is even better, I think. You should have seen all the beautiful peculiar poems my students penned after spending the first portion of class reciting and then imitating famous works. These were poems, by the way, that I didn't tell them to start writing. The students just did this spontaneously: finished their imitations and, swept up in inspiration, started in on their own compositions. The imitations led them to their own voices and gave them a sense of history, of the tradition of voices they were plugging into when they wrote poems of their own.

38.

Here is our mark, my friend, and let us hold closely to it: many are borne along inspired by a breath that comes from another.

39.

That the Romans felt no misgivings at all about submerging their individualities in the works of famous predecessors needs no demonstration here.

40.

Whenever I read a book or passage that particularly pleases me, in which a thing is said or an effect rendered with propriety, in which there is either some conspicuous force or some happy distinction in the style, I must sit down at once and set myself to ape that quality. I am unsuccessful and I know it; I try again and am again unsuccessful and always unsuccessful; but at least in these vain bouts, I get some practice in rhythm, in harmony,

in construction and the coordination of parts. I have thus played the sed-
ulous ape to Hazlitt, to Lamb, to Wordsworth, to Sir Thomas Browne, to
Defoe, to Hawthorne, to Montaigne, to Baudelaire, and to Obermann.

41.

This is the way to learn to write. It was so John Keats learned. It was so
Rainer Maria Rilke learned, and Langston Hughes, and Allen Ginsberg,
and Elizabeth Bishop. It was so, if we could trace it out, that all have
learned.

42.

When I was a boy, I took art classes with a painter in Berkeley. We met at
his house once a week. He had a scrubby gray beard and a basement stu-
dio. He would ask what I wanted to make, and I would show him whatever
I was interested in. At one point, I was obsessed with the *Tintin* comics
by Hergé, so my teacher had me create a comic book. He helped me repli-
cate the form and style and pretty much all aspects straight from Hergé's
work. My comic featured a young male reporter trying to find a treasure
map. There was a little white dog, and lots of chase scenes, and at least
one car wreck. It was even sixty-two pages, the same length as the *Tintin*
books. But in translating what I saw Hergé doing, I was never mindless.
I was learning a little about narrative, and drawing, and color—straight
from a pro. Later, when I was studying photography, I imitated the work
of Alfred Stieglitz and Henri Cartier-Bresson, picking out the kinds of
subjects they seemed to pick out, framing things the way they had, look-
ing for contrasts and light that they might have exploited. In doing so I
learned about each of these things by, in my rough and approximate way,
retracing the steps of the masters. Eventually I even took a few photo-
graphs that didn't look like Stieglitz's or Cartier-Bresson's, but rather like
my own, or at least like no one else's.

43.

I have often found myself in the midst of works executed upon principles with which I am unacquainted: I feel my ignorance and stand abashed. Imitation is an antidote to ignorance. Not to be too grandiose, but imitation might even be a precursor to empathy. All of us, young or old, might thus do well to more often imitate, imitate, imitate what is good—and thus learn, learn, learn from the inside out.

44.

Here's what I mean: In a time when the romantic notion of the inspired poet still has considerable credence, true imitation takes a certain courage. To submit oneself to imitation is to admit to needing to learn more. To submit oneself to imitation is to accept the anxiety of influence, to deny one's individuality, at least for a moment. This is hard for adults but, I think, rather easier for children, whose egos tend to be less developed. They are beginners at everything, and so to be a beginner at poetry writing or understanding, a beginner at Dickinson, Lorca, Whitman, Hughes, or de Burgos, isn't such a big deal. There is much to learn, and the students of 826 Valencia, like young people everywhere, are hungry. So in my workshop we walked through the construction of a few well-made poems in order to see better how they were put together. Then, when it was the students' turn to write, they knew a little more about how to build the foundations of a poem, how to build doors and windows, how to insulate them, how to wield the tools of the trade, the enjambments and rhymes and phrasings, because they had just gone through the motions of construction on a few great examples. From the inside out.

45.

This is why people sometimes say that genius borrows nobly. Or that good poets borrow but great poets steal. Or that art is theft. Take what you will with authority and see that you give it another, maybe even better life in the new context.

46.

In the workshop at 826 Valencia, the students who imitated the most directly came up with the weirdest, most vivid work. The direct collision of the student and the master artist is the most fertile smash imaginable. My students glowed.

47.

That's the way to the zoo,
That's the way to the zoo,
The monkey house is nearly full
But there's room enough for you.

STILLNESS

48.

Young and old, we are deluged with information, messages. Czesław Miłosz said somewhere that a life of total stasis is hell, but that so too is a life of constant motion.

49.

Stillness is not a lack of intensity. It is the sleep of the spinning top.

50.

What is indispensable about poetry, and what is thus most valuable to me about bringing it to young people, has to do finally with a state of being that it seems sometimes to inaugurate. A habit of mind it offers. A stillness.

51.

By "stillness" I mean something that happens while you read, a core trance that holds you, but also I mean the mental glow after you're finished, the pause before you blink and return to life around you. I mean literally that a poem insists (a little more, I think, than most things a person reads) that you be still and read it closely. I mean the breath held and the moment that breath is released. I mean, too, a stillness that sometimes takes hold after the classroom, away at home, seeping into you the next day or the next week. I mean stillness that is planted in the classroom but can't be noticed or measured till later. And not just literal, physical stillness. I mean that the act of reading a poem, of reading poetry regularly, of being inside poems, whether you are fifteen or fifty, is the act of equipping one-self for living, for navigating the convolution and noisiness of life.

52.

As my students worked, the room grew silent, full of stillness punctuated by bursts of pencil scribbling. I noticed as they worked that a student here or there would have an epiphany, a sudden laugh, a cascade of giggles, a big serious look. One student would lean over to another and show a permutation of a line from a poem he or she was imitating. They'd laugh together!

53.

The workshop finished out with students conducting all kinds of inspired poetry experiments. Some were still working on their imitations. Some, as I mentioned, had leapt from imitations directly into their own works. The students wrote individually or in small clusters, whispering and giggling. Many stared off through the ceilings and the walls, listening for lines or seeing images grow. Still waters, they say, run deep. I walked around, said a word here, asked a question there. They didn't need me too much anymore.

54.

Young people are as restless as any of us, and they have more energy. Stillness is not some medicine for jumpy delinquents; that's not what I'm proposing at all. Rather, I'm trying to suggest that stillness, one result of being in the presence of a masterful poem, results in a kind of engagement we get too rarely in this streaming world. That is to say, it creates within us a quiet empty room for a moment. Lets us hear the fly buzzing, the faucet dripping. And that drip becomes a sound reverberating throughout us, centering and focusing. Poetry is spirit nutrition. This, I think, is because of the stillness it generates in us.

55.

Nothing is more difficult for me, as a reader of poetry, than to describe why I am moved when a poem attains a certain intensity of quietness, when it seems to wait. This quietness that is neither quietism nor repression.

56.

Simultaneity—the awareness of so much happening at once—is now the most salient aspect of contemporary life. A good poem acts as a momentary reprieve from the grand sweeping movements of the universe, such that we are both aware of the simultaneity but also fully local. It makes us aware of the water right around us while not letting us forget that we're in a vast ocean of things.

57.

Poems are refuges, repair shops for the self, places of silence. Every child should have poems. The benefits seem immeasurable, and yet in our times unmeasured. The workshop ended and the stillnesses within faded and the students jumped up to pack their bags and meet their older siblings and parents for rides home. A few lingered with questions about the poems they were working on. Some asked for book recommendations. Some gave me book recommendations. Some promised to send me poems.

58.

One of the poems we used in the workshop was Federico García Lorca's

"The Little Mute Boy." It has a form that invites imitation. The group that read it out loud divided up the lines, delivering a crisscrossing chorus. Two read in one voice, two read in another. Two read one line, two read another. I went home with their haunting recitation echoing in my head. It inspired me to try imitating the poem, as I'd asked them to do. Though it was Lorca's vehicle, my imitation unlocked something I wouldn't have found my way into otherwise. Something I wanted to say, without knowing I wanted to say it, came through. It happened that I'd just lost a great love in my life. I felt lost from someone I had cared for deeply. The poem I came up with left me in a clear patch of illuminating stillness, like being in moonlight. The poem I came up with, though, seemed about more than broken love. It seemed also about the shock of the new, about the still, blank page of the self at the core of the self. It felt like mine, though I don't think it belongs to me:

The Little Mute Hand

The hand was reaching for the body.
(A man on the coast of summer had it.)
Inside a lemon
the hand was reaching for the body.

I do not want her forever;
I will let her break me
so that she can open time
finding blank notepaper.

Inside a lemon
the hand was reaching for the body.

(On a scorching day, far away,
she touches her new love's cheek.)

NOTES

This essay imitates the form used by David Shields in *Reality Hunger*. Some of the numbered pieces in this essay are direct quotes. Sometimes just a portion of the numbered piece is a direct quote. Other pieces I wrote entirely, or they're taken from somewhere but deeply massaged or completely rewritten. In any case, here are the sources they refer to or derive from.

1. and 2. http://826valencia.org/about

4. Ross Burkhardt, *Using Poetry in the Classroom: Engaging Students in Learning* (Lanham, MD: Rowman & Littlefield, 2006), 59.

5. Laura Apol and Jodi Harris, "Joyful Noises: Creating Poems for Voices and Ears," *Language Arts* 76, no. 4 (March 1999): 315.

6. Ruth Finnegan, *Oral Poetry: Its Nature, Significance and Social Context* (Cambridge: Cambridge University Press, 1977), 5.

8. Iona and Peter Opie, eds., *The Oxford Dictionary of Nursery Rhymes* (Oxford: Oxford University Press, 1962), 1.

11. Finnegan, *Oral Poetry*, 3.

12. G.S. Kirk, *Homer and the Oral Tradition* (Cambridge: Cambridge University Press, 1976), 202.

13. Eileen Murphy, "Ten Poems Students Love to Read Out Loud," www.poetryfoundation.org/learning/article/178700.

18. M. Fisher (1994), quoted in Apol and Harris, *Language Arts*, 317.

19. Apol and Harris, *Language Arts*, 317

20. Nancy Fraser in "Rethinking the Public Sphere," as quoted in Cynthia L. Selfe, "The Movement of Air, the Breath of Meaning: Aurality and Multimodal Composing," *College Composition and Communication* 60, no. 4 (June 2009): 616.

21. Krista Ratcliffe in "Rhetorical Listening," as quoted in Selfe, *College Composition and Communication*, 616.

22. Selfe, *College Composition and Communication*, 616.

23. Kirk, *Homer*, 4.

26. Ron Padgett, "Creative Reading," *Educating the Imagination: Essays and Ideas for Teachers & Writers* (New York: Teachers & Writers Collaborative, 2000), 246.

27. Padgett, *Educating the Imagination*, 249.

28. Finnegan, *Oral Poetry*, 242.

29. Padgett, *Educating the Imagination*, 250.

32. Finnegan, *Oral Poetry*, 24.

36. Theodore Roethke, *On the Poet and His Craft: Selected Prose of Theodore Roethke*, ed. Ralph Mills (Seattle: University of Washington Press, 1965), 69.

38. Longinus as quoted in Casper J. Kraemer Jr., "On Imitation and Originality," *The Classical Weekly* 20, no. 17 (March 7, 1917): 136.

39. Ibid.: 135.

40. Robert Louis Stevenson as quoted in Kraemer, *The Classical Weekly*, 136.

41. Ibid.

43. William Blake quoted in Christopher Ricks, *True Friendship* (New Haven, CT: Yale University Press, 2010), 1.

44. Roethke, *On the Poet and His Craft*, 70.

45. David Shields, *Reality Hunger: A Manifesto* (New York: Random House, 2010), 87, and Roethke, *On the Poet and His Craft*, 62.

47. Traditional verse, quoted in Finnegan, *Oral Poetry*, 4.

49. Thomas Hardy, *Jude the Obscure* (London: Penguin Classics, 1998), 112.

55. Harold Bloom, *Modern Critical Views: John Ashbery* (New York: Chelsea House Publishing, 1985), 64.

56. In this case, the referenced bit is this line: "Simultaneity—the awareness of so much happening at once—is now the most salient aspect of contemporary life." It comes from David Mazzucchelli's *Asterios Polyp*. No page numbers are given in that book, so, if you're interested, look for the quote in the last third or so of the book.

58. We used the translation by W.S. Merwin.

Fears, Truths, and Waking Life: On the Teaching of Kenneth Koch

Jordan Davis

To use Kenneth Koch's work with children as a model for your own teaching, you have to take children seriously—their feelings, their ideas of beauty, their ways of using language.

First, this means not talking down to them. You can't give a child a story about what you're teaching that's categorically different from what you would give an adult. Children understand when you're not telling the whole story. You do have to communicate your story clearly, which requires choosing direct words, stating the idea once, and finding instantly understandable examples of what you're talking about. Everyone in the room deserves for you to get through to them.

Second, this means responding sincerely and compassionately. When you praise student work, it has to be clear what you're praising, why it's worth calling attention to, and how anyone in the room could have come up with something like it, or, better, could use one child's discovery to make something of his or her own. When the students are going in a direction where you see nothing to praise, stop and start over. It's not the children's fault they found nothing inspiring in the suggestions you've made. Just as you can't falsely praise work that is trivial or lifeless or mean-spirited, you also can't criticize children for giving back what you've asked from them.

Third, because you're the teacher, the one who's supposed to know, the one the children will be looking to, it's crucial that you take yourself seriously and know your own feelings, ideas of beauty, and ways of using the language. If a writing idea isn't one that you can use yourself, you're not going to have an easy time showing nine-year-olds how to make it work. This doesn't mean you need to think and write like a nine-year-old, but it does mean, for example, that if you were happier reading *Richie Rich* and *Casper* comics than DC and Marvel, you're not going to have much to say on the subject of superheroes' origin myths and hard-earned grudges. But you may be able to use what all comics have in common— the wish to identify one's own special power—to suggest that the children write poems in which they try on several different kinds of magic or ability: to fly, to be invisible, to be able to create anything instantly, to go anywhere in space or time, to stop bullets or airplanes or bombs, to talk to the dead, to heal, to make people believe anything.

Likewise, if you don't particularly care for writing that pulls lots of different examples together in one small space but prefer to read and write narratives that work from a single premise or situation and feel their way through setbacks and conflicts to satisfying conclusions, you may have trouble suggesting that the children write list poems with different animals, colors, and places in each line. If it's not your idea of beauty, it's a lot trickier to make it work.

You may be able to adapt what worked for Koch into something better suited to your tastes. There are, of course, some preexisting limits you'll have to consider—the forty- to fifty-minute class periods, the difficulty of engaging twenty or thirty children on a single topic, the kinds of stories children are told and will think they are supposed to tell—knowing that even the most accomplished teachers struggle with them from time to time.

The best introduction to Koch's ideas about teaching poetry writing to children—and while I am using superlatives, the best work there is on the subject—is his 1970 book *Wishes, Lies, and Dreams*. Used correctly, it can help inspire children to write poems of strong feelings and lively images almost instantly. Opinion over the years on the correct use of Koch's methods has not been unanimous. There are purists and there are critics. I had the good luck to work with Koch for several years, and it seemed to me it might be useful to teachers and poets, or at any rate not too distracting or misleading, if I shared some of what he told me.

I worked as Kenneth's assistant from 1990 until his death in 2002. I began as a replacement for his graduate assistant (I was an undergraduate), responsible for mailing his bills and retyping his drafts. I remember thinking my duties would include library research—Kenneth's riffs on Tadeusz Kantor, Fernand Braudel, and Ludwig Wittgenstein in *One Thousand Avant-Garde Plays* had come out a couple years earlier—but learned gradually that self-conscious erudition was not Kenneth's default mode; friendly competition was.

I had been dating his previous research assistant, and as her graduate exams drew closer, she told Kenneth she needed to stop assisting (and me she needed to stop dating) and start focusing on studying for her comps. And she told him that I knew Kenneth's poems as well as or better than anybody, including Kenneth himself. This was a stretch, but in any case I'd read all of his poems and plays, and as he had told me, I was probably one of twenty people who'd read through both his novel *The Red Robins* and the play of the same name. I had also looked at one or two of his books on teaching. I got the job.

One of the main texts Kenneth taught from was Mayakovsky's *How Are Verses Made?* He quoted to students Mayakovsky's rule that the most important thing for a poet is to have a clean copy of what you've written when it's time to revise. What he did not tell his students is that he had assistants to make these clean copies for him, which he would then mark up in pencil, grease pencil, highlighter, ballpoint, and felt-tip, then cut up and tape, rearrange, and hand back to be turned into new clean copy. Kenneth's industriousness was not unlike a factory's. There were days when he generated forty or fifty pages of these drafts.

I was not the first assistant to make these clean copies using a personal computer with a dot matrix printer or laser printer, but judging from Kenneth's archives, I was probably among the first three or four, and he was pleased and surprised that I returned his work to him while it was still fresh in his mind. It was fortunate that I could do so because I resented the bill-mailing part of the job to the point of incompetence, with treachery lying just beyond. Dozens of young scholars, poets, and artists must have worked in a similar capacity for Kenneth over the almost forty years he taught at Columbia University. One of my first tasks was to accompany him to a rug dealer to find a carpet to furnish his office on the fourth floor of Hamilton Hall. Kenneth was very good at using his allocation of the English department budget.

A few months into the job, at the start of a long weekend break from school, I received from Kenneth a fifty-page draft of a poem in the form of fake book reviews, à la Gilbert Sorrentino's *Mulligan Stew*. I didn't know at the time that Kenneth had been let go by his editor, that he'd had a cancer scare, that the woman he considered the muse of the thousand plays had left him, or, for that matter, that book reviews were in those pre-Amazon days the main way authors could tell how they were doing. All I saw, as I read Kenneth's parody of the *Times Literary Supplement's* wonderful but obscure miscellany on the train home, was that it was not a good poem. The reviews were mean-spirited, the books were implausible, the jokes were flat. I didn't want to type it. Sunday came around, and it remained untyped. My parents, sensing that I was even more out of sorts than usual, counseled me just to tell him that the piece wasn't up to his standards and that I didn't want to take his money to do work he wouldn't use.

"You're fired!" he said, taking the poem from me. It wasn't the first time he'd said it, but it felt definitive. I walked down the long hallway from his living room, where he wrote, to the front door. There was an enormous Red Grooms canvas along that hallway, a backdrop from the stage production of *The Red Robins*, showing a plaza in Guadalajara with at least one man in a sombrero, shoulders hunched, caught mid-stride. I took a good last look at it as I walked, to memorize details to put in a short story about my brief time as a writer's assistant. I was at the front door when I heard Kenneth again.

"Fucko! Come back here." I walked back. "You're right. It's no good." There was a pause. "Why don't we try something different," he said. From then on, I was to listen to Kenneth read his drafts aloud, let him know which works were promising and which were not likely to work out. I was flattered and daunted by the increased responsibility. It took me a while to understand that I was actually being hired as a sparring partner.

A few years later, I was about to start my first residency through the Teachers & Writers Collaborative. One evening, after having discussed several long and short poems on diverse subjects and a play about a man who shows up for a duel in a giant bird costume, I changed the subject to ask for some advice on teaching. Kenneth paused, then reminded me that he'd written a few books on the subject. I allowed that I had read them several times and in fact had shipped off several orders for them that day as part of my job at T&W. "What I was hoping for," I said, "were some general instructions." Kenneth paused again, then smiled. "Some General Instructions" is the title of a poem he'd written at the height of interest in his work teaching children. (If you ever need a favor from a poet, it sometimes works to quote the poet's work casually in conversation.)

Shortly after *Wishes, Lies, and Dreams* was published, around when

I was born, the poems of Kenneth's elementary-school students at P.S. 61 in the Lower East Side made a splash. The children read on David Frost's TV show, and Barbara Walters interviewed Kenneth. The book was reviewed widely. And Kenneth found himself speaking frequently to groups of educators around the country. Sales of the book were good, and Kenneth proposed a sequel. *Rose, Where Did You Get That Red?* picked up a promising lead left undeveloped in *Wishes*: how to use great poetry— Blake, Lorca, Shakespeare—to teach elementary-school children to write poems.

Kenneth enjoyed success. The sixties had begun extremely well for him: a tenure-track position at Columbia, his first poetry book reviewed in *Time* magazine with more books of plays and poems following quickly upon it, collaborations with major artists and composers, and every sign suggesting he and his friends were finally being heard. By the end of the decade, though, his first marriage had fallen apart, his closest friend in poetryland, Frank O'Hara, had been killed in an accident, and poems, which had always come easily to him, were proving more and more difficult to write. The enthusiastic reception of work in one area of his life suggested an opportunity, and through trial and error, he found a way to use in his poems what was working so well with teachers and students.

In *The Art of Love*, published within a couple years of *Rose*, Kenneth pursued the thought experiment of addressing several subjects in poetry, beginning in roughly the same tone he used in his prose about teaching, leaving the restrictions of the schoolroom behind while taking his chosen subjects—love, beauty, poetry—as seriously as possible, which is to say, entirely seriously and with a little silliness. (He told me once that, regarding being silly, he took courage from Maud Gonne's referring to Yeats as "silly Willie," paraphrased by Auden.) He referred to these as his "instructional poems." One success led to another. Inspired in part by the increasingly adventurous all-inclusiveness of the work of his friend and rival John Ashbery, Kenneth decided to try an instructional poem about life itself. The following are lines from "Some General Instructions," the poem I mentioned earlier:

> Be attentive to your dreams. They are usually about sex,
> But they deal with other things as well in an indirect fashion
> And contain information that you should have.
> You should also read poetry. Do not eat too many bananas.
> In the springtime, plant. In the autumn, harvest.
> In the summer and winter, exercise. Do not put
> Your finger inside a clam shell or
> It may be snapped off by the living clam. Do not wear a shirt
> More than two times without sending it to the laundry.

Though the instructional poems derive their tone from Kenneth's work among schoolchildren, there's an important difference between them and the books about teaching. In his prose he's careful not to tell teachers what to do but describes what worked for him and how he found it, stays in the first person and the past tense, and sticks to specific classrooms and the obstacles he overcame in them. In the context of the constant explosive change of the poems and plays he had published up to this point, the coherent narratives of the introductions to the teaching books mark a change. The introductions to his books on teaching can be read as one thing after another, and reread as complex explanations of how to identify and remove problems in order to create ideal conditions for spontaneous discovery and collaboration. In his introductions, Kenneth takes the teachers in his audience as seriously as he does the children in his classrooms: all appearances to the contrary, he doesn't tell any adults what to do; he simply explains his goals, what difficulties he found, how he and the students found ways around them, and what they accomplished together.

I'd read the introductions. Young and foolish, I preferred the absurd certainty of the instructional poems to the pragmatism of the teaching books. I wanted an executive summary of the introductions, and I thought

I had figured out how to get it. "Well now, very funny, White Fang," Kenneth said, in response to my having quoted him. (Kenneth's instant nicknames tended to fall away like sticky notes on corduroy.) He proceeded to quiz me on my knowledge of *Wishes* and *Rose*, both the introductions and what others refer to as "writing prompts" but he preferred to call lessons, assignments, or poetry ideas. And satisfied, I suppose, that he could emphasize certain points in what he had written without sacrificing the sense of the work as a whole, he gave me a few suggestions. They are below.

When teaching poetry to children, it's important to start with a poem written in collaboration with the whole class. Write five or six lines from different students on the chalkboard so that everyone sees that everyone can do what is being asked and so there can be ideas to work from on the board.

Wishes are good to start with because they encourage children to connect writing with expressing what they're excited about and also because they allow children to feel comfortable sharing feelings and ideas in a friendly, competitive way. There will be wishes for world peace and a billion dollars; it may be useful to accept each of these wishes once and then ask what else the students wish. If the prevailing mood in the room is too far in the direction of trying to please you by saying what they think you want, make up a bunch of completely different kinds of wishes to relieve the pressure of having to say the "right" thing. It may not happen as much with children these days, but it can be scary to be told to say what your wishes are; wishes and fears are famously connected. You really don't have to tell the children that, though. The important thing in the first few lessons is to interest and excite them and to keep adding to what they can do in a poem.

Once the children have become familiar with the idea of putting a wish in every line, you can increase the difficulty modestly by asking them for a wish and one other thing in every line, such as a color or place.

The formal requirement is a slight distraction that can give access to surprising changes of association: What color are the leaves on the tree you want to be sitting under instead of at your desk, for example? What color do you make the invisible car when you need to see it to find it? What's something else that has that exact color? You'll know it's working if the poems are lively and surprising.

If you have weeks and weeks and the students are responding well, you can cover comparisons, colors, and noises one class at a time for each, but you may find that by bringing synesthesia into the classroom from the beginning, you can cover them all at once. Ask the children to close their eyes and keep them closed; then jingle your keys or ring the teacher's bell or pull open a shade and ask them what color they saw when they heard the sound. Some won't have seen any color, but some will. Ask them to name something else that has that exact color; if they say something general, help them be more specific. Then write a line based on what they've said and put it on the board: "The sound of keys is purple-silver like the little flowers by the blacktop." One thing that can work well is to compare the sound of a word in different languages—for example, which is darker, *night* or *noche*? *Green* or *vert*? *Five* or *fünf*?

Lies. There's a lot in the book to make it clear that writing in the classroom is a special situation in which giving children permission to do what comes naturally can be put to socially acceptable ends. The power of saying "put a lie in every line" is undeniably exciting; if it looks as though it might get out of hand, you can revise and have them put something crazy or unusual in every line, but it's not as good. What is always good, when the students seem stuck, is to encourage them to make their lines as real or as crazy as they feel right then.

The "Swan of Bees" exercise is a good fourth or fifth class. A spelling mistake in a poem a third grader was writing suggested this idea, as did that phrase in Frank O'Hara's poem "Easter": "the roses of Pennsylvania."

The idea is to put together unexpected combinations using the word *of* in the middle of them. You can also have them use *is* alongside *of* to connect apparently unlike things. It helps to suggest that students make the two things they connect have only one part in common: "a road of strawberries" would make sense because pavement is usually slightly bumpy like a strawberry, but "the forest is coats" may be too obvious. "The woods are a hallway of cubbies" might be a better example, where the spaces between the trees are like the cubbies of absent students.

If you try having students write to music, the examples mentioned in *Wishes, Lies, and Dreams* are all by classical composers, but jazz can work, as can songs in other languages. Songs in languages the students know can be a little distracting from the purpose, which, like the "sounds and colors" poems, is to have them write what the music suggests to them, to be aware of how it makes them feel and what that reminds them of. Different kinds of music lead to different feelings, from Wagner to Louis Armstrong to Gregorian plainsong.

Work on dreams after you've been in the classroom a few times. It may be good to prepare students for the next class by asking them to pay attention to their dreams. If they want, they can take notes when they wake up each morning so they remember, but it isn't necessary or required homework.

Having the students combine poetry ideas, once they're familiar with some of them, can be exciting, as can poems that encourage feelings of mastery and change. The "I used to, but now" poetry idea is good for that; having them begin one line with I used to and the next with but now, lets kids talk about memories and things they miss (and don't miss), as well as mistakes they've made and ideas they've outgrown.

It's almost always better to suggest that students write as if they are the things they want to talk about or as if they're talking to, rather than just describing, them.

Eat a good breakfast and drink some (not too much!) coffee before class. Wear nice, brightly colored clothes, show up on time, smile, and have writing paper ready to hand out to everyone.

Wishes, Lies, and Dreams and *Rose, Where Did You Get That Red?* include several student examples for each of these ideas and others, and if it seems as though the ideas aren't getting through, it may help to read from the examples. The best examples will usually be the freshest ones, though—yours, and those of the students in the room.

In my work as Kenneth's assistant, I was comfortable letting him know when I agreed and disagreed with his ideas about poetry and when I thought specific lines and entire poems were working or not. As a student of his teaching, though, it hasn't occurred to me to argue with his methods, which I've found produce remarkably consistent results in classroom after classroom. I'm aware that that consistency itself is, for some critics, a sign that the poetry ideas wash over children without being integrated into their thinking and practice, that the ideas just give back what Kenneth put into them. I've also heard the criticism that the children's poems included in Kenneth's books on teaching writing don't live up to the claims Kenneth made for them. I could not disagree more. The analogy I keep thinking of is to gym class or sports camp. The exercises suggested in *Wishes, Lies, and Dreams* develop some basic skills that much contemporary writing fails to demonstrate, writing that would be improved by a stronger sense of form, a greater variety of imagery, sensuousness, spontaneity, and deep feeling.

Teachers who have already applied Kenneth's methods will recognize that much of his advice to me in his general instructions derives from the introductions to his books. He did restate and repeat certain principles and ideas many times in his college classroom and in his writings. I think I heard him quote Paul Valery's line that "a poem is never finished, only abandoned" about a hundred times. My own advice to writers and teachers coming to these ideas for the first time is to read the introductions to Kenneth's books a dozen times. They are at once brimful instruction manuals and breezy narratives. It is very easy to mistake a necessary ingredient for a passing remark. And then, having read and reread his texts, try anything and everything that comes to mind as a poetry idea for the classroom, as long as it feels exciting and surprising and leads to lines of your own that you can look at coolly and find life in.

The Door Called Poetry[1]

William Stafford

Learning *magazine, for teachers in grade schools, asked
me to write about teaching from a poet's point of view. I felt
a surge of ambition—to help reduce that distance pupils
are induced to feel between themselves and "literature."
I reduced it by starting with a slight piece about first grade
at the beginning and an actual transcript from a preschooler
at the end; but my article was identified as "Exploring the
Wild, Surprising World of Poetry."*

First Grade

In the play Amy didn't want to be
anybody; so she managed the curtain.
Sharon wanted to be Amy. But Sam
wouldn't let anybody be anybody else—
he said it was wrong. "All right," Steve said,
"I'll be me, but I don't like it."

---

1. William Stafford, "The Door Called Poetry" from *You Must Revise Your Life* (Ann Arbor: The University of Michigan Press, 1987).

So Amy was Amy, and we didn't have the play.

And Sharon cried.

Is this poetry? In my view, yes. In my view, though, poetry, like breathing, happens all the time, but—like breathing—at its best it should get little attention.

In the classroom, any time anyone says anything or jots down anything, some of what is said or written is luckier than the rest—and poetry is language with a little luck in it.

Those lucky places—everyone stumbles upon them; they are homogenized into our lives. And in class I try to recognize what comes at me, not to commend or admire, and not even—usually not even—to mention it, but simply to feel it myself. The signals I give off when someone says or writes something that lucks into poetry will come naturally—in my eyes, in the way I lean forward, maybe even in my sudden look of envy.

It is that immediate response to language that counts. Sometimes it seems to me the best equipment for being a teacher of talking and writing and reading—of communication—would be a wonderful rubber face that would register every nuance; my role would not be that of approving or disapproving, but simply (and it's not simple) that of realizing, realizing everything, all those amazing, miraculous connections that language and the mind make with each other.

When we are with children we are constantly in the presence of these sparks. To do poetry is to read or speak or write or listen with a readiness for the surprises, the bonuses that come on the individual wavelength of any human being. To organize the response, to try to coerce it so that it will be correct or approved in any way is to violate the nature of what poetry is. And that is why—though I am a poet myself, and a teacher, and a student—I get very jumpy in the presence of many poetry lessons.

So—in the classroom I wouldn't even use the word poetry if I could help it. I would try to keep students from knowing how educators have codified and classified and labelized the approaches to this shimmering and unexpected field full of goodies.

If an alert student would look at a page of poetry and say it is fat or skinny, I would feel better than if the student said it was iambic hexameter.

OK—I know we have some disagreements about this. And of course many authorities, some of them awesome, would clobber me. Still, let me sing my song, for there is one to be sung about the sidling approach in the classroom.

The turn from the authority way in poetry came to me vividly when a student was reading her theme in class not long ago. The others began to talk about it, and I listened awhile (my best tactic) and then had to ask, "Megan, wasn't there something strange in the way you moved along in that first part?"

"Well, you see," she said, "I wrote this first as a poem, and then I made it an essay." Then she went back to talking to the others, while I brooded about what she had said.

I know this student well, so I dared interrupt again: "Do you very often do that?"

She briefly turned to me and said, "Oh, yes. I usually write an essay or a story first as a poem." And she went back to the more important issues she was discussing with the other students.

Naturally I had to interrupt one more time. "Why?"

She was patient with me. "Writing a poem is more direct and simple and easy. I can put down things as they come to me, and I like to let myself ramble along the way I feel while I am writing."

It was an ordinary afternoon, but I permitted myself to lean back and savor a historic moment, a moment like that when a monk in the Dark Ages first read a page without moving his lips. I had been present when a lucky young person let me glimpse a new generation's easiness with one of the arts. The occasion was all the more satisfying for my having come out of my own Dark Ages when we students were so instructed in poetry that we were ready for the literature of greeting cards: if you had a rhyme, you had a poem.

With this new class, I was meeting students who had found the freedom and opportunity there is in language: letting it carry you as you explore forward along the line that develops where your own sensibility touches a theme.

That line cannot be predicted, if you are to take advantage of what the language begins to offer the ready talker or writer. Our students, if we give them our company, our responding presence during their questing (the rubber face again), may be induced to accept their own discoveries and to feel the satisfaction of converging with those resonating helps in language.

Let's face it, though—poetry will always be a wild animal. There is something about it that won't yield to ordinary learning. When a poem catches you, it overwhelms, it surprises, it shakes you up. And often you can't provide any usual explanation for its power.

For all of us in our careful role as educators, there is something humbling in the presence of the arts. There is no use thinking hard work and application and responsibility will capture poetry. It is something different. It cannot live in the atmosphere of competition, politics, business, advertising. Successful people cannot find poems. For you must kneel down and explore for them. They seep into the world all the time and lodge in odd corners almost anywhere, in your talk, in the conversation around you. They can be terribly irresponsible.

In a class I visited once, the teacher had copied for the students on the board in front a "poem for the day," a pleasant verse by a successful someone who affirmed feeling lonely and liking to think about warm little animals. But on the board in back—where the teacher looked—was this:

> When I have fears that I may cease to be
> Before my pen has glean'd my teeming brain,

Before high-piled books, in charact'ry,
  Hold like rich garners the full-ripen'd grain;
When I behold, upon the night's starr'd face,
  Huge cloudy symbols of a high romance,
And think that I may never live to trace
  Their shadows, with the magic hand of chance;
And when I feel, fair creature of an hour,
  That I shall never look upon thee more,
Never have relish in the faery power
  Of unreflecting love!—then on the shore
Of the wide world I stand alone, and think
  Till Love and Fame to nothingness do sink.

So—there is a strangeness in our work when we deal with poetry. It ranges from high to low. We can find it in Keats, and we can find it, as I did, in the words of a preschooler telling his mother about his day:

This has been an awful good day.
  First, I found a snake
  then an old rotten dried-up mouse
  then a baby dead mole
  and then an old part of a gun.

The snake will probably get away.
  A cat will eat the dried-up mouse.
  The baby dead mole's mother will take him to her nest.
  But I'll keep the old part of a gun.

Making the Rounds

Jimmy Santiago Baca

Most poetry textbooks or guides for teachers focus on the elements of the craft—they describe in detail the workings of metaphors, rhyme schemes, and various aspects of poetic traditions. This, of course, is a must for any teacher of the art. But how can teachers conduct workshops for "bored kids"? How can teachers turn problem classes—every instructor's fear—into memorably beautiful ones?

Kids don't need to be taught the essence of poetry. No matter whether they are in a rez schoolroom, a Hopi hogan, or a prestigious private school such as Exeter—in New Hampshire, Oregon, or the hardcore but beautiful barrios of San Jose—they understand the language of childhood.

What follows are some illustrations of my experience with students, beginning with my experiences in prison. Though they live in adult bodies, many of the prisoners with whom I have worked appear imprisoned within their own minds and bodies—trapped as people who have committed crimes against themselves, as well as those in the outside world.

1.

My teaching "career" started when, as an inmate, I visited other convicts' cells. I sat on the concrete with the bars between us, reading them poetry.

I'm not sure why poetry was so popular with prisoners, but I have a guess. Many had no books in their homes growing up, yet often family members had memorized poems—Spanish speakers call those *dichos*, pithy sayings that give a lot of meaning for the few words the sentence uses. Mothers nursed their babies and hummed poetry to them, and when the children grew older, their mothers whispered bandit epics into their little ten-year-old ears. Those epics inspired them to want to become gangsters—in other words, to live flamboyant lives with drama and conflict. Too often, though, these lives were cut short.

2.

I was released from prison in 1979. After having had a couple of poetry books published, I started teaching elementary-school students through the New Mexico Arts Division (funded by the National Endowment for the Arts). My students reintroduced me to the imaginative language of childhood—the speech that carries the excitement of images, the fires of unpredictable vocabulary, the surprise word choices reeling with hilarious giants and talking ants and Santa Clauses who are not Nordic or Caucasian but Chicano and who burrow beyond San Felipe Pueblo deep into the nearby Sandia Mountains outside Albuquerque. A Santa Claus who has, instead of reindeer, a herd of mules he dresses up like reindeer for Christmas and who even likes tortillas, tacos y burritos, and beans and chili. When the instructor opens up to this type of imaginative language, the conversation about poetry with children becomes an adventure. But this adventure must first refer directly to kids' day-to-day experiences—that is essential.

3.

If we turn to a slightly older age group—adolescents, say, in a classroom for students at risk—we find some students who don't like school, will not study, refuse to collaborate with the teacher, and disregard lessons and curricula as if homework were a terminal disease. At this point, as a poet-teacher I know that I need to surprise them. How can I do this? What teaching tools can help me shake them into wakefulness?

Here is one example: I once asked violent students at a charter high school to consider a poem that asked for forgiveness for beating on poor people, for clubbing down Mexicans in the street for no good reason other than that it was entertaining. All the kids in the room got it, nodded their heads in assent, hung their heads low, and motioned with facial expressions that they appreciated the poem. They knew a woman had written it, and they wondered why. Why did she need forgiveness from them?

That's when the author—whom I had invited to the class—explained that she had been a police officer in San Diego for twelve years and had routinely beaten Mexicans for no reason. All the students were stunned, unsure how to react. A cop apologizing to them? No way. An ex-cop writing poetry? No way. Every student's mouth was agape. Their perspective on life was suddenly realigned. Bravo for poetry. The students felt more human after an ex-cop had apologized to them and written a forgiveness poem for them—and after they had accepted it.

Of course, it is not every day that one can bring an ex-cop to recite poetry to an inner-city high-school audience. But the point here is simple: the work must connect to the audience's everyday experience, cast a spell on the audience, and teach a lesson—something worth holding on to.

4.

We now fly from the Southwest to South Florida, where I'm teaching poetry to a class of middle-school kids. I have a list of themes (from my textbook for teachers and students, *Stories from the Edge*) that I want them to tackle. Among the mostly fun themes is a hard one: write about a painful experience. On this occasion, everyone wrote for an hour, and when it was time for the students to read their work aloud, one young girl rose and spoke of her father molesting her—that very morning it had happened, and it had been going on for years.

Suddenly it became an emergency. The librarian called the teachers, the teachers called the principal, the principal called the counselor, and the counselor called an off-grounds psychologist. While all this was happening, the kids were hugging the poor abused girl and sharing not only in her happiness that she had finally freed herself of the debilitating silence but also in the sorrow of her suffering.

Her poem meant a fresh start, a way to begin the recovery process. (The first order of the day was to arrest her father, which the police did.) It was a profound moment in that classroom and one of the most meaningful and consequential uses of poetry I've ever witnessed. Of course, it is not something that happens in my classroom—or any classroom—every day. Nonetheless, one must find a way to teach literature so students can begin to engage their freedom of self-expression, to write poetry that alerts them to their importance in the world.

5.

It is important to make poetry real for kids, available to all their senses. Here's what happens: I give each kid in my class an ear of corn (use anything you wish in yours; this is just an example), and I tell them to close their eyes and imagine everything they wanted out of their lives that had never materialized. Each corn leaf represents a memory. "Aggressively tear a leaf from the husk," I instruct them.

Once the corn (their souls or hearts) is stripped bare of bad memories, I ask them to feel and smell the kernels. I tell them to keep their eyes closed and imagine every kernel as a good memory, to find images and sounds and rhymes and rhythms and phrases and nouns and verbs that they think stand for and make up the elements of life—with the sun doing its part, the earth and water theirs.

When the kids open their eyes, I ask them to begin writing their vocabulary for joy, for sadness—to begin to work with language to express their emotions in images, assonances, alliterations, metaphors. This is just the beginning, of course, a starting point—but hopefully also a turning point in their learning to find poetic tools for expressing their voices.

6.

When a kid is caught in his or her version of no-man's land, with nothing to lose, it is usually interpreted as the kid having committed some terrible crime, as the kid having done something stupid to sabotage his or her chance for a normal life.

Poetry has the magic to transform that crazy energy for the person's benefit. Poetry can make use of desperation and hopelessness—and once that wild, passionate energy is harnessed, directed, and engaged with focus and purpose, real personal change is possible. No one can anticipate the magnitude of gifts the person will contribute to society's welfare. When poetry engages despair, it's a game changer.

Try it in your classroom with the so-called gangbangers, bored kids, troubled, wounded lads—it works wonders.

Radical Strategies:
Toward a Poetics of Play[1]

Karen Volkman

Some of my earliest teaching of poetry took place in elementary school classrooms. I spent five years working with schoolchildren in New York City through the organization Teachers & Writers Collaborative, founded in the lost years of humanistic idealism in the 1960s by Rosellen Brown, Kenneth Koch, Herbert Kohl, Phillip Lopate, and Grace Paley among others. One of T&W's key terms is "educating the imagination," and their ambition is to bring the imaginative freedoms of poetry and the ethical expansiveness it allows into the early experience of language, and so to the early acts of articulating experience and perceptions. I taught in public schools in neighborhoods ranging from the South Bronx and East Harlem to Belmore, an upper middle-class suburb of Long Island. And I discovered what happens between the first acquisition of writing (the very painful crafting of letters in kindergarten and first grade—literally physically painful—I have so many vivid memories of kids putting down their pencils and shaking out their sore fingers) to the point of writing

---

1. Karen Volkman, "Radical Strategies: Toward a Poetics of Play" from *Poets on Teaching: A Sourcebook*, edited by Joshua Marie Wilkinson (Iowa City: University of Iowa Press, 2010).

with relative fluency by sixth grade.

Working with hundreds of kids taught me that the weird and fascinating panoply of knowledge the mind receives in American grade schools—marine life, volcanoes, planets, numbers, colors—as well as neighboring streets, music, food, and the grandparents' donkey in Mexico are completely equal and exciting and allowable phenomena within a child's poem. The borders aren't there. They start to develop around the end of sixth grade when we are taught to define experience in terms of categories.

Like many poets, my deepest wish in teaching is to reawaken such a state of immediate engagement with language, as though we were first discovering the word *krill* or *lava*, and taking pleasure in the new realm of sensation it ignites in the mind. Velimir Khlebnikov, the great Futurist visionary and one of the most singular imaginations of the twentieth century, was fascinated by children's writing and its expressive and imaginative freedoms, its borderlessness. Dada sound poems, as well, sprung from a desire to return to an even earlier state of language experience, prior even to structuring sound into words. In these avant-garde movements, radical experimentation truly seeks a return to some fundamental root, rediscovered as a fertile, generative force—before the plant grew into a usable structure to be harvested and pruned.

To bring students back to this point, I use a range of methods, often drawn from experimental practices of different artists or schools. One course, "Radical Strategies," focuses on avant-garde movements of the twentieth century, starting with Futurism. In a recent version of this class, Futurism, Dada, Surrealism, students explored these three seminal movements (which can be collectively viewed as the childhood of the avant-garde) and wrote from experiments drawn from their works, including poems, prose, paintings, short films, music, manifestos, and speculative writings.

From the manifesto "The Futurist Reconstruction of the Universe," students imagined how language could respond to one of the various proposed reconstructions, including "The Futurist Toy," "The Artificial Landscape," and "The Metallic Animal." An exercise based on Khlebnikov's "Alphabet of the Mind" set into play an associative relationship with sound and letter and word, breaking out of traditional logics into a more extensive mode of relation. Another exercise made use of the "Surrealist Art Questionnaire," based on the example in Mary Ann Caws's anthology *Surrealist Poets and Painters*; questions posed for De Chirico's "Enigma of a Day" include "Where is the sea?" and "Where would you make love?" as well as more scatological queries. For this project, students worked in groups of three, each proposing questions about a work of Surrealist art, which they each then responded to and compiled (I also invited them to have friends, roommates, and partners contribute, widening the circle of response). This approach helped break through any reverence for or intimidation by the painting or sculpture, resulting in a greater intimacy and freer interaction with the relational energies of the work.

For another exercise, based on the section in André Breton's *Mad Love* in which Breton and Alberto Giacometti wander through a flea market chancing upon resonant objects, I asked students to go to one of Missoula's junk / antique stores with a partner, in search of some instigating Thing. As Breton describes, the presence of another person results in the receptive faculty being "primed"—a different field is opened and charged by the emanation of the other with his or her own references, associations, extensivities, hauntings.

As a form of "educating the imagination," a poetics of play provides a new set of engagements, de-emphasizing the I-centered perspective while still allowing a dance of sensibility, a tracing of a ranging intelligence touching and touched by phenomena—including language and sound relation as event and phenomenon—but not compelled to subvert these sensations to a reductive or boundaried conception of self. It prompts a shift of mind to the importance of encounter with the material of phenomena, of inhabiting not a self but a diversity of selves created by engagements with the sensuous. It is poetics as a process of initiation and invitation, alive with insights, hints, glimpses into new relational realms.

A Dream: The Poetry School

Dorothea Lasky

For a while I've had a dream of a Poetry School. This "school" would be many things: a writers-in-the-schools teacher-certification program, a professional development provider, an actual school, and eventually a K–12 system that could make poetry both the lens for learning and its focus. At the Poetry School, poetry would become the essential backdrop to a community of learning and a way to provide a major place for poetry within the educational system. It is my dream to help make a space for all young people to roam language wild and free and for poets to teach. Let me explain—and to do so, I want to begin by telling you where the idea started.

Two Memories of My Schooling

I tend to be hopeful about the future of public education, despite the current shortsighted emphasis on standardized testing and educational decision makers' inability to understand the importance of providing opportunities for arts learning to every student. My hope arises out of having had an excellent K–12 experience within a set of public schools in suburban St. Louis, Missouri, in the eighties and nineties, where I was afforded many learning opportunities that people tend to think happen only in private schools. It scares me—it literally keeps me up at night— to realize that my vision and version of public schooling does not exist everywhere.

One teacher who always sticks out in my memory is Mrs. Jayne Hanlin, my fifth-grade teacher at Spoede Elementary School. She was a strict force, with the sharpest wit. I can see her now, with her fierce eyes looking across the room at the sea of students in which I was a bobbing octopus. She had a fuzzy head of red hair (like me) and played the cello. She was the kind of teacher who was in charge. I once wrote her a thank-you card for something, and she corrected my alot. "No, that's a lot," she remarked, making the note with the cold grace of a grammarian. She gave never-ending gifts to her students, but her greatest gift to me was her love of classical poetry. She loved Latin and Greek, and I am forever grateful that she was in a school where she could demonstrate this love to her students.

Every day, during lunch, Mrs. Hanlin read stories from Ovid's *Metamorphoses*. I was a ten-year-old poet, and I had never heard anything like those stories before. They were so weird and brutal, and they cut into my soul. She also began a classics partnership with the district high school (where I would take Latin years later), and we all put on plays drawn from myths. In one play, I was Calliope, the muse of epic poetry. I belted out my lines and held a long (very long) paper scroll. I really was Calliope, just as all young actors really are the people they perform, and I can't ever thank Mrs. Hanlin enough for casting me in a role I would live out in so many ways in this lifetime.

Only much later did I realize that my school experience was not available to every student in the country. In high school, I was an absolute nerd because I was a poet and loved to learn. But there was a place for me in that handsome brick building. I liked to think of myself as Queen of the Nerds, with a band of trench coat–wearing comrades. As a junior, I did a physics project on radiant heat energy that was conceived with (but more by) my teacher, Mr. Miller. I then participated in a physics contest; I was ill prepared but somehow got a good score. Mr. Miller also had a partnership with a city school, whose students visited our school a few times. One time we visited their school, and it was an absolute shock: the place was bare, in a run-down building, and there were few students in attendance. The school felt listless. The science teachers had us do an exercise, and I remember how basic it seemed. I had never perceived the inequality of education more clearly than in that moment. I saw firsthand what I now know is the educational inequality that leads directly to the achievement gap. A little spark pushed me even then. I wondered what might allow the students in less privileged schools to experience the beauty of knowledge and the awe of learning that I had encountered. I have only begun to understand the answer to this question.

A Recent Educational Experience

I recently finished a doctorate in education, and for my dissertation I studied how teachers foster creativity in their classrooms. I studied five high-school science teachers in a large urban school system. I also visited numerous other science classrooms, and I studied the ways teachers nurtured their students' creativity. I looked at how teachers planned their lessons, how they responded to their students' innovative thinking, what perspectives on the importance of creativity they brought to their classrooms, and so forth. Although I looked at students in a science context, what I really found were many poets in those schools, students who loved poetry, and teachers who responded to this love. I saw teachers harness their students' learning in science through poetry. I saw teachers create assignments that allowed students to apply a "poetic skill set." For example, teachers asked their students to look for patterns in the world, to read for subtext, to invent new kinds of logic to explain natural phenomena, and to make careful observations and write about them. One teacher gave a student an alternative assignment when he failed an astronomy test. Because the teacher knew his student loved music and writing, he asked him to listen to a symphony inspired by outer space and write a creative response to it. The student did well and passed the class.

Many times, without even knowing I was a poet (after all, to them I was just "Ms. Dottie, the researcher"), the students shared their poems and hip-hop songs with me—reading me their work, giving me CDs, inviting me to their poetry readings. I saw that poetry had a natural place for so many young learners, even within a discipline such as science, which is often seen (unfairly, of course) as poetry's opposite. I also saw once again the limitations of and inequalities in our schools, where I did not meet another Jayne Hanlin nor find an environment that nurtured any teacher reading Ovid to her students during lunch. My dream of creating a better place for young poets seemed all the more important after these visits.

My Dream: A Way to Fight for
Poetry and Education (A New Direction)

In this book, the editors have set out to show you the wealth of poets-in-the-schools programs in the United States and a bit of their history. There are so many great programs out there and so many people who are doing wonderful work in schools. My dream, the Poetry School, would build upon this work by providing not just an opportunity for poets to visit and teach occasionally in schools, but also a chance for them to run a school.

The Poetry School would give students a chance to learn in and through the lens of poetry. Poetry would be the school's focus and would be the means by which students learned all subjects. Poets would be employed in every aspect of the school. They would not only be the teachers, but would also work in the cafeteria, as administrators, as the cleaning crew, as the dance teacher, the music teacher, the Spanish teacher, and so forth. A "poet" would be defined as anyone who loved and actively wrote poetry. The poets wouldn't all have to have books, chapbooks, or publications. They would simply have to write poetry, love poetry, be devoted to whatever task they were hired for, and be committed to the vision of the school.

To start off, the Poetry School would serve only a particular age group, most likely K–5. But as time moved on, it would include a group of elementary schools, or, ideally, a pre-K–12 school system. The pedagogical focus of the school would be object-based learning. For example, there would be a small museum onsite where students could have classes, do writing exercises, and host readings. Objects in the museum, gathered from historical sites and funded by donations, would be used as jumping-off points for lessons in any subject, to be seen with and through the lens of poetry. Children at the school could also contribute to the museum. Each child would have his or her own exhibit space (however small) to change and work with, depending on the year and school projects. Ideally, the school would have several sets of translucent Lucite or very strong glass walls, facilitating a natural collaboration in an architecture that does not always contain energy only within classroom walls, but also lets outdoor light energize the entire physical space.

Along with an emphasis on objects, poetry, and experiential learning, the school curriculum would be a collaboration among teachers, administrators, children, and families. The Poetry School would provide the same subjects offered at all public schools, and subjects such as math and physics—not just English—would be taught by poets, who would really teach these subjects, not some abbreviated version of them. The Poetry School's pupils would need to meet state and national standards. (I would argue that they would exceed these standards, but we would have to wait and see.)

In the classroom, poems would be used to teach concepts that extended beyond the humanities. I would build upon the work that great arts educators, such as Kenneth Koch, have done to bring into the classroom poems that are not written only for children. Koch demonstrated faith in his students by giving them "adult" poems and empowered them to be real readers. Poems would be used to explore ideas in every classroom. For example, the poem "Tulips," by Sylvia Plath, would not be simply a text used to understand the feelings or images she conveyed in her poem or to incite a discussion of her mastery of language, but would also be used as a jumping-off point for a lesson on botany or the history of mental-health facilities in the United States. In other classes, students would write poems to process concepts. For example, students might be asked to translate the quadratic formula into a poem or to act out the formula in a play written collaboratively in small groups. In an art history class, students could retell Paul Gauguin's biography in a series of poems, with each part of the series outlining a major event in his personal and aesthetic life.

This manner of incorporating poetry into all of the school's lessons is indebted to Visible Thinking, a method of integrating student thinking with content learning developed by scholars at Harvard's Project Zero. This approach to education values all forms of thinking and demonstrates to young learners that classroom concepts are not above them, but are rather something that they can constantly build upon. An hour in the Poetry School could bring about new answers as well as new inquiries. Some of these include the following: How does a young poet see the universe and its physical laws differently from a young scientist? What new dimensions of space can a poem uncover? What if there are entire new disciplines waiting to be discovered by a child?

The school wouldn't support only transdisciplinary leaps across the sciences and poetry. Poetry would be twinned with its more traditional partner in crime—the arts. Young poets would put on plays to understand moments in world history more clearly. Young poets would rewrite poems and stories in class. They would study the lives of composers and then make picture books of their biographies. Teachers would be supported to experiment with their curricula. Just as Mrs. Hanlin taught me in a school that gave her space to read Ovid to us during lunch, the Poetry School would give space for all its teachers to take risks in their pedagogy, to bring a love of poetry into the classroom. It would empower poets to be poets, who would empower young poets to be poets and creative thinkers. The power cycle would be endless.

Poets would run every aspect of the school, not just teaching. The cooks and administrative staff would all be poets, and if they recited "Song of a Man Who Has Come Through," by D.H. Lawrence, while they made the salad—yes, this would be allowed, if not encouraged. In the beginning, teachers would be funneled into the school through a fellowship program for MFA graduates, providing a professional track for a group of people with, currently, few options. Structurally the Poetry School would create a pipeline for its teachers through a three- or four-step process. The school would start with a few fellows (MFA graduates), and the fellows would be placed in partnering schools. With funding from these partners (similar to the way Teach for America fellows get their funding from school partners), the fellows would teach in the schools, earn certification in the process (through a partnering university), and then make a commitment to their sponsor schools for two to three years after the fellowship. As the reputation for the fellowship grew, the fellows and alumni could start offering professional development for teachers to bring poetry into classrooms. As the school's reach broadened, opportunities might arise for future Poetry Schools to start.

The professional development component of the school would allow for the school to maintain at least some of its own funding. Many public schools seek outside providers to fill teachers' professional development hours mandated by the state. As part of their funding package, Poetry School fellows could provide professional development to partnering schools. Through professional development, teachers in partnering schools could be taught how to incorporate poetry into their practices.

These methods would include workshops that emphasize cognitively-rich pedagogies such as large- and small-group collaboration while teaching poetry and ways to integrate opportunities for object-based learning. In addition, for funding purposes and sustainability, an educational researcher would be hired to be part of the school to help evaluate the health and success of its programs.

A place such as the Poetry School would foster a social culture that values poetry as learning. Although a lot of us grew up within school systems that nurtured our learning, many children do not. The Poetry School would provide an antidote to such a reality.

The Future for Poetry That the Poetry School Will Bring

Change in both education and poetry is often not as swift as one wishes it would be. A dream of a Poetry School might take a long time to bring into the world, but I would like to believe that it could one day be a reality. In my most idealistic way of looking at it, I think that something like the Poetry School could bring a new future for education, providing a new direction for MFA graduates, whose love and excitement for poetry is often not fully realized in the few professional opportunities afforded them. The Poetry School fellowship program would not only provide an alternative track to academic teaching, but also make use of poets' natural and trained skills for the benefit of society. A place like the Poetry School would train a (seemingly infinite) new generation of poets, both in the actual school and through the work of the professional development program. A place like the Poetry School would change the vision of what a school can do, and it could inspire all kinds of innovative educational reform. What an exciting way for poetry to bless a new century and to reenvision itself, its schooling, its poets! I'm in. Are you?

Part 2
Roundtable Discussion

What follows is a discussion with leaders at eighteen US organizations, from among the hundreds, that offer meaningful guidance, opportunities, and instruction at the intersection of poetry and kids. We picked operations we thought would represent some of the diversity—in terms of geographical location, size, offerings, management style, and ethos—of what's going on in communities around the country. To each one we sent a questionnaire with a handful of questions. From the many and fabulous responses we received, we assembled this conversational, roundtable-style discussion.

While the personality of each organization is unique, many of the aims and methods are the same. We hope this section is helpful not only for teachers but also for potential leaders looking to learn more about the nuts-and-bolts of setting up and running an arts organization of their own.

—*The Editors*

Meet the Roundtable

TERRY BLACKHAWK / INSIDEOUT LITERARY ARTS PROJECT

InsideOut places professional writers in Detroit schools and community settings to conduct creative writing residencies and engage children in the pleasure and power of poetry and literary self-expression. Poetry and creative writing spark imagination, inspire creative and critical thinking, and empower young people to express and understand their lives. The mission is to encourage young people to "think broadly, create bravely, and share their voices with the wider world." Since its inception in 1995, when it placed writers in five Detroit high schools, InsideOut has grown to conduct yearlong in-school residency programs for thousands of students annually in grades 1–12. Since 1995, InsideOut has published 363 separate titles for eighty-seven K–12 schools, serving more than forty-five thousand students.

MICHAEL CIRELLI / URBAN WORD NYC

Founded on the belief that teenagers can and must speak for themselves, Urban Word NYC (UW) has been at the forefront of the youth spoken word, poetry, and hip-hop movements in New York City since 1999. UW presents literary arts education and youth-development programs in creative writing, journalism, college prep, literature, and hip-hop. UW provides free, safe, and uncensored writing workshops to teens year-round, and hosts the annual NYC Teen Poetry Slam, the New York Knicks Poetry Slam, local and national youth slams, festivals, reading series, open mics, and more. UW works directly with twenty-five thousand teens per year in New York City alone and, as a steering committee member of the National Youth Spoken Word Coalition, has partner programs in forty-five cities. UW also has a vigorous community educator and teacher-training series that links inquiry-based classroom practices with student-centered pedagogy.

KEVIN COVAL / YOUNG CHICAGO AUTHORS

Young Chicago Authors aims to engage young people in their own lives and education process through the telling of stories, realist portraiture, and verse journalism, and to use the spoken word as a tool for community organizing.

DAVE EGGERS / 826 NATIONAL

Founded in 2002 by author Dave Eggers and educator Nínive Calegari, 826 is a national network of nonprofit writing and tutoring centers that help students ages six through eighteen improve their creative and expository writing skills. 826 centers in Ann Arbor, Boston, Chicago, Los Angeles, New York City, San Francisco, Seattle, and Washington, DC serve thousands of students every year with a variety of inventive programs ranging from storytelling and bookmaking to the Young Authors' Publishing Project.

MARTIN FARAWELL / GERALDINE R. DODGE FOUNDATION

The Dodge Poetry Program is an initiative of the Geraldine R. Dodge Foundation. It has three main elements: (1) the biennial Geraldine R. Dodge Poetry Festival, the largest poetry event in North America, which, over four days, regularly attracts audiences of sixteen to nineteen thousand, including more than four thousand high-school students and fifteen hundred teachers who attend free of charge; (2) the Schools Program, which sends poets into New Jersey high schools for single poet visits and mini-festivals that feature four to eight poets, and runs annual poetry exploration groups for teachers; and (3) the Dodge Poetry Archive, twenty-five hundred hours of audio and video recorded at previous Dodge Festivals that will soon be available online.

TERRI GLASS / CALIFORNIA POETS IN THE SCHOOLS

The main function of California Poets in the Schools (CPITS) is to place professional poets in public and private schools, afterschool programs, and juvenile facilities throughout the state in order to teach K–12 students an appreciation for poetry. The poets encourage the imaginative process while teaching specific crafting tools, such as metaphor, rhyme, and personification, and provide training and professional development for new poet-teachers with an annual conference and trainings at the statewide CPITS office. CPITS publishes an annual statewide student anthology, and many poet-teachers produce local countywide and school anthologies. CPITS works to facilitate Poetry Out Loud by using CPITS poet-teachers to mentor high-school students in the art of reciting and performing a poem.

SUSAN GRIGSBY / ST. LOUIS POETRY CENTER

The St. Louis Poetry Center (SLPC) was founded in 1946 when Mrs. Fred Armstrong saw the need to establish "a facility for writers as a means for stimulating the writing of poetry." Meetings were held on Sundays at the downtown public library, and writers Tennessee Williams and William Inge attended during the early days of the organization. SLPC still holds its free workshops monthly at a public library and also coordinates three poetry reading series, collaborative community arts events, fee-based writing workshops, and outreach programs for adults and youth. Even with no facility, their outreach programs serve hundreds of students every year. They have six to seven poets who work on an as-needed basis in the outreach program, teaching in schools, afterschool programs, community centers, children's treatment centers, parks, nature centers, and museums.

MIMI HERMAN / POETRY OUT LOUD

The North Carolina Arts Council, in partnership with the National Endowment for the Arts, the Poetry Foundation, and, recently, the Greensboro Public Library, has inspired thousands of North Carolina high-school students over the past seven years to discover and develop deep, personal relationships with great classic and contemporary poetry through the Poetry Out Loud National Recitation Contest. The program starts in the classroom, broadens to the state level, and culminates at the national finals in Washington, DC. In 2012, some 365,000 students participated nationwide in the Poetry Out Loud Contest through programs run by each state's art agency.

BOB HOLMAN / BOWERY POETRY CLUB

The Bowery Poetry Club is a full-service poetry establishment that includes a coffee shop, a performance space, and a full bar. The space is open daily, with "poetry as the generator," and offers kids' programming on weekends, afterschool poetry programming for high schools, and the Summer Institute of Social Justice and Applied Poetics. It is cosponsored by Urban Word NYC and designed specifically for graduating high-school students to transition to "grown-up" poetry—MFA writing programs, the slam scene, publishing projects, poetry activism, and more.

JAMES KASS / YOUTH SPEAKS

Youth Speaks (YS) works with thousands of young people each year through in-school and out-of-school programs that help young people find, develop, and publicly present their voices through various art forms, including poetry and spoken word. The organization is a force behind youth poetry slams and conducts thousands of hours of writing and performance workshops with thousands of young people in the Bay Area and across the country. YS also hosts approximately fifty performance poetry events each year and helped launch a network of more than sixty programs promoting poetry among students throughout the United States.

JEFF KASS / NEUTRAL ZONE

The Literary Arts Program at the Neutral Zone (Ann Arbor's Teen Center) has three components. The core program is the VOLUME Youth Poetry Project, a program that meets weekly with fifteen to twenty-five teenagers who read and write poetry together. The two other components of the Literary Arts Program are the Short Story Workshop, which meets once a week with fifteen to twenty-five students, and which holds four to five readings and events each year, and Red Beard Press, an independent publishing company that edits, designs, promotes and distributes four to five books a year. These books are by both teenage writers and well-known professional authors. All told, the Neutral Zone Literary Arts programs include about 150 annual participants and reach three thousand to four thousand high-school students with their work.

MATT MASON AND ANDREW EK / NEBRASKA WRITERS COLLECTIVE

The Nebraska Writers Collective, through its Poets On Loan program, sends teams of poets into middle and high schools. The organization also puts on youth literary events in the community and organizes and sponsors local and regional literary events by providing administrative support, staffing, and help with fund-raising.

MEGAN MCNAMER / MISSOULA WRITING COLLABORATIVE

The Missoula Writing Collaborative sends professional writers into school classrooms to teach creative writing in collaboration with classroom teachers. The Collaborative typically offers programming for students in third through fifth grade, but offers high-school residencies as well, and sometimes works with children as young as kindergarten age. The organization works in eighteen schools in western Montana, in Missoula and surrounding areas, and in Helena, Montana, east of the Continental Divide. Students in each classroom receive twelve hours of creative writing instruction.

PAMELA MICHAEL / RIVER OF WORDS

River of Words (ROW), based at the Center for Environmental Literacy at Saint Mary's College of California, promotes environmental literacy through the arts and cultural exchange. ROW has been inspiring educators and their students for almost sixteen years with an innovative blend of science, natural history, and the arts. Cofounded by former US poet laureate Robert Hass and writer/activist Pamela Michael, ROW, in affiliation with the Library of Congress Center for the Book, conducts a free annual international poetry and art contest for children and youth. Through professional development workshops, curriculum materials, exhibitions, and publications, ROW encourages students around the world to explore their own communities and imaginations and then synthesize what they observe and learn into line and verse.

PATRICK OLIVER / SAY IT LOUD!

Since 1997, Say It Loud! has provided opportunities for children and youth ages ten to eighteen to participate in literary arts activities and events designed to enhance their appreciation for literature as a tool for personal, educational, and career development. This is accomplished through creative writing workshops, rap sessions around popular culture, field trips, book clubs, visiting writers, publication of writings, readings, book signings, and more. Regularly held public programs include youth readings and performances, author talks, information forums, and developmental workshops.

ROBIN REAGLER / WRITERS IN THE SCHOOLS ALLIANCE

Writers in the Schools (WITS) sends poets, novelists, and playwrights into classrooms to provide long-term creative writing workshops to twenty thousand K–12 students each year. Since 1983, WITS has helped improve students' writing skills, enhance self-efficacy, and raise standardized test scores. The WITS Alliance helps similar organizations across the United States and Canada develop their own WITS programs. Through one-on-one consulting and small conferences, WITS shares best practices and assists with troubleshooting and strategic planning.

BERTHA ROGERS / BRIGHT HILL CENTER

Bright Hill Press and Literary Center offers literary and visual arts workshops for adults and youth throughout the year. Bertha Rogers and Ernest M. Fishman founded Bright Hill Press in 1992 and operated it out of their home until 2002, when funding enabled the purchase of what was to become the Bright Hill Literary Center in Treadwell, New York. In 2004 the organization built the Bright Hill Community Library & Internet Wing, home to more than ten thousand books. That year the organization also designed and built Patterns, a literary garden that contains a secret garden for children. In 2006 Bright Hill converted an attached garage into the Bright Hill Education Wing. The complex also includes the Word & Image Gallery, offices, and two guest rooms for visiting writers, some of whom enjoy brief residencies at Bright Hill.

AMY SWAUGER / TEACHERS & WRITERS COLLABORATIVE

The Teachers & Writers Collaborative (T&W) seeks to educate the imagination by providing innovative creative writing programs for students and teachers and by providing publications and other resources to support learning through the literary arts. Since 1967 T&W has worked with more than 760,000 students and more than 26,000 teachers, primarily in New York City, and has published more than eighty books and *Teachers & Writers Magazine*. The website offers a variety of free lesson plans, descriptions of best practices, and other tools to support classroom teachers and writers who teach in schools and at other sites in their communities. The vision of T&W's founders was that the classrooms in which our teaching artists collaborate with teachers would be laboratories to develop effective strategies to engage students in literature both as writers and as readers, and that the lessons learned in the programs would be disseminated via publications and other resources. These two functions are still at the core of the organization's work. Each year, thirty to forty T&W teaching artists work at forty-five to sixty sites, teaching poetry, fiction, nonfiction, memoir, essay, and other genres to K–12 students as well as leading professional development sessions for teachers.

What are the main benefits of teaching poetry to children, both in terms of an individual child's learning and development, as well as to the society at large?

MEGAN MCNAMER: Students discover the power of words, and they feel the joy of learning. They realize that their greatest resource consists of the details, simple and profound, of their own lives. They can extrapolate from this realization the experiences of others and apply them to all areas of learning. As creative writers, children have a chance to flourish spiritually, socially, and intellectually. They commune and connect—with themselves, with one another, and with the world around them. Teaching poetry is one important way to help children become human beings who are fully awake to the world.

JEFF KASS: We live in an age where communication is becoming more and more impersonal, where it's easy to text people with a kind of text-speak slang that minimizes actual commitment to language. Poetry presumes commitment to ideas, to words, to fresh, insightful, imaginative, and precise language. It's also low-tech and very often highly personal, very often one of the few places that people, especially young people, tell the truth about their lives. My students are bombarded by commercials in all forms of media that seek to convince them they need to look a certain way or buy a certain product in order to improve their lives. Politicians and news commentators practice a language of obfuscation and spin, as often do teachers and school administrators. When young people are confronted with a language so often grounded in true experience, and in honest reflection about that experience, they are startled by the power, by the low-tech human ability of a poet to connect to them on their deepest emotional levels. When we involve young people in poetry, perhaps that's what is most important for them to learn, that by disconnecting from their electronic devices they can form deeper connections to other people through our most basic and most important human invention: language.

MARTIN FARAWELL: There are the obvious ones: that it develops close reading skills, language skills, critical thinking, analytical thinking, and creativity, and that it teaches diversity and cultural awareness and allows for self-expression. Any society benefits from having more citizens with strong reading, language, and critical-and-creative thinking skills.

Anyone who has ever visited a poetry group for teenagers held in any inner-city church basement or community center has seen firsthand how much poetry matters. In such poetry groups, teenagers learn they can speak their own truths and address the challenges and fears they face every day, probably for the first time. They do this in a nurturing, nonjudgmental atmosphere, and become members of a group that supports them and celebrates their strength and courage. It may be the only place where they find such support, and where their need to express themselves receives encouragement.

This is true of any poetry or slam group, in or out of schools, and in urban, suburban, and rural areas. The friendships formed in these groups can last a lifetime or, at the very least, long enough to help these kids survive high school.

Reading poetry from diverse cultures invites students to experience the world from another's perspective, to take abstract concepts and make them specific, particular, and human. It's difficult to imagine that even the most homophobic teenage boy could hear Mark Doty read "Charlie Howard's Descent" and not have his perspective on bullying altered.

One of the crucial aspects of teaching poetry is that it develops the capacity for metaphorical thinking. Most of the measures of superior intelligence—the capacity to simultaneously hold two disparate ideas in the mind, the ability to take what is learned in one area and apply it to another completely disconnected area—are examples of metaphorical thinking. $E = mc^2$ is a metaphor. Creative thinking and all art are based on the fundamental unit of the metaphor. Being able to make connections and comparisons, to see that this is like that, is essential to everything from software design to sculpture.

As with language acquisition, it appears there is a period in human development when people are most receptive to this kind of learning. If the capacity for metaphorical/creative thinking isn't nurtured early in life, learning flexible thinking later becomes increasingly difficult.

Creativity is essential not only for how we perform specific tasks, but also for enhancing the quality of our lives. If we can think only in linear, logical ways, then when the lives we have methodically planned for ourselves are wrenched violently off-track—we lose our jobs and pensions in a stock market crash, or we're diagnosed with a neuromuscular disease—we may lack the creative capacity to see ourselves in our new lives. Adapting to changed circumstances requires creativity.

Teaching poetry also increases what Keats called "Negative Capability," the capacity to be "in uncertainties, Mysteries, doubts, without any irritable reaching after fact & reason." Another way of saying this is our capacity to dwell in the unknowable, to live with unanswerable questions.

This is crucial because the kind of knowledge that determines the quality of our lives is not based on fact and reason. For example, how do we know what we are willing to die for? Unwilling to die for? That this person is the one we want to spend the rest of our lives with? That we should or shouldn't sign that do-not-resuscitate order? This is the realm of poetry and art. The humanities remind us what it means to be human. We must be constantly reminded. History shows us how often we forget.

No standardized test prepares us for the qualities of mind required to be successful in life by any measure. The arts came into existence to teach us to be human. Imagine a society in which none of its citizens possessed the creativity, open-mindedness, curiosity, and compassion the arts engender, and you have some sense of the importance of what poetry brings to the world.

TERRY BLACKHAWK: Ongoing evaluations of InsideOut's in-school programs show statistically significant improvements in students' writing behaviors, confidence, understanding of poetry, attendance, and school achievement. The findings also suggest mental health benefits as youth communicate feelings and experiences through writing.

PAMELA MICHAEL: Teaching poetry to children opens their ears, their minds, and their hearts by honing their observation skills and by encouraging experimentation, invention, introspection, playfulness, and daring. Poetry often provides a right-brain respite in a left-brain world. Children who learn to write poetry begin to develop a heightened relationship to language and the world around them. The increased adeptness with words that poetic craft bestows enriches children's prose writing too, of course, and gives them new ways to explore and interpret the landscape of childhood and their own lives. Poetry nurtures creativity and imagination, which are necessary qualities of sustainable societies, qualities that support not only artistic expression but also scientific innovation and, indeed, all intellectual undertakings.

Poetry and the arts in general seem to have particular success in reaching and teaching children who have learning challenges. Over the years, River of Words has seen many children with serious challenges (both to learning and healthful living) achieve well beyond expectations—their teachers' and their own—when they begin to write poetry and to think of themselves as poets. Our annual contest has had an inordinate number of prizewinners who were severely autistic or learning delayed or who faced tremendous socioeconomic or physical obstacles to learning. The recognition these children received for winning a high-profile international competition also did wonders for their self-esteem and for their relationships with their schoolmates.

MATT MASON AND ANDREW EK: Poetry works through exploring the connections between worlds. What simile and metaphor do is just that: they find the interconnectedness between things that people don't always see as connected. Applying this to our personal experiences and emotions, we can discover connections within and between ourselves and the world in which we live.

BOB HOLMAN: Language is the essence of humanity; poetry is the essence of language. Those who teach poetry are teaching social justice, where the words themselves resonate and illuminate. It's creation juice. It's making the future.

SUSAN GRIGSBY: When we teach students poetry, we provide them the earned opportunity to believe in themselves as writers. And we provide them a safe place, among fellow poets, where they can sculpt a vessel and channel into it their feelings about real and often difficult topics of their lives, including issues of self-identity and of circumstances beyond their control, such as crime, death, and family problems.

JAMES KASS: I could talk about this for hours, but I'll just say this: I have met thousands and thousands of teenagers who have looked me in the eye and thanked me for being a part of changing their lives. When they understand that their voices matter, they understand that they matter.

What past efforts to teach poetry to kids have inspired your organization, and why?

AMY SWAUGER: T&W's founders included some of the pioneers in teaching poetry to children, including Kenneth Koch, June Jordan, Herb Kohl, Anne Sexton, Grace Paley, and Muriel Rukeyser. We have also benefited from the expertise of people like Phillip Lopate and Ron Padgett, who taught for T&W in the 1970s and 1980s. Padgett then served as the organization's publications director in the 1990s. Kohl, Lopate, and Padgett continue their involvement with T&W by serving on the board of directors and by interacting with current teaching artists to share their expertise and experience.

BLACKHAWK: InsideOut grew from my experience teaching creative writing in a high-school classroom from 1989 to 1995, when I started writing poetry myself and found that my classroom could be a great laboratory for creative writing and teaching. I tried out prompts and approaches to teaching poetry, which I found through publications from the Teachers & Writers Collaborative, the Heinemann publishing company, the National Council of Teachers of English, and elsewhere. I participated in the annual Detroit Institute of Arts Student Writing Project, which supplied sets of slides for classroom discussions and sponsored subsequent field trips that always led to remarkable writing.

KEVIN COVAL: Young Chicago Authors is a twenty-year-old organization, but in 2001 these things happened: the towers fell and the world went crazy—again. Brown people around the planet were criminalized. And the city of Chicago was busily enforcing a newly passed anti-gang, anti-loitering law and locking up kids of color for hanging out in groups of more than one. In this moment of fear and madness, we wanted to bring the stories of young people together to offer a culture of hope, which was when we created the poetry festival Louder Than A Bomb.

JEFF KASS: I founded the Neutral Zone's Literary Arts programs after having attended the very first Youth Speaks Teen Poetry Slam in San Francisco and having been involved with some of Youth Speaks' earliest events in the mid-1990s. I've been inspired both in my classroom as a public high-school teacher and in cultivating the programs at the Neutral Zone by the work of Nancie Atwell and her book *In the Middle*, as well as by efforts demonstrated by the group Young Chicago Authors and their Louder Than A Bomb Youth Poetry Slam.

MASON AND EK: We've talked with folks at 826 Valencia, WITS, and Young Chicago Authors, all of whom have bent over backwards to answer our questions and help out. It can be tough to put a program like ours together, but it's wonderful to see how the communities who do this sort of work aren't guarding "shop secrets" or things like that. They've been nothing but helpful to us as we find our way.

FARAWELL: Almost all the staff and poets who designed, developed, and produced or worked for the Dodge Festival and Program over the last twenty-five years have taught literature, poetry, and/or creative writing at some point in their careers. We have firsthand knowledge of how much pressure teachers are under, especially in these days of mandated standardized tests. Teachers need opportunities to feel respected, to be treated as adults, to have their imaginative and creative inner lives nurtured, and to be reminded of why they wanted to teach in the first place. Dodge has tried to create these opportunities through poetry discussion groups for teachers. We have always acted under the assumption that one of the best ways to teach poetry to kids is to give teachers experiences with poetry that are so refreshing and revitalizing that teachers are eager to share them with their students.

EGGERS: We were influenced by a San Francisco group called Youth Speaks. They teach poetry to kids, with an emphasis on performance and poetry slams. They're fantastically good about getting kids to be confident and socially engaged, and to express themselves with incredible courage. When 826 Valencia started, we decided to be more of a print-oriented partner to Youth Speaks, concentrating on the words on the page, on books, magazines, newspapers.

ROBIN REAGLER: Every project we have done since 1983 has had the potential to inspire. All it takes is a participant who can tell that story and make it come to life. Of course, particular stories stand out. Some dramatic examples show the possibility for transformation:

-» A deaf child performed in sign language—in her poem,

she prepared her baby doll (also deaf) for what she could expect in her life.

-» A young man in juvenile detention used his WITS time to write his autobiography, the recurring theme of which was fire.

-» A girl in a homeless shelter published a poem about a magical circular staircase. She attended the prestigious McCombs School of Business at the University of Texas at Austin on a full scholarship, and graduated in May 2012.

We rarely know the true long-term results of our work with kids, but we carry these stories with us to remind ourselves that this work matters.

Do you think there are any advantages to teaching writing to kids outside a traditional academic setting?

BERTHA ROGERS: Yes and no. Yes because it's less formal, and it's friendlier—without the rules and tests that transitional academic settings require. No because even though a traditional academic setting has more requirements, it's really up to the teacher to instill the love of the subject in the children. What's important is that the children feel that their opinions are valued and that the work they do is important, not just to them but to the adults who participate as well. I always tell the children I teach that we'll be working hard, and I ask them if they're up for that. They always are. But that should happen in a traditional setting as well, shouldn't it?

EGGERS: Sometimes, sure. Growing up, I learned well within my public school environment. I had great teachers, and they were given wide latitude to come up with great lesson plans for writing. But now, in many public schools, teachers don't have that freedom. So that third place—not home, not school—comes into play. And no matter the circumstances, learning from community members, some of them professional writers, is always a nice way to augment what's happening in school.

MICHAEL CIRELLI: The advantages of poetry instruction outside the traditional classroom are boundless. The cornerstone of our work is creating safe, student-centered, and uncensored spaces for young people to engage, develop, and cultivate their powerful voices. Schools are, for the most part, unsafe, teacher-centered, and censored spaces, where young people are rarely challenged to engage, develop, or cultivate. This may not be true for all schools, but the schools that most of our students come from are set up to fail, and they marginalize the young people in them. Therefore, when we have space outside of the classroom that is driven by a social-justice pedagogy, culturally relevant poetics, and a commitment to the full development of the young person (not only the young artist) the results we see are astounding, from engaging poetry to accessing college scholarships.

SWAUGER: The main advantage to implementing any writing program for kids outside the regular school day is that there is typically more time available with fewer distractions. In New York City, school-day class periods, often filled with classroom distractions, are sometimes as short as thirty-seven minutes, leaving at best thirty minutes for a teaching artist to focus on the day's writing lesson. In our out-of-school programs, sessions are usually at least sixty minutes and sometimes as long as two hours. During afterschool or weekend programs, there are fewer people in the school and not as much competition for program participants' attention. Our teaching artists view the extended time and the chance to work with students in a quieter, more focused setting as a gift.

FARAWELL: Yes. One of the great things about High School Student Day at the Dodge Poetry Festival is that it takes poetry out of the confines of the academy. Readings and discussions are held in churches, theaters, art galleries, tents—all decidedly nonacademic settings. It gives kids a sense that poetry exists outside the classroom, in the real world, and is actually vitally important to more people than just their English teachers.

MCNAMER: Not really. That is, we think that poetry, and all creative writing, creates its own exceptional space, which is not dependent on a setting. We believe firmly that the "traditional academic setting," insofar as that refers to public school classrooms, is the ideal place in which to teach poetry to kids. That sends the important message that poetry, poetic experiences, and the creative ways of using words that respond to and inspire poetic experiences are all basic to human existence, as important to know as the square root of nine or the capital of France. Paying special attention to poetry helps any person develop a poetic sensibility, and a poetic sensibility opens up the world. Suddenly poetry is everywhere, and when it comes to enjoying this wealth, each child is potentially as rich as the next. We do want to support the idea of creative writing as an endeavor that is not dependent on a rarified atmosphere for its existence.

COVAL: Traditional academic poetry is mostly boring, dead, and white. To excite anyone about poetry, language, the world—anything—contemporary, reasonably accessible verse is the place to begin. Traditionally, poetry is taught as if it existed in a museum: look and don't touch. We want poetry to be real and malleable, have students dig in and get dirty, down to the nitty-gritty minutiae of their own lives. Using the world(s) around them, putting that into poetry. Paulo Freireian poetics. Education is failing young people, and poetry can be a part of the process that helps alter that scenario. Part of the process is also bringing young people together in spaces outside traditional academic settings. A new place can jar new awareness. A theater, a park, public transit, a youth writing conference at a community center, a master class in the conference room of your organization with five kids from five different schools, an ALL-City open mic, a Louder Than A Bomb festival. These are some ways to promote interest, engagement, and participation in the rigor of craft and education.

JEFF KASS: Absolutely. Outside of an academic setting, kids are free to use language and address topics that are often off-limits in schools. We are also more in control of the environment we can create for writing. We can eliminate, for instance, the interruption of a workshop by the principal making an announcement over the PA system. We can create warmer, more welcoming spaces in which to write, with couches or large conference tables. We can provide refreshment and we can also dispense with some of the formality of the institutionalized teacher-student relationship.

Outside of the school setting, we can challenge students to take risks they wouldn't necessarily try to take in school because we can create an environment that encourages and rewards those risks instead of instilling in students the need to perform a task well in order to achieve a particular grade. Perhaps that is the biggest advantage of writing workshops outside of school: kids who engage in such workshops do so solely with the goal of improving as writers. All the motivation is intrinsic instead of extrinsic.

PATRICK OLIVER: We don't want our participants to view our organization as an extension of school even though we have a history of school-based recruiting and site location. Therefore, we develop a meeting place reflective of youth culture—walls adorned with art and posters, bookshelves with books by noted authors (fiction and nonfiction), comic books, graphic novels, and young-adult novels for pleasure reading, video games for free time, and kid-friendly seating arrangements during particular writing exercises.

Selection of reading material is important. The majority of the reading material must mirror students' environments. This is particularly important for students of color. Most school districts don't have books that reflect the surroundings of students of color. When students see and hear their experiences in literature they really enjoy it, and they respond to writing activities associated with those books.

HOLMAN: They love it. The café reeks of poetry. This is a place where language doesn't have to go to the edge of the page.

REAGLER: The advantage of teaching in a nonschool setting is that the relationships among students and writers are different and often more personal. In those settings, writing is understood as self-expression more so than in school, where it is often associated with rubrics, grades, and testing.

GRIGSBY: Teaching in museums, parks, and gardens opens up obvious opportunities that we don't have in the classroom for students to observe, discover, and respond through writing. Nontraditional settings also allow for greater flexibility and more time for writing, conferring, and sharing. Unfortunately, most traditional classrooms are on these forty-five-minute cycles, and just at the point where kids are immersed in the groove of what they're doing, a loud buzzer rattles their souls and it's time to switch gears to another subject. We especially treasure the summer opportunities to work with the Green Center's "Science & Art Summer Experience" programs, in which groups of students each spend a week exploring prairies, wetlands, rivers, and woods and responding through poetry and drawing.

Another benefit of moving beyond the four walls of a classroom is that it provides youth (or writers of any age) the impetus to look beyond themselves as they respond to paintings, prairies, insects, music, or the clouds drifting across the sky. However, if students are "classroom-bound," you can bring bits of the outside world to them through library books, print media from museums and conservation departments, the Internet, and so forth.

What is the best way to create a thriving poetry education organization? What are good mechanisms for sustaining such an organization?

ROGERS: The first mechanism is dedication. You have to be dedicated to the project; you have to want to make it work. You have to have employees and volunteers who love it too and are willing to commit to a long-term goal. You can't worry too much about money, but you have to be practical enough to keep it going. You have to be willing to cut back on things that maybe aren't so important and work hard to keep the necessary programs going.

GRIGSBY: In our situation, we've created a thriving organization through mutual support and collaboration with a wide range of community institutions and small businesses. We have no facility of our own, but happily go to other sites to bring poetry to youth and adults. Teaching professional development workshops is another method of spreading the magic of poetry. We also participate in many multidisciplinary events that open other organizations' hearts and minds to the possibilities of weaving poetry into academics across the curriculum—into visual arts, musical, dramatic, and dance events, and into science, nature study, and history.

We are sustained by the willingness of poet-educators to volunteer their time when funds are not available for stipends, by institutions and businesses that volunteer their facilities and resources to us, and by the ever-growing number of schools in our area that realize the benefits reaped by arts integration in the classroom. When organizations work together to bring the arts to youth in the community, interest in such activities grows, and demand often follows.

CIRELLI: The best way to create any organization is to have a firm grasp of your mission and vision and not to deviate from these. The mission is ultimately the conduit for actualizing your vision. Despite urges to deviate from it, for funding or grants or donations, it is imperative to stay the course.

FARAWELL: The answer is deceptively simple: surround yourself with good poets and good teachers, and listen to them.

No matter how brilliant, original, or exciting you may find your own ideas about teaching poetry to be, the impact of any program you create will depend on the quality of the people going out into the field and doing the work. It can be easy to lose sight of that if the program is successful. Never forget that praise and success deserve to be shared because everyone's contribution keeps the organization running. Your goal should be to create an organization that can function without you.

You need to find poets who enjoy being around young people, who are good communicators and sympathetic and attentive listeners, and who feel strongly, even passionately, that poetry matters and that it can make a difference in the lives of young people who have so much emotional turmoil to deal with, who so often feel isolated in their suffering, and who have no way to communicate it or believe others have gone through similar experiences.

It is also crucial that you remember that teachers are your partners and allies. In these days of standardized tests, creative teachers are under siege. Any teacher who takes the time to offer students opportunities to encounter poets deserves respect, admiration, and compassion. Think hard about what you need to know, and give careful attention to the feedback you receive, especially that which makes your hair bristle.

BLACKHAWK: First off, a thriving poetry education organization needs the buy-in and commitment of a talented, zany, dedicated, accomplished, diverse group of writers. These writers need to be nurtured. They need to earn a decent rate of pay, they need support and structure when going into schools, and they need to feel that they are part of a community of writers. InsideOut celebrates the accomplishments of its writers inside the classroom and out. We host a regular reading series at a local art gallery, which puts our writers before the public and builds esprit de corps. We provide a handbook with lesson ideas and teaching tips, and we give mentoring and feedback to those who are new in the classroom. We work hard to build relationships at the school level among principals and teachers so that writers are welcomed as members of the school community. A thriving poetry education organization also needs community partners in the media as well as within other cultural organizations.

MIMI HERMAN: I'm a great believer in revising, both in my own writing and in creating programs. The first year of any program is an opportunity to see what works and what can be revised to make it work even better. The more you're willing to see what's not working, and to find creative ways to make it work, the more your organization will thrive.

MICHAEL: River of Words applied organizing techniques traditionally used by activists to create and grow our organization. Among these strategies are:

-» Collaboration/partnering/networking
-» Leveraging of resources—use wisely; don't reinvent the wheel; repurpose, reuse, recycle
-» Savvy use of media, technology, social networks
-» A willingness to follow (and a belief in the efficacy of) an organic unfolding of organizational structure and leadership
-» Decentralization/diversity—River of Words has built an extensive network of (unpaid) state and regional coordinators who implement and promote our program in their respective states/regions based on the needs and resources of their individual constituencies. This strategy

serves (at least) two purposes: it allows us to extend our reach and effectiveness despite a small staff and budget, and it creates resilient and relevant locally supported and administered programs. Most of our state coordinators are employed by state agencies—departments of natural resources, humanities councils, et cetera—and (so far) have a more stable funding base than most nonprofits.

-» Talking directly to "the people"—River of Words' success in getting into classrooms is due, in part, to reaching out to teachers rather than to principals or school districts. Though, over time, those bureaucrats and bureaucracies have become fans of our work, it is the individual teacher—the person who actually teaches poetry to children—who most needs and deserves our support and attention.

COVAL: Determine who the stakeholders are and bring them to the table: students, teachers, teaching artists, capable administrators, active board members, and community partners. Think all-city, and bring a city's resources to the table to help sustain the organization: public/private dollars and resources, essential partnerships with other organizations and institutions. We have young people. Young Chicago Authors interacts with and engages tens of thousands of young people each year. Other institutions, theaters, universities, and companies want the attention of those young people as future consumers. Ask those established institutions for partnerships that can help sustain your organization. It's sometimes about asking for dollars, but it's also about space, printing and other costs, and resource sharing that will allow your work to happen and grow.

JEFF KASS: You will need somebody who is skilled at graphic design so you can create posters, flyers, handbills, and electronic announcements that will attract young people to workshops and readings. Once you have all that, you need to work hard at constantly trying to get new kids excited about being involved. You need to keep reaching out, keep listening carefully to what kids write, and keep caring about helping them. You have to believe in the magic of what you're doing. You have to believe that the voices of young people are powerful and important. You have to commit to trying to make your broader community believe that too.

MASON AND EK: Focus: our resources are limited (time, money, and labor), so it's important that we devote ourselves to doing a few things really well, rather than a bunch of things poorly. For us, this means stripping our functions primarily to our Poets On Loan program and the Louder Than A Bomb literary festival. These are more important to us than other worthwhile expenditures, like running other festivals, hiring staff to raise our Twitter presence, and so on. The organization spent a lot of time figuring out the shape and direction of its mission, and while it changes as circumstances change, we stick to it as much as possible. This means declining a lot of opportunities, but that's a necessary trade-off.

JAMES KASS: Well, we've always made sure to put the voices of the young people first. We have a very specific pedagogy that drives our arts education work, and that pedagogy allows our teaching artists (whom we call poet-mentors) the freedom to build their own curricula. I've always told our poet-mentors that they can't be afraid to show the kids why they write, why they need it, love it, and take it so seriously. It's very important that we don't try to pretend that poetry is this thing that's far away from us.

OLIVER: I highly recommend starting very small, with minimal staff and an extensive group of volunteers and parent supporters. The poetry project should be headed by someone who:

-» loves literature and can lead by example and reflect the mission of the organization;

-» is a youth advocate with a record of working in diverse environments;

-» is a great communicator and team builder who can organize volunteers and develop community partnerships;

-» can write grants, sponsorship letters, project descriptions, organization newsletters, and general correspondence; and

-» has a working knowledge or understanding of budgets and budget narratives.

Sustainability is related to several factors:

-» Identifying key areas of the poetry project and staying with it (i.e., mission statement, goals, objectives, and curriculum)

-» Developing a board that wholeheartedly supports all of the above and the organization's fund-raising efforts

-» Recruiting young people who enjoy the arts, especially writing

-» Promoting parental support—encouraging volunteering, attending public programs, and assisting with fund-raising

-» Establishing a relationship with the local school district to recruit students, get classroom space, start public programs, and monitor student achievement and volunteers (academic and nonacademic)

-» Forging partnerships with institutions of higher learning to recruit volunteers from language arts/English departments and student mentors, finding classroom and public program space, hosting events, cosponsoring public programs, and funding college scholarships for youth

-» Creating relationships with local museums and cultural

centers, and making use of these resources via field trips, individual student projects, and public programs

-» Forming relationships with local and state elected officials who are interested in the arts (funding is often available through various local and statewide youth intervention initiatives)

-» Creating a strong social media presence, so that parents, volunteers, supporters, funders, and potential funders can always be abreast of what the organization is doing; build a website, write an e-newsletter, and join Facebook, LinkedIn, and Twitter.

HOLMAN: Acknowledge that the poetic economy is a gift economy—no one's buying anyway. And by sustaining a field of generosity, you begin to have the proper environment between poet and audience, whether text or oral. Not expecting money means having a supportive community of people who volunteer. It means the administrators delegate to people who bring energy and ideas, not necessarily connections. Poetry's deep meanings and reach toward utopia are for real and need to be honored in all aspects of the organization.

REAGLER: Each of our board of directors meetings begins with a volunteer reading a poem by a WITS kid. Every staff member, including those on the business side of our work, visits our classrooms once a year. At staff meetings, program staff members share anecdotes every week. These rituals remind us why we are doing this work. Through their poems, the children remind us.

When
I write,
I imagine.
I use my heart.

I listen to my
soul-mind.
I use my hands
and touch the tip of the pencil.
I write words.
I imagine things I want to do.
I listen to myself.
I feel free.

—Nathan, age eight

What are some funding opportunities available for starting a program to teach poetry to kids outside a traditional academic setting?

ROGERS: It's my experience that funders want a track record before they open their wallets. You need to launch the program first and prove that you can do it; then they will help. That means that the first couple of years are going to be dicey. In New York, the New York State Council on the Arts is a potential funder (we are funded by NYSCA, and we bless them every day); there is also the NEA. We get some funding from the County Youth Bureau, through the auspices of New York Child and Family Services. And most communities have small private foundations that focus on the good of the community, i.e., the children. They will fund youth programs because they're interested in keeping the community viable (which can be difficult in rural communities, where too often the most ambitious leave). If the organization is lucky enough to be able to employ a grant writer, that goes a long way. Supplies, programs, and equipment are available through TechSoup, Academic Superstore, and other agencies.

JEFF KASS: Often, local community foundations or family foundations can be good options for a few thousand dollars to help get things going.

Initial moneymakers can also be books, CDs, DVDs, T-shirts—things that can be produced relatively cheaply and sold at a pretty good profit margin. You can also charge nominal amounts for people to attend readings, but I'd be wary of doing that early on when you have an unproven product and the goal is to bring people into the room and introduce folks to your program. Once you get rolling and have built some kind of credibility, then you can charge admission at slams and readings (I'd still keep prices low, though) and hold benefit parties where people from the community make donations. However, you have to build solid programming first.

JAMES KASS: We get about 65 percent of our $2 million budget from foundations, but it was a long time coming. Our first grant was $5,000 from the local community foundation, and we grew from there. Public arts agencies are good. Raising money from people you know is where fundraising professionals tell you to start. When I founded the organization, small grants and individual fund-raising drives kicked it off. Now we get much larger grants, some of them multiyear, but it's rare for that to happen when you're starting an organization.

When fund-raising, the most important things are to be clear about what you're asking for, to be proactive in describing the need you want to fill and why you're the person/program to do it, and to be as specific as possible in saying what you're going to do with the money. If you believe in something, you can inspire others to believe in it too.

The best advocates for this work, though, are the young people themselves. Their voices speak loudly when they describe what this work means to them.

OLIVER: I highly recommend solidifying local funding before going after national funding. You want to show national funders that you have developed a local base for funding support and that you have the capacity to raise matching funds and receive significant in-kind grants.

REAGLER: We have found that in the Houston area, hospitals, museums, and community centers are often willing to raise the funds to pay for our services. Typically our collaborators are also nonprofits, but we have managed to maintain this model because of the high-quality professionalism of our program. What this means is that the collaborator writes the grant to pay WITS. This situation is ideal, but it may not be possible for young organizations. However, it's a great goal to work toward. When we initiate a new project with another nonprofit, we often write the initial grant ourselves.

What's one really effective fund-raising secret you would be willing to divulge?

EGGERS: Patience. Sometimes it takes a donor or foundation a few years to act. But if you keep people informed of your progress, very often they will think, Wow, they just keep doing great work. And they'll donate. One more suggestion: creating books has been very helpful. When you can hand a potential donor an actual three-dimensional book—a collection of student work—it's very powerful. It sells the program for you.

SWAUGER: Use every opportunity you can think of to let potential funders see kids participating in your programs, whether it's sitting in on a workshop, attending a poetry reading, or seeing a short video on your website. Even providing copies of final "products" (e.g., anthologies of student writing) helps make the work real to people who aren't part of your organization. Nothing is more effective for getting funders' attention than seeing young people who are excited about what they're doing.

FARAWELL: Never forget that programming and development require two very different skill sets. Asking a person who may be absolutely brilliant at programming to write grant applications means both your programming and fund-raising will suffer. You're taking away time needed to do programming well and spending more time than necessary on development tasks that an experienced person would accomplish more efficiently. You're likely to wind up with inferior grant applications that way, because writing good ones is a highly specialized skill.

In small start-ups, the founder, director, and fund-raiser might be the same person. Recognize that if you want to do development well, or even adequately, you'll need professional help. If you don't believe you can hire a freelance consultant who can bring in enough grants or donations to make his or her compensation worthwhile, consider pooling resources with other nonprofits to hire a development person who can work for you all. If no such cooperative exists in your area, initiate one. Co-ops can combine marketing plans; share legal fees, space, et cetera; and find many ways to cut costs for individual members while increasing revenue for all.

BLACKHAWK: Say thank you. If you don't get a grant, call and ask for feedback.

COVAL: Universities and colleges have money. They need students. Holler at admissions and marketing departments about cosponsorship. We can bring many college-bound students onto a campus for an open mic, a poetry festival, or a conference. Schools pay for that kind of exposure. Encourage them to pay your organization to do this work.

JEFF KASS: More important than anything else is the process of building really outstanding programming. People will put money behind something when they see evidence of its good work. If you are conducting workshops that a lot of young people are excited about and are showing up for, and if you are presenting work to the public through dynamic readings and quality print materials, then you will be able to get people to see how important your work is. If the growth of young people is evident in their writing, if they are opening up the minds of the public, if parents and teachers are seeing real growth and development, then it will be much easier to secure continuing support, from both institutional sources (school districts, universities, and granting organizations, et cetera) and private funders (parents, community philanthropists, et cetera). It's kind of a catch-22—you need money to get things started, but you need to get things started in order to bring in money.

The good news is that as long as someone is willing to put in a lot of volunteer time at the outset, you can make things happen without a huge budget, at least at the start. All you really need is a microphone, a small stage somewhere, and some kids who want to write. If you give those kids quality instruction, they will inevitably create moving and powerful work that will engage the public, and then you can begin to build a reputation as an organization that's making a positive difference in the community.

MASON AND EK: This one isn't really a secret: build relationships with your donors, and tell them about what you're doing. If they like it, if they feel you're doing good work, and if they feel you care about them as more than just a source of cash, they'll keep donating to the best of their ability. Fund-raising is difficult and takes a lot of time, but it's not complex.

OLIVER: In the past we've hosted quarterly public programs featuring noted writers. Past public programs cost around $2,000 to $4,000 to cover honorariums, hotels, and travel. I drafted a donation letter for each public program and sent it to thirty to fifty people asking for $100 to $150 donations. They are told that their names will be listed on the program. Local businesses donate refreshments for the receptions, and parents provide potluck.

Low-documentation mini-grants are another option. Local businesses, banks, government agencies, and humanities organizations often have mini-grant applications for small community projects. These mini-grants range from $1,000 to $5,000. Because the applications are so similar, the same information can be used in all the proposals.

REAGLER: The secret to fund-raising is the site visit. We find that if we can get prospective funders to immerse themselves in an hour of WITS, we can usually get support. Some of these suggestions will seem obvious, but here are a few pointers for getting the most out of a site visit:

-» Choose one of your best writers teaching his or her best class.
-» Prepare the writer with a briefing about the funder. Is she interested in education, creativity, school reform, literacy, or writing? Does she represent herself, a private foundation, or a corporation?
-» If a classroom teacher or other partner is working with the writer, ask the writer to let him know ahead of time about the visit. Explain what is at stake and how it will ultimately be to his benefit. Having a person outside your organization "testify" about the power of your program is always a huge help.
-» Always meet the funder and attend the workshop together. Your job is to help interpret what the funder observes in the classroom.
-» Encourage the funder to write with the students. If she writes, you should write also.
-» In addition to asking questions about the funding organization, ask the funder more personal questions. How did you first get involved in philanthropy? What other exciting work do you see taking place in our community?
-» Be prepared to discuss money, if asked.
-» Follow up the visit with a handwritten thank-you note and any other information requested during the visit.

If your budget were cut by 90 percent but you still wanted to continue the majority of your programs, how would you go forward? What are some creative ways to thrive in the face of shoestring budgets?

ROGERS: Our budget has been cut in these past few years but not by 90 percent (please, no!). If it were cut that much, I would ask writers to read their work in our reading series for very little remuneration. I would also continue the kids' workshop series and the high-school poetry competition, asking teachers and judges to contribute their work, with the understanding that we would do everything we could to make the situation temporary. As it is, we've made our youth programs virtually free because we are in Delaware County, a rural area in upstate New York, which is one of the poorest counties in the state. We charge only a small fee for materials and transportation (when we go to museums). We get supplies from TechSoup, Academic Superstore, and other organizations that provide equipment and supplies free or cheaply to nonprofits.

EGGERS: We've always run on a shoestring. We have two hundred volunteers for every staff member. It's actually crucial that an organization like this run leanly, because donors want to know that the majority of their donation is going to programming. So we keep overhead very low.

CIRELLI: Partnership is the name of the game right now. The only real way to thrive in this challenged economy is to engage the various networks, expertise, space, volunteers and personnel of like-minded organizations. For example, Urban Word gives away more scholarship money to college-bound teens each year than exists in its actual annual budget. We do this through dynamic and profound partnerships with world-class organizations such as the New York Knicks, and by leveraging those types of high-profile relationships with colleges and universities who may be interested in offering scholarships to the young people we serve. This model is most likely the only one of its kind in the nation, and it is an example of leveraging the resources we have in-house.

We have incredible young artists and leaders who are savvy, political change-makers—people who, as one sponsor of ours, Nike, says, are "game-changers." We also have relationships with high-profile sponsors such as the Knicks and Time Warner. We use all of these to gain greater access, whether it be through promotion or through further relationship-building. This ultimately leads to a model that various partner colleges and universities use to promote their brand and get these "game-changers," and we in turn get to offer more than half a million dollars in scholarship money to our youth each year.

FARAWELL: The hardest thing to do in the face of drastic cuts is to avoid desperation mode—a frantic state of perpetual panic in which you're so consumed by what you think requires your immediate attention that you don't step back to plan what your next steps might be. Such times require that you do the opposite of what your instincts tell you to.

Step back, take a deep breath, and make time for a long, hard look at what you actually set out to do, what you really think is most important to do now, and how it's possible to do that with far fewer resources. You may have the same goals, but how you achieve them may be radically revised. Don't waste time hearkening back to the way things were in the past, and don't simply think in terms of doing the same thing but on a smaller scale. Accept that everything you took for granted about how you do what you do is out the window. Put aside your ego and your attachment to all the things you've already accomplished. You're starting from scratch now, with only so many dollars. What really matters? What's the last thing that can be sacrificed? What are you willing to give up? There is no one-size-fits-all solution to drastic budget cuts.

MCNAMER: We were forced to do some serious contingency planning in 2008–2009. We chose to keep our overall programming intact, but to reduce all individual residencies by half. That way we didn't have to choose one school over another, and all our writers shared the hit equally. That was a budget cut of 50 percent, but 90 percent is a tougher call. At this point, I feel that we have board members who could step in and run the program quite effectively; in fact, some of them already function more as staffers than as members of a board. But we pay our writers well, and I'm not sure that many of them could forego 90 percent of what is, for them, significant income. Rather than take such a big cut in all writers' salaries, I think we would have to pare down to serving only one or two schools and rebuild from there.

MICHAEL: This scenario actually happened to us during the recent economic collapse—or came close: we lost more than 75 percent of our funding. We saw it coming and spent almost two years seeking a likely partner/safe haven. We ended up dissolving our nonprofit and becoming the flagship program of a new Center for Environmental Literacy (which was founded to house us) at a small liberal arts college in California. During the transitional period, we furloughed our staff to a shorter workweek for more than a year and ultimately laid off everyone but our executive director. We cut some programs and services, negotiated a deal with our landlord to pay half our rent, and took other drastic measures to keep the doors open while we navigated our way to a more sustainable future.

JAMES KASS: We couldn't have our budget cut by 90 percent, as we now have about a $2 million dollar budget. Most of that goes to the people who do the work, so we simply wouldn't be able do the majority of our work. I think if it came down to it, we'd go back to what we started with: free writing workshops and performances so young people could share their work.

But I want to say this: this work is important. If budgets for programs such as ours were cut by 90 percent, I'd raise a serious racket. How dare this country not invest in young people? This ultimately is not about poetry as a luxury, as Audre Lorde famously said. This is about giving young people a place to find their voices and to shape and project those voices. This world needs the voices of young people. For whatever reason, poetry has become something that young people respond to in really significant ways. Young people are telling magnificent stories, deconstructing the world around them, dreaming of a future, and revealing themselves in very interesting and deep ways. These budgets cannot be cut. This work is way too important.

HOLMAN: Ha! Poetry budgets are already 90 percent less than those of most arts organizations. And don't forget that the annual US budget for military marching bands is larger than the NEA's.

Any suggestions on where or how to find supplies?
Where do you get your pens, paper, computers, tables,
chairs, books, projectors, staplers, crayons, et cetera?

EGGERS: We get a good deal of them donated, from individuals and from the companies who make them. We bind books using a tape binder, for example, and the company who makes the tape binding gave us enough to print twenty thousand books.

SWAUGER: If you're starting small or have a limited number of program participants, there's a good chance that a local business, such as an office supply store, will be willing to provide in-kind donations of equipment and supplies.

Think about collaborating with others in the community to deliver your programs. For example, public libraries or youth-serving agencies often have a lot of programming time to fill and might welcome you as a partner in providing programs. Perhaps your poetry program could be one of the local library's offerings for the community: the library would provide space and equipment, and you would be responsible for program content.

BLACKHAWK: As an in-school program, we consider the use of school space as in-kind support. Our supplies budget is relatively low, but we have benefited from pro bono contributions in a number of ways. Before it closed, Borders conducted a book drive at all four of its Detroit Metro Airport locations. At checkout, customers could select books from a list of high-quality children's and young-adult titles that InsideOut compiled and the store made available. We received countless wonderful deliveries of books, stuffed animals, and other gifts that we took into the classrooms we serve. We have also received pro bono services from a number of graphic designers, recruited online, who help us bring out the twenty-five to thirty separate titles we publish each year—one professionally printed for each school served. This is a tremendous gift, and we are extremely grateful to our volunteer graphic designers.

MICHAEL: We are very good at dumpster diving—a good bet in a place like the Bay Area. We also utilize various "repo depot" recycling centers for teachers, university-run warehouses for excess equipment, Internet resources such as Freecycle and Craigslist, plus a "wish list" on our website.

OLIVER: Local businesses and major chain stores will often donate paper, journals, notebooks, and other small supplies. We wrote grants to local foundations to get funding for computers and related items. Foundations typically provide funding for organizations that seek to better the community. Grant proposals to foundations must be written to show how literary arts programs develop productive students, model citizens, and future employees and entrepreneurs. I highly suggest looking at foundations for technology and computer hardware needs.

We opened a writing lab in one community, and a used-office-supply warehouse provided all the furnishings. The lab looks like a twenty-first-century workspace—thirteen computer stations, a projector, and a printer.

I'm also an advocate for organizations having libraries, even though this is the age of electronic media and e-books. I see a significant number of students master smartphones and computers, yet they are functionally illiterate. Required reading of books and participating in book discussions are also part of satisfying some grant-proposal requirements. To stock our library, we send fund-raising letters. We also receive significant discounts for purchasing new books by contacting publishers and bookstores.

HERMAN: When I'm looking for supplies and my budget is somewhere between minimal and nonexistent, I ask my friends. And I ask them to ask their friends, and their friends' friends, and so on. Somewhere there is someone with an extra ream of paper that's taking up room in a closet, or an old printer that still works, or more books than shelves. Create a charming e-mail that's easy to forward, and send it out to everyone you know.

GRIGSBY: We believe strongly that writing journals are like golden tickets to the world of believing in oneself as a writer. The journals allow the children to carry their newfound enthusiasm for writing beyond the workshop doors. Many parents have remarked that they have had trouble getting their kids to bed because they just wanted to stay up and keep writing! Yet journals can be pricey. We scour the various dollar stores, grabbing up all the quality journals they carry. Some of the better-endowed sites we work with, such as major museums, often provide journals and pencils. An investment in clipboards will reap rewards. In addition, with enough recycled cardboard, kids can even fashion their own journals and clipboards. The necessity is to provide students with portable, sturdy surfaces on which to write, and the ideal is that they are something kids can call their own.

What resources, aside from financial, are available for starting a program to teach poetry to kids outside of a traditional academic setting? (This can be in terms of education, general advice or support, et cetera.)

ROGERS: All you need is a space, pencils and paper, and a small library of poetry books so the children have good resources. You must love the children and genuinely want to lead them and help them understand the point of poetry and the power and beauty of words. The space you use and the people with whom you work must be above reproach. The people you hire must understand the social contract successful adults have with children; they can't condescend or be superior, sarcastic, et cetera. They must love the children.

EGGERS: Schools, teachers, libraries...there are so many extant partners out there waiting to be tapped. Before you go starting your own organization, always check around to see who's already doing anything like what you're planning. Chances are you can save yourself a lot of time and money by partnering with, or working within, the existing network.

CIRELLI: The best thing to do before starting an organization is to assess the field, the way people are framing and talking about the work, and to have that inform the process with which you work with young people. I have found that this was the most important thing as we've grown exponentially over many years, and our pedagogy was the only thing that kept us grounded. There are numerous teacher-education programs, nonprofit-management programs, and artist support groups that can help burgeoning nonprofit administrators or educators on their path to actualizing their vision.

SWAUGER: Lesson plans and other resources are available on the T&W website, in *Teachers & Writers Magazine* ($20 for a one-year subscription), and in T&W books (available on Amazon and barnesandnoble.com). A book catalog, available on the T&W website, includes many ideas for teaching outside of the school setting as well as in a regular classroom.

FARAWELL: Finding space outside an academic setting can often be a challenge, and a very expensive one, if you think your program must have its own space. Build the program first. Many inner cities have cultural centers run by city agencies, nonprofits, or churches that are hungry for programming and educational opportunities to offer young people. These can sometimes be found in suburban and rural areas as well. There might be classrooms, performance spaces, or even office space available at little or no cost. This can also be true of local theater companies or performing arts centers. Public libraries also often have meeting rooms they will open to literacy or reading programs. Does a coffee shop in town run an open mic? Maybe it will let you use the same space earlier in the day for an afterschool program at no cost.

BLACKHAWK: In 1998 I attended a colloquium of a national group of programs similar to InsideOut. It was convened by Writers in the Schools of Houston, Texas, which has since grown into the national WITS Alliance. The resources, advice, modeling, mentoring, and friendship that I gained from WITS was invaluable. I recommend seeking out and participating in national networks of youth arts organizations or other groups engaged in this work. The President's Committee for the Arts and the Humanities features groups that are finalists and semifinalists for the committee's annual award and are worth becoming familiar with. The National Guild for Community Arts Agencies and the Association of Writers and Writing Programs are also great resources.

MCNAMER: Houston WITS mentored us. A mutual funder arranged for members of our staff and board to go to Houston and observe their program in action. (Later, we played that mentoring role for an emerging program in Hawaii.) I regularly ask advice from the staff at Houston WITS on a number of topics. Additionally, we are a member of the WITS Alliance, a consortium of writers-in-the-schools programs across the country. Many, if not all of these organizations offer programming outside the traditional academic setting, as do we with our Talbot Youth Home workshops.

I also think it's a good idea to try to attend the AWP Conference, held annually in various major cities. I have always returned inspired by the panels on teaching creative writing to children.

We have received a number of grants from the National Endowment for the Arts. Even in the years we didn't, or when the amount was smaller than expected, we benefited from our conversations with the NEA and with the wealth of material on its website.

MASON AND EK: First, find someone who is doing similar work. It doesn't need to be literary; you could approach someone who runs a community center or afterschool programming. Even better, find several such people. The fact that you are teaching poetry rather than, say, art or dance or unicycle-riding is somewhat cosmetic at this stage, as what you actually need is a venue of some sort and people to populate it.

Definitely consider talking to libraries, both school-affiliated and public. Contact local creative writing teachers and ask about summer writing programs whose leaders might make good allies for your own programs.

More than anything, most of your resources will come from within. What do you want to do? What do you want to accomplish? How? What experience do you want the youth who come to your program to have? Coming up with these answers may be difficult, especially if you are in the gestational stages of planning, but these are worthwhile questions to begin exploring.

Find people whose common sense you trust, who will be honest with you, and who will ask challenging and difficult questions. These contacts may be your most valuable resource. If you treat them well, they'll keep you from making too many mistakes.

Finally, talk directly to the youth whom you intend to serve. They have plenty of sweet ideas, and if you get them invested early, they'll reward you for it many times over. Nothing would be worse than doing a year of work only to find that no young people know that you exist. Talk to them. They're the ones you will most directly serve, so they're the ones whose input you should get first.

OLIVER: Collaborations and partnerships are critical in the process of developing a start-up organization. Educational institutions, local museums, cultural centers, and businesses are perfect. Volunteers from these organizations can sometimes assist with identifying resources through their network. These volunteers can also help facilitate activities related to our curriculum, which cuts down on the number of paid hours to writing instructors without compromising quality and quantity.

How do you attract volunteers?

EGGERS: We've always been dedicated to making it easy to be a volunteer. I remember signing up for a volunteer program in college and they wanted me to commit to two days a week for two years, which wasn't possible for me—or for most people. Our services are centered around two-hour blocks. A two-hour block might be a tutoring session, a field trip, an evening workshop, or an in-school project. Almost all of them are two hours or less, so if a volunteer can commit to just two hours a month, or even two hours a year, those two hours will be used well. And they'll have a profound effect. If you've ever spent two full hours on one student's work, you'll know how deep you can go in that amount of time.

BLACKHAWK: In addition to recruiting graphic designers via Craigslist and elsewhere, InsideOut is now centrally located in the Detroit cultural community. We have offices at Wayne State University with strong ties to various departments, especially the Honors College. Students from the university earn service-learning credits through InsideOut by working on projects in our classrooms, assisting with events, proofreading magazines during publication time, and taking on other projects.

COVAL: Good events and college interns. When most people think of poetry or youth poetry, they want to jump out of a tall building. We are changing that perception by putting on some of the most dynamic public programming in the city. The programs are crisp (nothing should be more than two hours—an hour and a half is pushing it) and include a mix of styles, voices, faces, and ages.

Colleges also have a ton of programs that attempt to place students into community organizations. For instance, you could develop twenty job descriptions that don't require too much management and distribute them to departments, professors, and former students in an attempt to engage them in the organization.

MASON AND EK: Don't think of it as finding ways to "attract" volunteers. Think of it as finding ways to invite new volunteers. Surely people will find you and will want to help. But more often than not, you're going to have to find people you'd like to work with, and then ask them to work with you.

The Nebraska Writers Collective is lucky in that we are able to pay most of our volunteers, which is a nice incentive. More than anything, though, we're involved in the local writing communities and so know whom we want to ask. That is, we actively recruit new volunteers, and we keep sending work to the old volunteers as long as they are willing to handle it.

Seriously, if you know of someone you want to work with, just ask. Maybe the person will say no, but if you ask in the right way and continually show your organization's worth inside your community, he or she might say yes in the future.

HERMAN: People love a barn raising, an opportunity to create something grand, useful, and visible where it didn't exist before. When you can frame your request for volunteers in this way, the volunteering becomes festive and worthwhile. If you can throw in some pizza and sodas, well, you have yourself a work party.

The teachers who sign up for Poetry Out Loud tend to stay with the program. Many have been involved for years and have helped to mentor other teachers who have become involved. With a good barn raising, the initial people you invite end up sharing their enthusiasm, and before you know it you have a crew large enough to accomplish the task.

JAMES KASS: Attracting volunteers is similar to attracting donors. Do good work. Publicize it well. Invite people to participate, and then continue to cultivate that participation. Visibility is important. Show off the brilliance of the young people and you'll have to turn away more volunteers than you can handle.

HOLMAN: Attracting is not the problem—it's keeping! To keep volunteers, you must make them part of the community, with real responsibilities. They should be treated as staff and have all the perks that staff members have.

What ways have you found to attract kids to your organization? Also, once involved with your programming, what have you found to be the most effective ways to excite children about poetry?

ROGERS: The kids love the workshops; they come and stay for years. Their parents love what's happening with the kids, and their teachers notice the difference. For our high-school kids, we offer the Share the Words

High-School Poetry Competition. I also offer a free online mentoring service, working with kids in our area and from all over New York State. I teach my high-school and college poet interns how to assemble a chapbook, edit it, typeset it, and reproduce it in a limited edition under their own imprint.

My translation of *Beowulf* was published in 2000, and that led me to the study and translation of Anglo-Saxon riddle poems. That in turn led me to teach riddle poems to students, which may be the most successful poems I've ever taught. The kids love the riddles, and they learn the uses of metaphor and simile along the way. We have in-workshop riddle-poem contests, and this year we're doing a regional one. Big hit all around!

EGGERS: It was never very hard. And that's because we operate behind these strange storefronts. If you start with bizarre and fun storefronts, you have an advantage over a more sterile environment.

SWAUGER: T&W programs often end with a student reading and/or publication party. The experience of reading their work to an audience is meaningful to kids, but the book seems even more important to them. It's tangible evidence of their accomplishment and is something they can keep and share with family members and friends who weren't able to attend the reading. We make sure that the school or another site receives extra copies of the anthologies to keep in the library or another central location where future program participants will see the books and have their interest sparked by realizing that kids like them have been published in a real book.

FARAWELL: We work almost entirely through teachers. We ask them to do more than simply involve their classes, AP students, or kids who are successful on campus in the traditional sense. We urge them to look deeper for kids who might benefit most from the experience of meeting a poet. Anyone who has ever worked with high-school students knows that the most creative ones are not necessarily the most academically successful, and some of the most troubled are those most in need of what art can bring into their lives. It's important to cultivate relationships with teachers who can help you reach these kids.

I'm not sure the goal should be to excite children about poetry. I suspect slams, open mics, performance competitions, prizes, and publication excite kids about getting applause, approval, prizes, and attention. Instant gratification from praise for work that is usually given little serious effort belies the difficulty of making art and does little to nurture the quality of mind that flourishes in a lifelong connection to poetry.

I'm not interested in exciting students about poetry so much as I am in giving them experiences of genuine substance and in helping them navigate the emotional turmoil of adolescence, which will allow them to mature into adults whose inner lives are rich enough to endure difficulties, challenges, and even tragedies. The suicide rate among teenagers is harrowing, and seems always to be getting worse. They have plenty of diversions in their lives, in the form of computer games, movies, television, and other entertainments that distract their attention from their fears, insecurities, and very real problems. They have enough excitement, or perhaps stimulation is a better word. What they need is something that helps them not to turn away, but rather to turn toward the conflicts they face in their everyday lives. This is what art, what poetry, does. It helps us look more closely at our lives, our experiences and troubles, and gives us the creative and emotional resources to respond to them.

These experiences with poetry include direct encounters with living poets who can speak to kids. Whatever activities are planned, respect must be given to what kids need from the art itself. They need to know that others see the world as they do, feel what they feel, have engaged in the same struggles. Kids too often feel that no one has ever endured what they have, that no one can possibly understand them. There's a reason so many teenage girls adored Sylvia Plath when I was in high school: what she said spoke directly to their own experiences and inner lives.

So find some poets whose work will speak to students: Matthew Dickman, Sharon Olds, Lucille Clifton, Mark Doty, Marie Howe, Sandra Cisneros, Patricia Smith. Give students the opportunity to experience personal connections to poets without having to prove their analytical skills or defend their preferences. This will create lifelong readers. Such readers know what a deep resource poetry is. Helping kids discover this is more important than getting them to dabble in writing poetry for a week or two, a phase they might look back on fondly but dismissively when they're adults.

BLACKHAWK: I can't overstate the impact of publication and performance in building pride and a sense of accomplishment among kids.

MCNAMER: We get kids where they live, at least for six or seven hours each day: at school. Our summer program is an extension of this experience; almost all our enrollees have participated in our school program and want to continue it during their vacation.

We think that the power of language is itself the most effective way to excite children about poetry. When children write about their worlds in language they own and then share this original writing with their peers, the result can be an invigorated sense of the uniqueness of all literature, an acute feeling about the "human-made" nature of writing that brings words alive. Children might hear the poem "Nantucket" by William Carlos Williams and be asked to imagine the place of the poem, the room, the curtain, the breeze, and to think about their own ordinary places that feel special, framed, important. The writing that results is astonishingly varied—from descriptions of a grandmother's kitchen smelling of cinnamon to a father's pickup truck "with the bullet hole in the door."

A big feature of our everyday instruction is the sharing of original writing. Students take turns reading their poems, and everyone is applauded. At the end of a residency, there is a public reading, with the sharing broadened and the applause amplified. Each residency culminates in a printed anthology of student work, and every child receives a copy. (This is probably more important, overall, than the experience some of the kids have of being published in submission-based collections.) Each child in the program, through these readings and these anthologies, is able to achieve not only a strengthened self-image, but also a public persona as a writer, which can be a powerful incentive to keep writing.

GLASS: We don't have to attract the children; we work in classrooms where the poetry sessions are required. Effective ways to excite children about poetry are to have an excited teacher teach them, to read great poems they can relate to, to have a performance poet come in and recite a poem, and to work collaboratively with musicians and visual artists.

Having their poetry published in anthologies or displayed in public settings, such as in libraries or on buses, as well as participating in readings and slam competitions at local venues, are other ways to get kids excited about poetry.

COVAL: A huge, dynamic spectacle—like the citywide youth poetry festival and slam called Louder Than A Bomb. In our audiences and on our stage over the course of the four-week Chicago festival, we will see thousands of young people and their teachers. The festival is representative of the year-round work we do as an organization and is also a feedback loop, allowing us to attract more and more writers and partners. Having the festival means we also have an organizational calendar and goal that can govern how our programs manifest.

We also run weekly open mics, weekend writing classes, publication and journalism programs, summer spoken-word camps, in-school residencies, and professional development programs—and all of it feeds all of it. The work is the work of building a citywide (worldwide) movement of young people being heard and hearing one another. Kids are undeniably attracted to spaces in which their voices are valued in concert with other voices—where they will be seen and also where they will see worlds that are typically hidden because of myriad circumstances, including segregation. We create intentionally mixed spaces where people can see the whole of the city. That is exciting, enticing, a way for young people to feel engaged and motivated.

JEFF KASS: We attract kids to our organization primarily through word of mouth and flyers that we put around schools and in downtown areas where high schoolers hang out. It also helps that I teach high-school, so I can constantly provide information about our programs to my students and to other teachers so that they can get the word out to their own students.

What's most effective, of course, is to create a high-quality experience for the students involved. If they're getting a lot out of the workshops, they'll want to keep coming back. It's also important for us to maintain a welcoming environment within the workshops so people can make friends and feel included. We like to do open mics as well and give students a chance to perform, but you have to be careful about burning students out on those kinds of opportunities. You want them to treasure chances to perform, but if those chances come along every week, students will take them for granted, or even come to see them as a burden. We've found that a couple of open-mic events per semester is the right balance, along with a couple of larger readings for bigger audiences, such as poetry slams or our annual early-winter extravaganza, Poetry Night in Ann Arbor.

JAMES KASS: We've built incentives into our programming. In 1996, the first year of Youth Speaks, we received some donated computers and gave them out to the first twenty kids who came to at least forty hours of workshops. We've employed various tactics like that over the years. We hosted what turned out to be the first teen poetry slam in the country. Since then, we've hosted the national youth poetry slam in a different city every year.

We've also been fortunate to get some high-visibility attention in the media—from PBS documentaries and HBO shows to CNN news stories and trips to the White House to perform for the First Family. All of this is really about the same thing, though, which is that nothing attracts teenagers to programs like other teenagers. Young people themselves can become the best advocates for the work—both as direct outreach partners and as inspiration. Hearing and reading the poetry of teenagers inspires other teenagers to join the conversation.

But yes, offering opportunities for presentation and publication is great. We do not offer cash prizes, but there have been incentives, including trips to perform at the Sundance Film Festival.

OLIVER: The author-in-residence program is the biggest attraction for the students. We make an effort to identify authors who write about life experiences similar to those of the youth. This commonality helps students develop immediate relationships with the authors, and students then become interested in the authors' literary works. Young people subsequently feel comfortable writing about their personal experiences.

GRIGSBY: We don't actually recruit kids directly, but we do need to engage and excite both the students and their teachers, especially given the sad fact that all too often poetry has earned the reputation of being something to dread—like poison ivy. Additionally, it is the students' enthusiasm that helps our organization grow, through referrals and invitations to return.

One thing we love is a microphone. Some classrooms have these. We've purchased simple microphones that we use with karaoke equipment or used guitar amps for a total cost of less than $60. They're relatively lightweight and can be carried from school to school. At the end of each class, some or all of the students read their poems aloud. Small voices become strong and clear and gain the attention of other students. The microphone imparts a notion that poetry is important and honored as an art, as is singing or playing an instrument. The microphone also helps listeners stay tuned in to the reader. If the poems being read are still in the revision process, listeners are invited to share their views as to what worked really well ("Something I liked was...") and to ask questions about lines needing more clarification ("I want to know...").

In a recent class, the third graders took an interesting turn with this exercise as they listened to their classmates' self-portrait poems. Instead of asking questions like "Where was the party?" or "What kind of cake did you eat?" they asked, "Why do you say you're a dark cloud?" and "Why do you sound like fireworks?" Rather than redirecting them, we listened, and the poets' responses, all willingly given, illuminated a deep understanding of both themselves and the power of words and images to convey many depths of meaning. Whereas an adult or adolescent might have shirked an honest response to such questions, the third graders joyously opened the windows to their inner lives.

Choral readings and creative movement can also be naturally paired with many poems, and both can excite younger children. The shared poem can be on a poster and echo-read by the students—which assists emerging and struggling readers. One such favorite is "Fog," by Carl Sandburg; half the class recites the poem while the other half moves across the room, imitating the content of the poem. This movement is a beautiful way for new students to grasp the concept of metaphor and internalize the physical connections Sandburg created.

We sometimes ask young emerging writers and beginning ESL students to draw their poems' images before they write them. If students appear frozen with fear over writing on the page, we let them tell their poems to people who can write them down, and then the original authors copy them. This builds confidence, and shy students are usually ready in the next session to write on their own.

There seems to be something extraordinarily special, almost sacred, to children about making a book, and students from K–6 exhibit great enthusiasm for this venture. Pages are stapled or tied with ribbon, yarn, or plant fibers, and students add their own illustrations. They are encouraged to read the books to their families and to students in lower grades. At the end-of-term poetry concert, they read selected works from their favorites. For K–2 kids, the books are shorter and might be themed or consist of just one poem, with a single line per page.

We love the River of Words annual anthologies and use many of those poems to demonstrate various themes with students. When students see that children their age have written poems, it seems to serve as an invitation to join the circle of poets. They also love selecting their best work and preparing it, like professionals, for the annual River of Words contest.

If you were to write a book on teaching poetry to kids, what would be the three main points of the book?

EGGERS:

1. Every kid has the potential to write effectively, but it's a process. When you can disabuse students from thinking that their first draft has to be perfect, you're halfway to making a competent and even inspired writer. When they understand that even professional writers go through three, four, or twenty drafts, it's an entirely different dynamic. They get down to business very quickly.

2. Subject matter is important. When we ask a ten-year-old to write an inspired paper about the cotton gin or steam engines and they deliver a boring or even plagiarized paper, we shouldn't be so surprised—the subject matter is crushingly dull. If we want young people to enjoy writing, we have to give them opportunities to write about things they care deeply about, even if that's Kobe Bryant or World of Warcraft. Doesn't matter. As long as they like to

write, you're on your way. But when kids associate writing with dull, make-work assignments, we quickly extinguish the flickering love of writing inside them.

3. You have to throw away the rules on the front end. That is, if you tell students their papers have to be five paragraphs long and each sentence has to have twelve words, four commas, and three clauses—all that—you will most assuredly be creating reluctant and uninspired writers. But if you tell kids, "Write whatever you want, in whatever way you want," then at least you get them started. You can always impose the grammar and structure on the back end (I'm a stickler for grammar), but saddling a kid with all the restrictions at the beginning is disastrous. It's utterly paralyzing.

CIRELLI:

1. Students are only going to go as far as you are willing to go. If you go simple, their work will be simple. If you get vulnerable, then they will, too. If the poetry you bring in is challenging, they will be challenged to create complex work.

2. Students already know tons of poetry by heart—tap into that. For many, it's called rap (the oral poetic tradition of hip-hop).

3. It's not bad to write about love, the heart, anger, your grandmother—the key to making it compelling is in the approach. How do I approach writing about an eggplant parm hero in a way that no one would expect or has ever written about an eggplant parm hero before?

FARAWELL:

1. Begin by creating as open, nonjudgmental, and non-threatening an atmosphere as possible. The simplest way to do this is to create an initial encounter with poetry that is nonhierarchical. Invite students to spend some time in a circle silently reading a shared packet of poems or an anthology. Ask students to pick poems they feel like hearing read aloud. Kids don't need to offer elaborate reasons for their choices. You should do this activity along with students. Spend some time just listening to one another read poems, without discussion. Listen to them more than once. Then invite students to talk about why they chose their poems. Don't challenge them or ask for analysis or explanation. Their reasons can be as quirky and personal as they want. You should offer truly personal, nonacademic reasons for your choices. That's it. Just enjoy hearing some poems aloud together.

    Invite everyone in the group to contribute poems (not their own) for discussion. If you have to use an anthology, try to pick one that covers a wide range and has a generous selection of contemporary poets. If you have no choice regarding which anthology to use, supplement it with more-contemporary poems that might have a stronger appeal for students. Whatever the configuration, get everyone involved in selecting the poems that are discussed. Here is a possible early exercise: flip through the anthology and pick two or three poems for discussion. Then have the group gather, and ask each member to share at least one of those poems.

    Don't worry yet that there are certain poems, literary devices, analytical tools, et cetera that you want students to learn, or that you might be required to teach them. There will be time for that. As a member of the group, you get to pick some poems too, so there will be ample opportunity to point the group toward poems that illustrate styles, approaches, forms, or concepts. But at first, allow for this personal engagement, this sharing, and open conversation. Once students are engaged, you can build on that. Their curiosity about how poets do what they do will inevitably lead to discussions about technique.

This is more challenging than following a prepared reading list. You may feel as though you're working without a net. A little fear is a good thing. It lets you know you're trying something new. Trust that eventually you will get to poems that allow you to teach the core curriculum standards. But if you begin by inviting connection and respecting students' choices and feelings, you'll have a much easier time getting them to follow you into other conversations.

2. Model "reading as process." Writers and teachers accept that writing well requires multiple drafts. Kids need to know the same is true of reading well. This means taking the risk of allowing students to bring in poems you may have never seen before. Better still, deliberately bring in poems that confuse you, or that have passages you don't understand. Let students see you go through the process of reading and rereading a poem. Admit that there are parts you just don't get. Maybe the students can help you. Maybe some passages are ultimately irreducible. This is a good place to talk about ambiguity, multiple interpretations, why paraphrasing can take writers and readers only so far, why certain poems refuse to be narrowed down to a single interpretation, and how some even seem

to take readers out into the unknowable by raising questions instead of answering them. Most important of all is for students to see that their teachers need to read poems more than once, that literary interpretation is not a trick, that analysis is not a game of guessing what a teacher thinks, and that multiple readings are rewarding.

3. Back into technical terms. Students may have to know literary terms for mandated standardized tests. The best way to teach such terms is through the poems themselves. For example, after everyone has listened to a poem read aloud, have students quickly jot down any lines or phrases they remember. Inevitably, a number of students will choose the same passages. Talk about what makes a line memorable. The qualities described almost always have names, such as *imagery* or *alliteration*. Asking students to choose a favorite line from a poem can spark the same conversation. Talking about why or how a particular poem makes an impact can lead into discussions of point of view, voice, rhythm, rhyme, et cetera. For standard forms, such as the sonnet or haiku, read the poems first and then define the forms through examples.

BLACKHAWK:

1. Trust yourself fully.
2. Imagine wildly.
3. Craft carefully.

COVAL:

1. Be fresh! Don't be wack and corny.
2. Build the bridge from Lil Wayne to Gwendolyn Brooks.

3. Be a student of contemporary movements in poetics. Hip-hop is poetry, and there is a generation of hip-hop poets perfect for this moment in the classroom. Immediately relatable, likeable, and teachable. Read and teach Patricia Smith, Willie Perdomo, Roger Bonair-Agard, Aracelis Girmay, Patrick Rosal, Kevin Coval, Idris Goodwin. Bring the work into the classroom and go!

JAMES KASS:

1. Don't focus on teaching young people poetry; focus on facilitating spaces in which young people write. Those spaces include being exposed to all kinds of poetry and understanding the traditions of poetry, but don't focus on "teaching" poetry. I'm not even sure what that means.

2. Poetry can be what people need it to be. In an interview, T.S. Eliot said, essentially, that once he was done with a poem, he was no better a critic of it than anyone else, that he'd be no better at describing its meaning than anyone else. He could explain his inspiration, even his intention, when writing the poem. But its meaning? That's up to the reader. It's critical that young people be exposed to all kinds of writing to open up their frame of reference and to give them as many tools as possible, but poetry needs to be something without limits. Poetry always needs to be defined by the next writer.

3. Create spaces in which young people can write. Just write. Write a lot. Allow themselves and their writing to be both challenged and celebrated. But get them to write. To take it seriously but love it. And enjoy it. Most of all, write. Writers write. That's what they do.

HOLMAN:

1. Nurture the poetry that's already present in the child's thinking.
2. Poetry is fun.
3. Respect and use all mother tongues in the class.

REAGLER:

1. Writing poetry is fun.
2. Poets' poems are all theirs.
3. By writing poetry, people make their lives more interesting, complex, and beautiful. They learn to understand themselves and others more deeply. Later in life, writing will be there when they need it most.

What are some ideal goals for the first year in the life of a new poetry organization?

JAMES KASS: Find a handful of young people who really believe in what you're doing, and ask them to help you build it. Partner with teachers. Write down what you want to do over the next five years. Do not discount the importance of a five-year plan, no matter how informal.

EGGERS: I think publishing student work should be right up there with the first goals. Students love to be published, and by putting their work out there, you give them an authentic outside audience. And as mentioned before, the books become a calling card for the organization.

SWAUGER: In the first year of a new poetry organization, I would focus on implementing a limited number of programs—perhaps one to three—very well, and use the opportunity that starting small provides to track results and assess what worked and where changes might be needed. At the same time, I would focus on getting to know the people who have some connection to those first efforts, such as parents of participating children.

CIRELLI: Create a sound vision, one that is ambitious. Develop a mission that will act like the coal to the vision's engine. Immerse your organization in pedagogy, in practice, in teaching, in learning, in (slowly) growing. Forget about fund-raising until all of this is mastered.

REAGLER: To run a great organization, you will need money. It's a lot easier if you understand that fact up front and plan for it. But there's no one way to grow an organization. When I survey the twenty-two WITS programs in North America, each is unique. That is a beautiful thing. The specific goals of each new organization will depend on the local environment and the skill sets of their leadership. In fund-raising, for example, if your city has numerous private foundations, your goal might be to develop a grant template. If there are corporate sponsorship opportunities, you might create a marketing plan. If you live in a gala-driven city, you might try planning a fund-raising event. In raising money, you always want to assess the skills on your leadership team. Of course, try to choose the methods that will bring in the greatest revenue for the least effort—assuming they are not at odds with your mission!

HERMAN: Find allies. Help people see why working with your organization is beneficial to them.

JEFF KASS: First you have to recruit a core group of students and keep them interested. You also have to be really organized in terms of what you present for students when they show up. Whether you're running a reading or a workshop or a slam or any other kind of event, you want students to be able to feel like they're part of an organization that knows what it's doing. As things move along, you want to be able to turn some of that organizing responsibility over to the students themselves to help them feel personally committed not only to the idea of improving their own writing, but also to building the poetry community. If you can accomplish that much in your first year, you will have done a lot. You also want to be able to put on at least one high-profile public event so people in the broader community can gain an appreciation and understanding of what you're doing.

It's also good to develop relationships with local businesses that can be useful to you. For example, create relationships with bookstores that can host readings, carry your publications, and even offer gift certificates as slam prizes; create relationships with coffee shops and libraries that can host readings or workshops. Such partnerships help build credibility for your program and establish your presence in the community. Some of those businesses might ultimately wind up as sponsors of major events as well. It's also a good idea to build relationships with local schools by trying to find teachers who are open to having poets come visit their classes or to promoting your program and events.

I would also suggest researching local community foundations and granting organizations. You might not be ready to apply for big grants yet, but it doesn't hurt to find out who's involved in these organizations and to start building relationships with them. But all that is secondary, once again, to building great programming. Present terrific workshops. Put on electrifying readings. Get kids excited, and the other stuff will follow.

MASON AND EK: Money does not matter beyond a certain point, nor do fancy business cards, websites, or any of those other things. Instead, do as much as you can to build something where you get kids coming to write poetry with you, and where they keep coming back on a relatively regular basis. The benefit to this approach: when you begin soliciting donors and volunteers, and when you begin growing your organization, you will have a body of work, so to speak, and an organizational history.

HOLMAN: Survival.

How do you sustain interest in your organization from your various communities (local and/or national)?

COVAL: Remain relevant. Poetry is a contemporary art, alive now. It's about the worlds people inhabit at this moment. The work and words should reflect, refract, represent, and re-present these realities. And the accompanying programming to highlight these words should be dynamic and fresh. Think BIG! All-city everything.

REAGLER: We show tremendous respect to the people who do the real work for WITS—the writers. We pay them well and provide them with the resources they need to excel. We nurture their talents, encourage their growth, and promote their successes. This may sound like a strange answer to the question, but with 125 teachers and writers a year, this cultivation has an enormously positive ripple effect in communities.

FARAWELL: We write a weekly "Poetry Fridays" blog on a variety of topics related to our work: upcoming events, poets who have worked with us in the past or who are coming to a future Dodge Festival, opportunities for teachers and students, or essays on poetry in a broader sense. We started a YouTube channel to post videos of poets who've been to the Dodge Festival. We do regular postings through Facebook, Twitter, and e-mail about our programs and the festival, but we're careful not to bombard people. We have annual events for teachers and keep in touch with them pretty regularly. It's crucial to have events for teachers, not just students. Teachers suffer from this age of standardized tests as much as their students do.

GLASS: The valuable connections that poet-teachers make with schools and classroom teachers keep our reputation alive and ongoing. When classroom teachers see how students light up when "live" poets transmit a love of language, when students get excited to write, ripples form and expand to local communities. Our biggest selling tool is the quality of poems in our statewide anthologies, which we distribute to libraries and sell through our website.

BLACKHAWK: We use social media, e-blasts, high-profile events, and as much publicity as we can muster to put the message of InsideOut before the public. In 2010–2011 we conducted a Big Read Across Detroit, featuring the work of Emily Dickinson. We also sponsored an all-city youth writing conference, with Jimmy Santiago Baca as keynoter and a year-end multi-arts/poetry showcase. Our youth were especially active in organizing support for their slam team, which traveled to Brave New Voices—and won fourth place!

MICHAEL: We try to participate in as many festivals, conferences, symposia, and the like as we can. We attend (have a booth/table, give a workshop, host a panel discussion, have children read, et cetera) about two dozen public events per year, everything from TED, the National Book Festival, and AWP to local library events. We also publish an annual anthology of children's poetry and art, which we give to public and school libraries, and we have two widely distributed full-color anthologies published by Heyday Books and Milkweed Editions.

We also have a vibrant, frequently updated (at least we try) website, with content of interest to teachers, students, and the general public. Visitors to the website can subscribe to our electronic newsletter, which is free. We call it "Poem of the Month" and send out not only the children's poems and artwork but also general information about the organization's recent and upcoming doings. A company called Constant Contact, which we also use to create and distribute the newsletter, maintains the listserv. We forward the completed document to them to send to our list, and they send it out in a way that optimizes the format and look of the newsletter for the varying individual screens of the recipients.

HOLMAN: Always be open. Write letters to everyone who has done something with or for poetry in your community, and invite them to participate in your program. Say yes.

ROGERS: We do massive public relations. I learned press rules when I was a student at the University of Iowa and worked in PR in New York, so I understand the value of having your name and work out there. We send e-releases to every newspaper, radio, and TV station in our region and beyond. If the local news outlets don't run them, I call and ask why. We make sure our releases contain, in the first paragraph (you'd be surprised at how many people just don't get this), the who, what, where, when, and why of the story; then we elaborate. The press appreciates this. We keep regional teachers in the loop, sending information that will be of interest or benefit to them and to their students.

MASON AND EK: Simply put, if you continue creating opportunities for people, and then continue letting those people know that opportunities exist, interest will be sustained. It all comes down to doing interesting and worthwhile work.

What detail about the process of beginning an organization do you wish you'd known when you were starting out?

EGGERS: I didn't know a thing when we opened 826 Valencia, so every single thing we had to learn the hard way. But that made it fun. If we had planned it all out and just followed an outline, it would have been dull. We let it all unfold naturally, even chaotically, and that kept it vital and surprising. And of course, if you go into it with too rigid an idea of what you'll do, then you can't adapt very well to the needs or wants of the communities you're working with. It's best to have a certain idea of what you want to do but know that your plans will bend and might even be completely reshaped.

FARAWELL: Make time for planning ahead. You have to think beyond what needs to get done right now. You have to make time for sitting back and getting an overview of where you are, where you hope to be, and what steps are necessary to get there. This won't happen by itself. You have to open your calendar and write in blocks of time over the year when you are going to do nothing but think long-term, big picture, and examine where you are in relation to your long-term goals. Protect that time. Don't give it up. Use it for planning. Otherwise, short-term thinking will eat up your time, energy, and resources, and you will be in perpetual crisis mode.

MASON AND EK: The Nebraska Writers Collective incorporated as a 501(c)(3) nonprofit organization in 2008 and made two fundamental mistakes: we tried to do too much, and we didn't do a good job of building a strong board of directors, which meant that most of our initiatives succeeded or failed based on the one volunteer who undertook them. We eventually had to do a lot of work refining our mission, cultivating our programming, and building a collaborative and supportive environment. Even now, we are still learning so many things.

ROGERS: You have to stay with it. You can't ever give up. That's the simplest and most significant detail. You have to let people know about the organization. Many people will tell you to let it go, and many people will sample what you offer and then go about their business. Many writers won't understand that their attendance and participation help the organization continue. You have to keep your own enthusiasm.

Are there any aspects of the physical environment that you find help teach poetry to kids? (E.g., lots of light, art on the walls, beanbag chairs, big purple markers.)

EGGERS: I'm a proponent of nonclinical environments. I like old wood, chandeliers, ladders, trees, strange details. If the environment is imaginative, the writing will likely follow suit. If the environment is corporate, sterile, pedestrian, then there's a chance the students will think that way, too. But that's not a hard-and-fast rule. Obviously kids, and anyone, can create magnificent work in any context. But even small, inspired environmental elements can be significant.

KASS: Dry-erase boards and privacy. A dry-erase board is key in engaging students in conversations. Create a shared vocabulary and a shared blank page that you fill up together.

REAGLER: Most often, we have only limited influence on the physical teaching environment, i.e., the classroom. However, we do offer field trips for our students. We have found that location-based learning can jump-start the writing process for even the most reluctant or resistant young writers. Our destinations have included an art museum, a nature reserve, and a historic neighborhood.

ROGERS: Here's a really important thing that's been very successful for us: I cover the tables with white paper and encourage the children to draw and write on them. The kids absolutely love that feature of our workshops program, and it hardly costs anything. Each child also gets his or her own folder with a pencil, lined paper, plain paper, and extra erasers. A few years ago we wrote a grant and got a projector and an electronic projection camera; these tools are very helpful in putting poems on the board for workshopping.

FARAWELL: Anything that can break down the feeling of hierarchy in the room is important, and anything that can make the space feel less like a classroom is valuable. Is there adequate natural light to allow for leaving the fluorescent lighting off? If not, can some lamps with warmer light be brought in to use instead of fluorescent light? Can some colorful but inexpensive rugs be strewn around the room? Mobiles, artwork, weavings, or other wall hangings can break up the monotony of monochromatic spaces.

Any open, airy space can help by offering a change of pace. Reading poems aloud in a field or park results in a different kind of attention. No one can go to sleep if everyone is standing around listening to one another.

Finally though, amazing encounters can happen in even the most hideous, unwelcoming spaces if teachers and poets give their full attention to the kids and are present, emotionally available, genuine, and respectful. Generosity of spirit goes a long way toward creating a warm and welcoming atmosphere.

NOTE: *Readers interested in further discussion of all these topics are invited to check out* Blueprints: Bringing Poetry into Communities, *a copublication of the University of Utah Press and the Poetry Foundation. Noted poets and community leaders discuss innovative ways they have introduced poetry to diverse communities. Topics such as becoming a nonprofit, planning an event, working with a board of directors, promoting projects, and fund-raising are addressed in a toolkit loaded with practical advice and resources for founding new programs or for sustaining or transforming existing programs. Elizabeth Alexander, Robert Hass, and Lee Briccetti are just three of the dozen poets and artists who drew on a wealth of poetry community experience in the essays they contributed. Please visit the Harriet Monroe Poetry Institute (www.poetryfoundation. org/foundation/poetryinstitute) on the Poetry Foundation website for more information about* Blueprints.

Part 3
Lesson Plans

Dream Machine

Michael Dickman

"Out here, I can say anything."

—Larry Levis

Introduction and exercises to be adapted for your class or given to students as a take-home assignment.

Dreams are like poems.

In a dream, anything is possible. You can fly, you can travel to foreign countries or unknown universes. You can experience your wildest fantasies and face your most terrifying fears. In this way, dreams are like poems. They have their own stories to tell and their own music to sing, and they play by their own rules.

I think the secret to how dreams work is the word yes. Dreams never say no to anything, no matter how weird. Like great improvisational theater, our dreams keep saying *yes*.

I'm flying? Yes.

I suddenly have three heads? Yes.

On Mars? Yes.

And Mars is the size of a cell phone? Yes.

Mars calls me and wants to talk to my three heads? Yes. Yes. Yes. A strange dream!

So what happens if we keep saying yes in our poems? Where will that take us? I think it will free us to say some things we feel we can't say given the rules of our actual lives and the physical world. It will sharpen our imaginations in a culture where everything seems already imagined for us. It will lead to some interesting and exciting poems.

Here are some prompts in that direction.

Neruda

First let's look at a poem that is not about a dream but about a pair of socks. The poem is called "Ode to My Socks" and was written by the Chilean poet Pablo Neruda. Although it's not expressly about dreams, it says *yes* to dreamlike imagery. The narrator's feet are transformed by his socks, becoming one thing after another: sharks, blackbirds, and cannons.

EXERCISE

Write a poem about an object you love. It could be something very common, such as Neruda's socks. In the poem, describe this object in as many ways as you can. Try to move freely from one image to the next. Don't worry about how strange or odd it might sound. Just keep saying *yes*.

Clifton

Lucille Clifton's poems "my dream about being white" and "my dream about falling" take on very different circumstances. In the first poem, the narrator tells about a dream in which she experiences the world through another's race. In the second, she tells about the act of falling.

EXERCISE

Write two poems. In one, try to communicate what it would be like to be another person. In your second poem, try to convey a physical action—but one set free by the lawlessness of dreams. Anything can happen. In Clifton's poem, the speaker becomes an apple. What do you become?

Hugo

Richard Hugo's poem "In Your War Dream" is a great example of saying yes in a poem. The logic and story change quickly, but the poem feels whole, united. Notice also that it's a poem not about *Hugo's* war dream, but about *your own*. Hugo gives readers the experience of a dream in the form of a poem.

EXERCISE

Write a poem that invokes a particular kind of dream. A good dream, a bad dream, a red dream, a blue dream, a fish dream—you name it. How can you ensure that readers really experience the dream you have in mind? Feel free to jump around a lot in the poem, from sentence to sentence, and see where all that jumping takes you.

Paley

In Grace Paley's poem "I Invited," the narrator invites her deceased parents into her dream so that she can see them again and also see them together again. Her parents are allowed to speak.

EXERCISE

Write a poem that invites someone into your dream. It could be a friend or family member you haven't seen in a while. It could be someone you greatly admire but have never met. Let the person speak in the dream. Invite as many people as you'd like into this dream-poem party. See what happens.

Strand

Finally, let's take a look at a poem that ends with someone falling into a dream. The poem is called "The King" and was written by Mark Strand. In this poem, the narrator has a small exchange with a king who quickly falls asleep and "entered his dream / like a mouse vanishing into its hole."

EXERCISE

Write a dream-poem for your own king. What kind of dream would he have? Where would he go? Whom would he meet?

That's it. Keep saying yes, and enjoy the journey!

POEM SOURCES

"I Invited" — Paley, Grace. *Fidelity*. New York: Farrar, Straus and Giroux, 2008.

"In Your War Dream" — Hugo, Richard. *Selected Poems*. New York: W. W. Norton & Company, 1979.

"The King" — Strand, Mark. *Man and Camel*. New York: Knopf, 2006.

"my dream about being white" and "my dream about falling" — Clifton, Lucille. *Next: New Poems*. Brockport, NY: BOA Editions, Ltd., 1987.

"Ode to My Socks" — Neruda, Pablo. *Selected Odes of Pablo Neruda*. Translated by Margaret Sayers Peden. Berkeley: University of California Press, 1990.

Attending the Living Word/World: Using *Haibun* to Discover Poetry

Elizabeth Bradfield

"What makes *this* a poem?" A person's first response to poetry is often something along these lines. With students, the key to both writing and enjoying poetry is to engage this question. But where to start? *Haibun*, a classic Japanese form that combines poetry and prose, provides wonderful opportunities for students of all ages.

Haibun traditionally recounts events from everyday life or travels, using prose that is scattered with small bright poem-gems. The best examples are found in the writings of Bashō, the seventeenth-century master of the form (examples follow this lesson plan).

Haibun prose is informal and diary-like; the poetry is in haiku form and can come at any point in the writing—beginning, middle, or end. A haiku is a short, vivid poem that paints a picture of a single moment and often incorporates references to the passing seasons or the natural world. The haiku structure can be, roughly speaking, simplified to this: three lines with syllable counts of five, seven, and five. Some haibun have more than one haiku within them.

The poetry and prose of haibun do not tell exactly the same story; rather, they provide different windows into one story. Think of haibun prose as a panoramic landscape and the haiku as a focused detail from that broad swath. The prose moves; the haiku embodies stillness.

LESSON PLANS

Ask students to write a journal entry—just a paragraph or two—about something that happened recently. A trip to the grocery store, a time they walked the dog and it did something strange, someone in the hallway who dropped an armful of books and papers, et cetera. Tell students to use regular language, as if they were speaking to friends or family. Complete sentences are not required, but students should spend time trying to get the details right. They should be specific. Give them ten minutes or so to write, limiting them to one or two paragraphs.

Then ask the students to think about one vivid moment in the experience. It should come not from the central core of the story but from something a bit peripheral. For example, if a student writes about a family dinner, a piece of art on the wall or flowers out the window might be ideal. Have students write haiku about their moments or things.

Next, give students a couple of examples of haibun. I recommend selections from Bashō for older students in particular. (Examples and resources follow the exercise.)

Have students read the haibun example you've chosen. It's best to read it aloud a couple of times before discussing. With younger students, you might have to do the first reading, but it is important to allow the students to speak the poem, to take it in at the pace of speech.

Ask students what they notice about the prose. Some important aspects to point out: the shorthand style, as if the writer is jotting down notes; the focus on physical, external details more than personal reactions; the simple and perhaps even irreverent tone.

Then ask students what they notice about the haiku within the haibun. Aside from the short length, ask them how the haiku fits in with the prose. Does it retell the entire story, or does it capture one moment? How directly tied to the story is it? How do the images or ideas in the poems bounce off and speak with the images and ideas in the narrative?

After the discussion, ask the students to write haibun on their own. Have them use a moment from their walk/car ride/bus ride home. Encourage them to note at least three odd or interesting details in the prose part of their haibun. To encourage the jotted style of haibun prose, have students begin three sentences with phrases taken from the following list: "Went to (x place) and...," "Saw (x person) doing (x activity)," "Thought of (x person) and the time that (x happened)." Their haiku should include one image from the natural world (flower, tree, sky) and at least one color. Add any other constraints or requirements you think will be useful.

The next day, have students share aloud what they've written. Because their haibun will have come from similar experiences, they will be able to see the many variations that can arise from their own visions.

CONCLUSION

Students will discover through this lesson that their own daily, ordinary lives are perfect subjects for poetry. What's more, even without being aware of it, students who write haibun must think about the difference between poetry and prose and thus about "what makes *this* a poem." The choices they make about what to "journal" about and what to turn into haiku are also a first step toward revision. Revision, in this case, means looking hard at a piece of writing, deciding what is vital and important within it, and then trying to keep the language as compact and evocative as possible. The practice of reexamining what they've written will serve your students well in any written effort they might make: e-mails, love letters, speeches, job applications, essays, and even poems.

HAIBUN EXAMPLES AND RESOURCES

Seeing Nambu Road a good ways off, stayed over at village of Iwade. Went on via Ogurozaki, Mizu-no-ojima, and from Narugo Hot Springs made for the Shitomae Barrier and on over into province of Dewa. This route few travellers ever take, so guards eyed us suspiciously and barely let us through. Climbed high mountain there, sun already down, and happening on a border-guard hut sought shelter there. For three days winds and rain fierce, forced to hang on in that dull retreat.

what with fleas and lice
the horse's having a piss
right at the pillow

Bashō Matsuo, *Backroads to Far Towns: Bashō's Travel Journal*, trans. Cid Corman and Susumu Kamaike (Buffalo, NY: White Pine Press, 2004)

Finding Good Soil

A few petals have fallen away from the vase that rests on the patient's night table. I add water to rejuvenate the stems, but it's hopeless. The flowers are dead. The elderly woman tells me that she enjoyed watching the flowers change. She always grew roses in her garden. She drifts into detail—of pouring boiling water over the soil to sterilize it, of covering flats with a screen to protect the grains from mice and ants. Sometimes, the containers would spend a second winter outside to give the slower seeds another chance to germinate. At the beginning of autumn, she'd return each tool to its proper hook in the potting shed, then relax on the porch swing with her husband. By now, she is unable to stay awake. The light changes, as she naps, and I notice that the roses donated by our church have dried perfectly.

bells
beyond the garden
the garden beyond

Tish Davis, "Finding Good Soil," *Modern Haibun & Tanka Prose*, no. 2 (Winter 2009): 15.

Milledgeville Haibun

Beat. Beat. Beats beat here. The sound of the train on the Georgia road, the measured claps of the wheels at the gaps of the joints of the rails is the beat of the hammer on iron and anvil at the smithy, Sol's shop, shaping shoes for mules and horses; and the sizzle of red metal in water is the train's whistle, and all echoes resound and effuse, and the last word returns like watermelons here with summer heat, beat with a hammer, beat when he, a boy, broke into the garden at the county jail at night when the beat men were asleep because theirs were the sweetest, so bust one open, the dull thud just before the crack, and eat the heart and move on to the next; and he moved on to women and settled eventually on one and finally busted her with finality, thud before crack, and he measured time raising the sweetest watermelons for a time and time served he returned, a man, and he lay on the tracks of the Georgia road cradled by the rails. Heart stopped.

Old railroad, abandoned—
between crossties trees grow,
a feral pig roots below branches.

Sean Hill, *Blood Ties & Brown Liquor* (Athens, GA: University of Georgia Press, 2008)

OTHER RESOURCES

Modern Haibun & Tanka Prose—this literary journal has issues online that can be downloaded as PDFs and contains many examples of haibun.

"Haibun Defined: Anthology of Haibun Definitions," *Haibun Today*, December 16, 2007, http://haibuntoday.blogspot.com/2007/12/haibun-defined-anthology-of-haibun.html (offers further explanations of haibun).

Bashō Matsuo, *Backroads to Far Towns: Bashō's Travel Journal*, trans. Cid Corman and Susumu Kamaike (Buffalo, NY: White Pine Press, 2004)

Eavesdropping
on a Figure at Work

Yusef Komunyakaa

I spent 1984 crisscrossing the Big Easy teaching workshops in the New Orleans Poetry in the Schools Program for elementary- and high-school students. This was my first time working with young writers, and I was both eager and anxious. As I began to create lesson plans, I tried to go back in time, to conjure a place in my early imagination. My exercises varied: Students wrote poems about the experience of making toys or fashioning Mardi Gras costumes. They were asked to write poems about a member of the family cooking their favorite dish. They were told to imagine an extinct animal and then attempt to bring the animal to life through words. One exercise that always succeeded began with a tune by a Japanese flute master on the *shakuhachi*—a bamboo flute. When the tune ended, I'd let the silence own the space for a moment, and then I'd say to the students:

> Close your eyes. Take a deep breath. You are now stand-
> ing before a closed door. Your hand is on the doorknob.
> You can still hear a hint of the bamboo flute in your mind.
> Turn the doorknob slowly and enter the room. Someone is

sitting in a chair or on a stool—or standing—doing something with his or her hands. Who is this person?

He or she doesn't see you. Light comes into the room through a window. Let the hues and shadows of the room wash over you. Now focus on the person's hands. Look at the person's eyes, hair, ears, clothes, and shoes, taking in the smallest details. What is the person doing with his or her hands?

One last time let your eyes observe the entire room. What can you see through the window?

Return to the person. Take another long, hard look, then slowly back out the room. Close the door. Open your eyes. Now, write down everything you observed in that room— in lines of prose.

The students would write for about ten or fifteen minutes, and then I would ask them to share their work. As they read their prose poems aloud, I was always elated by how varied the writing was: some captured moments of music, fingers stitching clothes or untangling a strand of worry beads, hands working and playing, et cetera. I remember one particular poem that held everyone's attention in a workshop: a Vietnamese boy, within ten or twelve minutes, traveled across the sea and visited his grandmother sitting in an austere room in a small village somewhere outside Da Nang, his grandfather laid out for burial rites. I don't remember the lines or exact imagery, but I can still remember the monumental feeling his poem cast over the workshop.

Syllabus

Meghan O'Rourke and Liam O'Rourke

Each of the four sections below is organized into two parts: a reading component and a writing component. We designed this lesson so that you can add or subtract from what follows, expanding each section into a few classes if you wish or adding specific poems and poetic terminology that suit your class's age-group.

A great addition would be memorization exercises: have students memorize and recite poems. Combining all three activities—reading, writing, and memorization—would give students a strong sense of poetic structure as well as the visceral, musical quality of poetry.

Introduction: What Is Poetry?

Ask your students what they think defines poetry. What qualities do they associate with poetry? Consider linguistic qualities such as rhyme, musicality, compression, heightened use of figurative language, and use of image, line breaks, rhythm, and meter.

READ

Ezra Pound's "In the Station of the Metro."

DISCUSS

Ask students what they think makes this a poem. Consider the structure. Guide them to articulate (or point out) that the poem is written in only two lines—with an equation implicitly drawn between the lines—and a light rhyme. Can the students see this? Ask them what the line "Petals on a wet, black bough" refers to and why Pound compares the two images. (We suggest touching on the historical context of the poem—such as the growth of urbanization, and Pound's belief in making poetry new by including subjects/spaces that wouldn't have been considered traditionally "poetic," such as an underground metro station.)

WRITE

Have students compose two- to four-line poems comparing two unlike things. If you want to be more specific, ask students to come up with a metaphor for a crowd of people. For younger kids, write out the first line of "In the Station of the Metro" and have them fill in the blank of the second line.

Image as Metaphor

Images in poems are often symbolic—they reflect something beyond themselves. Images can create moods, establish tones, or point to something previously mentioned in a poem or to something entirely new. (Teachers of older students can talk more broadly about figurative language.)

READ

George Herbert's "Prayer (I)," Terrance Hayes's "The Mustache," and/or Wallace Stevens's "Thirteen Ways of Looking at a Blackbird."

DISCUSS

Consider with students the ways that each poet arranges these lists of images-as-metaphors. Ask your students how they think this serves each poem.

IN-CLASS ASSIGNMENT

Have students create between six and ten metaphors for something concrete, such as a mustache. Challenge them to make their metaphors as outlandish as possible while still evoking the original object.

WRITE

Ask students to arrange their lists of metaphors into full poems. They can do this either in class or as homework. Remind them that they should feel free to elaborate or give shape to their poems as needed.

Adventures With Lines

Ask your students what one difference is between poetry and prose. Guide them to the idea that prose is usually organized according to sentences and paragraphs, and the most basic and visible element of most poems is the line.

READ:

Walt Whitman's "O Captain! My Captain!" Examine Whitman's use of short and long lines. Have students read the poem aloud.

DISCUSS

Ask students where in the poem they find themselves taking breaths. Where might they become out of breath—almost as someone weeping would? Note that the only periods and full stops come after the word *dead*. Ask how the poem's punctuation intensifies its visceral effects.

READ

William Carlos Williams's "This Is Just To Say." Have different students read the poem aloud according to how they hear the tone and mood.

DISCUSS

Ask students why they think Williams broke the lines of his poem where he did. Introduce the term *enjambment*—from the French, meaning "to throw one's leg over" or "to step over." (With younger students, you can have fun demonstrating this physically if you wish!) Consider with the students how the first two stanzas work *grammatically* or *syntactically*. (With older students, you can pause to introduce the idea of syntax—the particular ordering of words in a sentence.) Where do students hear the thought *carry over* from one line to the next? Where do they feel it *pause*? What are the different effects of these two techniques? How might line breaks contribute to creating meaning or emotion?

IN-CLASS ASSIGNMENT

Select a poem (your choice—it will vary depending on the age group), and remove the line breaks so that the poem is written as prose. Write this new prose poem on the board, or type it up and hand it out. Ask your students to put the prose back into lines and to discuss why they broke their lines where they did. This can be done collectively or in small groups.

WRITE

Have your students write poems about things they have lost or that no longer exist. They should use lines, punctuation, and sentences creatively to *intensify* their poems' meanings. For example, someone might write a poem with no punctuation that relies on line and stanza breaks to help create meaning and emotion.

Making Music

One common differentiation between poetry and prose is poetry's tendency to focus unusual amounts of attention on the *musicality* of language. In this section, you will ask students to think about how various poems create music.

READ

A selection (your choice) of Bashō haiku, Marianne Moore's "The Fish," Gwendolyn Brooks's "We Real Cool," Emily Dickinson's "A Bird came down the Walk," Elizabeth Bishop's "Sandpiper," and Lewis Carroll's "Jabberwocky."

DISCUSS

Discuss rhyme, rhythm, and meter to whatever degree students can explore these concepts, getting more specific with older students about the use of *syllabics* (in Bashō and Marianne Moore) versus *accentual-syllabic* meter (in Dickinson) and rhythmic free verse (in Brooks). Explore how nonsense words and regular rhythm and rhyme in "Jabberwocky" nonetheless create a specific tone and mood.

IN-CLASS EXERCISE

Ask students to write poems using nonsense words that are highly rhythmic and that rhyme.

EXERCISE TWO

Starting with a simple word, such as *man*, have students come up with a full rhyme (*can, toucan*), several off- or slant-rhymes (*men, mantis*), and several "outlandish" rhymes (such as Bishop's rhyme *obsessed* and *amethyst* in "Sandpiper").

WRITE

Ask students to write poems about an animal—poems that are highly musical and that use especially surprising rhymes (they can be either *end* rhymes or *internal* rhymes). Their poems could be about looking at such an animal (as if for the first time) or even being that animal. Some animal-poems that you might have your students read for inspiration include Federico García Lorca's "The Old Lizard," William Blake's "The Tyger," and Alfred, Lord Tennyson's "The Eagle."

Three Imaginary Soundtracks: Projecting Prose Poems

Eric Baus

EXERCISE OVERVIEW

Students listen to three pieces of instrumental music as if the music were from the soundtrack to a film. While listening, students write complete sentences describing imaginary scenes the music might accompany. This exercise gives students an imaginative starting point for writing that begins with their own perceptual experiences and associations. The music should have enough variation and novelty to hold students' attention; it should also suggest a particular atmosphere while being ambient enough to allow students to write without becoming overwhelmed. I have used a number of actual soundtracks from films as well as other instrumental pieces that evoke a strong mood.

TOTAL TIME

One hour minimum—ninety minutes to two hours is ideal.

MATERIALS NEEDED

CD player, three recordings of instrumental music, a chalkboard or whiteboard for writing guiding questions, and instructions

AGE GROUP

This exercise works well with high-school and middle-school writers.

GOALS

-» To practice evoking a strong mood/atmosphere
-» To generate powerful and surprising imagery
-» To create a substantial amount of raw material to revise
-» To suggest a process that students might repeat on their own
-» To introduce the genre of the prose poem

SUGGESTIONS FOR SOUNDTRACKS

-» "Introduction," *Dutch Harbor* soundtrack. The track is five minutes and one second. *Dutch Harbor* is a documentary about the lives and work of people who fish for Alaskan king crabs near the remote Aleutian Islands. The piece uses minimal percussion, some field recordings of sounds from crackling and beeping walkie-talkies in which the speech is distorted, and various stringed instruments.

-» "Cloudscape," by Philip Glass, soundtrack to *Koyaanisqatsi*. The track is four minutes and thirty-two seconds. This piece works well as a holding pattern for writers so they can develop ideas. The intense, frenetic quality of the repetitions is often suggestive of physical movement.

-» "Saeta," *Sketches of Spain*, by Miles Davis. The track is five minutes and six seconds. This instrumental flamenco piece sets distinctive solos by Davis against the background of an intermittent marching momentum. There is a sadness and beauty that most writers pick up on when listening. The piece feels powerful and immediate and consists of several identifiable movements.

Sequence of Events for the Exercise

INTRODUCE THE EXERCISE (MINIMUM TEN MINUTES)

Explain to the students that they will be listening, and writing, to three pieces of instrumental music. Invite them to imagine that the musical selections are from a film soundtrack. You might want to write the following on the board to guide the writing:

As you are listening, imagine and describe the scene this music accompanies.

What is going on?
Where does it take place?
Are people there?
What does the scene look like?
What images do the sounds make you think about?

ASK STUDENTS TO LISTEN AND WRITE (MINIMUM FIFTEEN MINUTES)

Encourage students to answer the questions for all three musical selections and to write in complete sentences, without interruption, as they listen. Tell them that they may choose to write three distinct pieces or to combine their writing into one piece with shifting landscapes and atmospheres.

If you notice that most writers finish early or that a particular piece doesn't seem to work for the group, you might want to fade out the recording gradually and move along to the next one. I have found that most students start writing about thirty seconds into the first recording. Because students tend to become immersed in each piece and in their writing processes, it's natural for them to express some surprise or frustration at the quick transition between pieces. Encourage them not to stop writing during the transitions, but you can talk over the music for a few seconds to remind them that they have the option to continue the same piece of writing or to begin another one. After a brief adjustment period, the writing tends to take on a new direction, either by gradually moving the imaginary scene in a new direction or by abruptly shifting the scenario entirely.

HAVE STUDENTS REVISE (MINIMUM FIFTEEN MINUTES)

After the initial writing period, ask students to revise their work. Spend a few minutes making brief comments and suggestions about what kinds of cuts or alterations might be most helpful. For example, you can talk about the benefits of cutting language that explicitly acknowledges the writer (phrases such as "This sounds makes me think of ...") in order to give readers a more direct window into the world of the poem. Sometimes, on the other hand, the voice of the writer takes on the quality of a voiceover/narration, which can be engaging for readers. Most revisions tend to focus on paring down and clarifying the writing. Students who might have felt constrained by the time limits of a particular track have an opportunity to revisit and flesh out their earlier ideas.

SHARE AND DISCUSS (MINIMUM FIFTEEN TO TWENTY MINUTES)

Ask writers to reread their writing and to try to remember which sounds sparked particular images or ideas. For example, the crackling walkie-talkie sounds from one of the pieces might suggest two astronauts talking to each other while walking on the moon. The energetic, repetitive patterns of some of the stringed portions might suggest someone running or dancing. Invite each student to read aloud one favorite sentence without any additional commentary. The ways the pieces connect to one another may excite students. Go around the room quickly, making sure everyone has a chance to contribute to this impromptu collective poem. Encourage volunteers to discuss their thinking and writing processes: how did the sounds affect them? Ask students to consider whether the pieces created a narrative or more of a prose gallery of interesting impressions. This sharing period can begin or end with a brief time for writers to get together in groups of two or three to discuss their impressions, frustrations, and results with one another.

DISCUSS MUSIC (OPTIONAL, FIVE TO FIFTEEN MINUTES)

Identify the origins and contexts of the musical selections after students finish the writing, revision, and sharing portions of the exercise. Ask students to guess what kinds of scenes the music actually accompanied. When they learn that one of the tracks is from a documentary about deep-sea fishing, there is always surprise and laughter. You might want to discuss some contexts for Spanish flamenco music or show a brief clip of *Koyaanisqatsi*. You'll find that the gaps between their guesses and the real sources and contexts of the music often amuse the writers.

MAKE FINAL COMMENTS

Tell students they can repeat this exercise on their own with a friend. It's best to select music for another person so that each writer can approach it from a fresh perspective. You can repeat this prompt periodically in shorter or longer versions. Beginning a writing class with a five-minute piece of music can be an engaging way for young writers to generate quick bursts of raw material. This exercise is an excellent experiential introduction to the prose poem.

A Perfect Creature in the Imperfect World: Zbigniew Herbert's "Pebble"

Valzhyna Mort

LESSON PLAN

In this class, your students will read and discuss Zbigniew Herbert's poem "Pebble" and debate some aspects of its translation into English. The discussion will culminate in one or both of the suggested writing assignments at the end. You can use the writing assignments as in-class exercises or as homework.

Each student will need a copy of the poem, translated by Czesław Miłosz and Peter Dale Scott. You might also ask students to bring actual pebbles to class (unless you think it's too hazardous) to use as inspiration for the first writing exercise.

PART 1

After reading "Pebble," lead your class in a discussion of the poem. Ask students to consider these questions:

-» Is the poem about nature, or is it about human nature? What are the differences?

-» Which lines describe the pebble as a thinking creature?

-» In what circumstances do humans act like the pebble in Herbert's poem? Why?

Discuss with your students how often, in order to withstand the pressures of daily life and to survive, people are required to acquire the qualities of a pebble, which retains its composure under any pressure. Draw your students' attention to the unsentimental language of the poem.

ADDITIONAL QUESTIONS

-» Why is Herbert's language Spartan? Does this austere diction reflect the nature of its subject—a pebble "mindful of its limits"?

-» Can heat and drama still exist in such a poem?

-» Is the poem's drama in the fact that one often has to act like a pebble in circumstances that feel inhuman?

PART 2

Explain to students that "Pebble" was originally written in Polish and later translated into English by another Polish poet, Czesław Miłosz, and a Canadian-born poet and English professor, Peter Dale Scott. Ask students whether they think the poem was easy to translate. You have already discussed the precise, austere diction of the poem. Ask students if the translation likely seems more "accurate" to the original than that of, say, a poem with more ornate or traditionally poetic diction.

Ask students to look at the text of the poem again and try to guess which words or lines might have given rise to disagreements between the two translators. Direct students' attention to two occurrences in particular.

The first is with the definite article at the very beginning of the poem:

"The pebble ..." Explain what an article is, and then let students know that the Polish language doesn't use articles, so Herbert didn't have to choose at this point in the poem. In English, however, a choice must be made (unless, of course, one uses the plural: *pebbles*). Miłosz insisted on using *the*. Scott would have preferred *a*, but eventually he deferred.

QUESTIONS TO DISCUSS

-» What is at stake in this distinction? How important is it?

-» Which article do your students prefer for this stanza? Why?

The place of the second disagreement might be less obvious. As it turns out, it was over the word order in the last line of the poem. If this line were translated word for word, as Scott initially did, it would read "with an eye calm and very clear." Miłosz, however, chose to translate it as "with a calm and very clear eye."

QUESTIONS TO DISCUSS

-» How does Miłosz's translation of the last line change its nuance?

-» How does this affect the poem as a whole?

-» Does Miłosz's word order reflect the vernacular?

Point out that in any poem, the last word carries unusually significant weight. Ask students what they think works better for this poem as the last word: *eye* or *clear*. Remind students of the issues at stake in terms of meaning and suggestion. Would they prefer that the poem end on *clear*—that is to say, the idea of clarity? Or do they think it is better to end on the noun *eye*, which turns the pebble into an eye-pebble?

ADDITIONAL QUESTIONS

-» Ask students why the English translators might have decided to use the word *pebble* instead of *stone*.

-» Which of the two words do they think more accurately

293

describes this "perfect creature"?

Explain that a pebble is defined as a small stone made smooth and round by the action of water or sand. Ask whether this quality of being smooth and round is a key to understanding the translators' choice. If so, why?

PART 3: WRITING EXERCISE ONE

Leaving the authoritarian world of Herbert's pebble behind, lead students in imagining a world of passion, a mischievous and curious world in which they will probably feel more at home. In this world, perfect creatures long to go beyond their limits in search of new experiences. They arouse desire and sometimes can frighten or remind people, with their smell or texture, of the things they love. Have students write poems in which a pebble is the most imperfect creature in this world precisely because it's so calm and austere.

QUESTION TO DISCUSS

-» Which other qualities of a stone make it into something potentially negative in this new world?

Suggest that students consider, for instance, that a stone can be used as a weapon and that stones are incapable of growing. Ask students to begin their poems with this line: "A pebble / is an imperfect creature ..."

PART 3: WRITING EXERCISE TWO

Invite your students to think of another object that is, in their opinion, perfect in all circumstances. Then ask them to write poems focused on that object, using Herbert's "Pebble" as a blueprint.

Poems Are for Everybody

Alex Dimitrov

Poems happen every day and in the everyday. Poems are made of life. Frank O'Hara, one of the leading figures of the New York School poets, knew this and wrote poems on his lunch break. Those poems turned into a book called *Lunch Poems*, which City Lights Books published in 1964. It is a book full of love, life, and complicated emotions. Can't everyone relate to that?

You and your students can write poems this morning or this afternoon. Maybe it's early evening as you read this. A poem has already happened to you today. Speaking of today, perhaps you can start your class with "Today," by Frank O'Hara, as a way to get your students excited about writing poems.

Today

Oh! kangaroos, sequins, chocolate sodas!
You really are beautiful! Pearls,
harmonicas, jujubes, aspirins! all
the stuff they've always talked about

still makes a poem a surprise!

These things are with us every day
even on beachheads and biers. They
do have meaning. They're strong as rocks.

THE PLAN

To begin, for homework, ask your students to make lists of five things that are meaningful to them in their everyday landscapes, such as objects in their bedrooms or things they see on the way home from school. Have them answer these five questions:

Who was the last person you thought of before going to bed last night?
Who was the first person you thought of when you woke up this morning?
What song lyric can't you get out of your head right now?
What was the happiest day or moment of your life?
What was the saddest day or moment of your life?

When the class meets again, students will have made their lists and answered the questions. Organize them into pairs. Ask each pair of students to swap lists and answers so that everyone has a different person's list and answers. Ask students to write five- to ten-line poems using three words, objects, or descriptions from their partner's lists and three of their partner's answers to the questions. Essentially, they're making poems out of lived experiences and using their imaginations. Why not? But let's not stop there.

When the students finish their poems, ask them to read the poems to each other in pairs. Next, each set of pairs will write one poem collaboratively. How will this happen? Each student should pick three or four favorite lines from his or her partner's poem, which was written from his or her own list and answers. Then each pair should work together to put the six to eight chosen lines from both poems together into one poem or, as I like to call it, "remix" the lines into one poem.

Encourage the students to share their collaborative poems with the entire class by reading them aloud.

To take collaboration to the next level, set up a class Twitter page and let the students have fun coming up with a name for it. Some possible names are "Sixth-Grade English" or "Poets of the Future."

Lines on Twitter are limited to 140 characters. The goal with the Twitter page is to create an Exquisite Corpse and incorporate one line from each pair's remix poem into a class collaborative poem. If you don't know what an Exquisite Corpse is, or for more information on the technique and its origins, check out the Wikipedia entry for it: en.wikipedia.org/wiki/Exquisite_corpse.

It may be fun and interactive to have one student from each pair go to the computer or laptop at which you will be tweeting and tweet one line while also seeing the lines that came before. In the end, the class poem will be available for the whole world to see and can be shared with anyone.

Poems happen every day and in the everyday. Poems are for everybody.

Cartogram

Anthony McCann

Explain to students what a cartogram is: it's a map that is distorted in favor of a certain feature. Many examples can be found on the Internet.

Ask students to draw cartograms of their lives. In other words, ask them to make maps in a creative sense of the word, inviting them to distort space according to a single feature that is important to them. They should make maps of their lives that exaggerate the physical spaces (indoors or out) that are most meaningful to them. Such spaces could include their walks or rides to school, their rooms, the rooms of their friends, the family kitchen, a classroom at school, a park they spend a lot of time in, public transit, et cetera.

Once students have drawn their maps, have them select what they think are the five (you could vary this number according to the time constraints of the class) most interesting spaces in which to imagine their poems happening.

After that, students should do one of the following exercises:

1. Write a short poem (*haiku*, epigram, *tanka*, or sonnet) for each chosen space. Tell students they should imagine themselves in each space.

2. Write a poem of any length for each space, in any form they feel is appropriate.

3. Write one long poem that connects all the spaces. When working with college-aged students, I have used Eileen Myles's poem "Kid's Show: 1991" for modeling this variant.

Students could easily do 1 or 2 as an in-class exercise or a long-term homework assignment. Three tends to work a bit better as homework. Giving the exercise as homework, whether you assign variant 1, 2, or 3, allows students to write their poems in the actual spaces in which they are imagining them happening.

NOTE: *You might want to introduce the device of apostrophe. Students could address their poems to the actual spaces in which they imagine them taking place or to objects within those spaces.*

The Image List

Michael McGriff

Whether you're writing a poem for the first time in your life or working on your tenth award-winning book, starting a new poem is often an intimidating and daunting task. "What am I supposed to write about!?"—this is the question that often stops writers before they start. The exercise that follows, which I call the "Image List," is one I've used in every class I've ever taught, from graduate-level courses to elementary school classes. It's also a process that I use when I'm starting a new poem or feel as though I've run out of ideas.

One thing: this is a timed exercise. It's important to stick to the time limits because this writing exercise is based on the idea that your first thought might be your best thought.

FIVE MINUTES

In five minutes, make a list of *at least* fifty objects that are important to you. Remember, these are objects that are important to *you*—they don't need to sound special or "poetic." For example, your list might include things such as "the grass by our fence, Dad's boots, the old woodstove in our living room," to use a few examples from my own image list. There are no right or wrong objects to include on this list. Everyone is going to have a very different list containing a wide range of objects. The key to this exercise is to keep from overthinking—make a list of whatever comes to mind first. Keep your pen moving (or your fingers typing) until you've reached five minutes. Once you get started you'll quickly see that you can generate far more than fifty objects.

TEN MINUTES

Now that you have these fifty objects in your mind, it's time to make a second list. Take ten minutes to list the first twenty memories that you associate with the objects on your list. These memories don't need to be elaborate; think of these as notes to yourself. Your list might look something like this:

-» Visiting my mom in the hospital
-» Noticing the way the rain sounded against my window the night I got in trouble with the cops
-» Listening to Chopin for the first time

And so on. Again, there is no right or wrong way to make this list. Everyone is going to have different memories. Some memories might be serious, some might be funny, and some might seem very ordinary. Again, the key to this list is to write down anything and everything that comes to mind. After all, there is no subject too ordinary, too outrageously funny, or too serious for a poem.

FIVE MINUTES

For the third and final list, select two memories from the list of memories you just made. For each memory, make a list of as many sensory details as you can think of. Remember, a sensory detail is a detail that pertains to how something looks, feels, tastes, sounds, or smells.

Combine all three lists, and you have what I call an image list, a blueprint that contains everything you'll need for making a poem. The image list is full of things you know, full of things you have a personal connection to, and full of sensory details. Just as important, the image list is devoid of abstractions and generalities. Abstractions and generalities can often feel vague, unconvincing, and unimportant to a reader, whereas the contents on the image list will feel personal, intimate, and convincing. The more a writer can *show* an experience, the more the reader will sympathize and understand it. The contents on the image list can be used to make a small poem, such as one of Buson's great haiku, or a large, detail-stuffed epic such as Walt Whitman's *Leaves of Grass*.

To see how this exercise can be used, check out the following poems, each of which use the kinds of details and plain language that you'd find on an image list: "Things I Didn't Know I Loved," by Nâzim Hikmet; "Nostalgic Catalogue," by Garrett Hongo; "Getting It Right," by Matthew Dickman; "We Went Out to Make Hay," by Stephan Torre; "To a Friend," by Zubair Ahmed; and "Inventory" by Günter Eich.

Elsewhere

Katie Ford

What is remote becomes near, what is dead lives...

—Wallace Stevens

GRADE LEVEL

Six and up.

SUMMARY AND PEDAGOGICAL RATIONALE

There are places, distances, and times poets regularly exclude from their poems. Poets tend to write about what is in their own lives, things they can see, feel, smell, touch, and hear. But a poem can be greatly enlivened and deepened when a poet engages what can be experienced only in the mind's eye, the imagination. Teaching poetry is, very often, teaching students to interrupt their habits as writers and thinkers. In this exercise, students will be encouraged to stray "elsewhere," toward times and places outside of their poems' first drafts, making them time travelers or archaeologists who dig beneath ground or photographers who see outside the initial frame.

In this exercise of unbounded roaming, students will extend their points of view into unexpected and, perhaps, hauntingly strange or beautiful places. In the end, this exercise is meant to bring surprise to the writer. "No surprise in the writer," wrote Robert Frost, "no surprise in the reader."

INSTRUCTIONS AND PREPARATION

This is an exercise in revision to be done after students have already written a poem. In preparation, ask students to bring a typed poem to class that they would like to revise on the day of the exercise.

Copy part one of the exercise below so students have it on their desks.

When first explaining the exercise, review with the students the idea that an image is not only what is seen, or a "word picture," but also anything that is brought in by the five senses. So an image might be the description of a sound, taste, tactile feeling, sight, or smell.

Ask the students to reread their own poems silently in preparation for the exercise.

Read aloud each prompt of part one, allowing one or two minutes for the students to craft an image in response, an image that might later be added to the revision of their poem.

Make your way down the list. The exercise should take ten to fifteen minutes.

IN-CLASS EXERCISE: PART 1

- → Imagine your poem is a photograph that you have taken. What image is just outside the photograph? In other words, what is barely outside the text of the poem?
- → What is beneath the ground of the poem?
- → What is going on in the mind of the speaker of the poem?
- → What is something from the near past of the poem, say within five years?
- → What is something from the far past of the poem, say within a hundred years?
- → What is in the sky of the poem?

-» Imagine an animal in a foreign country. What is that animal, who is not in your poem, doing?

-» What is going on inside the body of the speaker? Be very physical: imagine human bones and systems.

PART 2

As a class, go through each prompt and have two or three students describe their images.

PART 3

Now, moving on to the revision process, invite students to read back over the poems they brought in.

Next, have them choose which of their images from the prompts they believe to be the most creative and imaginative and find places in their poems where they can unhinge the poems to insert the images.

How will students insert their images? With transitional words and phrases, such as *elsewhere*. For example, "Elsewhere, the wild horses of Asia have nowhere to go." "Up above, the sky is full of summer gnats, or maybe it's ash." "Ten feet below, there might be decaying leaves or lives." "Inside of me, my rivers pass my bones."

An optional part of the exercise is to brainstorm on the board words and phrases that can help a poem move through space and time. Students of all ages can make use of such a list: elsewhere, once, before, someday, "somewhere I can't see," "in fifty years," "up above," et cetera.

For ten minutes, allow the students to revise their poems using their new images. Encourage them to let their images transport their poems somewhere else. Encourage them to embellish or expand their images as the revisions lead them to do so. Encourage them to try finding natural but surprising locations for them.

Have some students read aloud from their revised poems. Alternately, ask the students to take their poems home and edit them thoroughly using some of the images they have created in this exercise.

VARIATIONS

-» If students have not yet written poetry for your class, begin this exercise by having them bring a photograph to class that means something to them. They can write a first draft of a poem triggered by the photograph and then proceed to the exercise.

-» Students can be required, in a later poem, to include this technique in the first draft.

-» When published poetry is read and studied in the classroom, ask students to point out when they see this technique used by the poet. Ask them to remain alert to the technique and to mention it when they see it. This will help students see masterful examples of shifts in time and place throughout the history of poetry.

-» A teacher can add as many prompts to Part 1 as desired. As a brainstorming exercise, students can be asked to think of where else the poem could go.

CONCLUSIONS AND OUTCOMES

This exercise seeks to expand a student's concept of what revision can become. Revision doesn't include only fine-tuning of diction, music, and ideas but can also involve the process of asking the poem to see again what possibilities await if the imagination is fully engaged. The senses can be broadened to include more of the world and its history. Although the revision might sometimes produce an awkward outcome—students might say, for example, "My elsewhere passage doesn't fit or make sense"—it is, nevertheless, preparation for future poems, in which this technique can be employed in a poem's first draft.

Bad Titles

Matthew Zapruder

This lesson plan was originally designed for a class of tenth graders, though it can be adapted for younger students. It is intended to free students from any limiting ideas they may have that "good" poetry has to be boring, completely serious, or totally planned out in advance.

The exercise is designed to give students a pleasurable, creative, and independent experience while also encouraging them to work together as a group. It should take about an hour and can lead to students' writing poems in class or as a homework assignment. Poetry is best when writers are breaking rules, and this exercise is designed to encourage some of that sort of behavior. So obviously, you need to have a class that can be trusted to enter this place of potential chaos.

STEP 1

Read (or ask a student to read) the following titles of published poems. Have them make notes while they're listening about all the different kinds of titles they hear.

"Zeus: A Press Conference," "Anecdote of the Squid," "Poem Without Voices," "My Wife Is Shopping," "The Paste Man," "A Milk Truck Running into a Crazy Maid at the Corner of Getwell and Park," "A Man in Blue," "Rooms," "I Run with a Pair of Compasses Stuck in the Back of My Head,"

"At the Hairdresser," "America," "Laura Cashdollars," "Breakfast," "No One Will Write Poetry," "The Little Box," "Black Horsemen," "To My Dead Sister," "Terror Is My Business," "The Death of Checkers," "Good Morning Little Schoolgirl," "The Underpant," "O Cleveland," "Yes, Señor Fluffy," "The Recipe," "Prime Numbers," "People Are Tiny in Paintings of China," "At an Elaborate Summer Barbeque Without You," "The Plural of Jack-in-the-Box," "Farm Implements and Rutabagas in a Landscape," "What Comes Naturally?" "Don't Get Too Personal," "Poor Britney Spears," "The Story of White People," "Is This Why Love Almost Rhymes with Dumb?" "Having a Coke with You," "First Dances," "In the Movies," "Anxiety," "Do Not Mind the Bombs," "Inside the Jacket," "Crescent Moon on a Cat's Collar," "Let Me Tell You About My Father, She Says," "A Small Table in the Street," "Are You Ticklish?" "So Long, Santa," "Things to Do in New York City," "American Express," "People of the Future."

Ask your students to describe all the different kinds of titles they heard. (Likely they will say that some are serious and others are funny, many contain the names of places or people, some are parts of sentences or entire sentences, and so on.) Do they find them funny, surprising, silly, trivial, exciting? Ask them to imagine what some of these poems might be about. Can they imagine a funny poem with a serious title? Vice versa? How are these poems similar to, and different from, the titles of poems they have read in the past?

STEP 2

After talking for a few minutes about these titles, ask each student to quickly write twenty impossible titles, titles so awful, so ridiculous, so silly, so unpoetic and unprofound that the students could never imagine them belonging to any poems. The worse, the better—but nothing profane or offensive. Ask students to write as many different kinds of titles as possible: one-word titles, sentence fragments, complete sentences, questions, negative constructions, jokes, titles with abstractions, titles with concrete objects in them. The more variety, the better.

STEP 3

Now ask the students to pass their titles to the person next to them. (If you have time, or a relatively small class, you can have each person read some or all of their titles aloud, though it is better to have the students read aloud in the next step.)

Each student should then pick the five most ridiculous titles from the paper they have been passed and write a first line for each.

STEP 4

Ask students to read their five titles and first lines aloud. Students should read them together, as if they were the beginnings of poems. Discuss with the students why they might have gravitated toward certain titles and what made them think of particular first lines. Do any of these seem especially promising or fun? Why? Ask students whether they have ideas about how they might continue the poems. Invite the entire class to share in the discussion.

STEP 5

As either an in-class writing exercise or a homework assignment, ask each student to finish one of the poems he or she has started. Have students read their poems aloud at the end of class or at the beginning of the following class.

Note: If your class is small enough, have students write their twenty titles on the board. You can talk about all the different sorts of titles and ask the students to think about what sorts of poems might come out of them. Then have students pick numbers out of a hat and choose their five titles from the board in that order, one at a time. (Ask them not to choose one of their own titles.) It's exciting to see which students like which titles and to watch students react with dismay when one of the titles they really wanted is gone or with delight when one is still available.

Street Sonnets

Deborah Landau

OVERVIEW

The Street Sonnet exercise—part writing assignment, part field trip—always provides a lively and exciting adventure in poetry. Students take a walk in a nearby neighborhood while carefully observing the world around them. Upon returning to the classroom, they create fourteen-line poems using language they have "harvested" from the walk. This exercise can be given a seasonal theme for focus, and it works especially well in the spring and fall, when seasonal change is most noticeable.

AGE RANGE

Suitable for poets of any age

TIME FRAME

One thirty-minute walk, one thirty-minute writing session. The activity may be expanded to fill larger and/or more blocks of time if desired.

MATERIALS

Each child will need a notebook and pencil and should wear appropriate shoes and clothing for a neighborhood outing.

OBJECTIVE

To encourage students to become closer observers of the world around them and to demonstrate how the ordinary can be transformed into the extraordinary through the art and craft of poetry.

INSTRUCTIONS

1. To begin, students take a thirty-minute walk with notebook and pen in hand, paying close attention to the outside world. Typically, the walk would take place in the neighborhood surrounding the school; the assignment can work equally well in urban, suburban, and rural environments.

2. While walking, encourage children to be very aware of their surroundings. What do they see? Hear? Smell? What is available to taste and touch? What kinds of language are visible (on signs, in shop windows, on bumper stickers, on T-shirts, et cetera) or audible (bits of conversation, cars honking, construction noise, birds chirping, music from a window, et cetera)?

3. Allow students to stop as often as necessary to record their observations. These notes will be essential to the poems they will write upon returning to the classroom.

4. After thirty minutes or so, the group returns to school, notebooks filled with language harvested from the neighborhood. Once back in the classroom, ask students to create fourteen-line poems from the harvested language. It's helpful to give them plenty of freedom at this stage so that they can experience the process of making poems as a form of play. It should be fun!

5. Once they're finished writing, ask students to share poems in small groups or in a large group workshop. Often it works well to ask students to read their poems aloud.

6. As a final project, the class can compile the poems into a Street Sonnet book to be shared with other students in the school and/or parents and families on visiting night. Drawings or photographs of the neighborhood might be used for cover material and illustrations.

Autobiographia Litter-Aria

Christina Davis

T.S. Eliot may have been on to something when he declared Ezra Pound to be *"il miglior fabbro"* ("the better craftsman") for his work as editor of *The Waste Land*. Pound notoriously culled and cultivated Eliot's original draft and helped reconstitute it into a new whole.

Almost one hundred years later, an inundation of information and a concomitant attention deficit that would have sent J. Alfred Prufrock, T. Stearns Eliot, and all their collective teacups over the edge characterize the times. Poetry is an art form that can help students home in on, attend to, and extrapolate pertinent and resonant material from the mass of data readily available to them.

To get into the practice of exercising that muscle of selection and to help young writers to appreciate that their manner of selection is always already unique, I like to introduce them to the following exercise, which I first encountered in a class taught by poet Kathleen Ossip. In honor of Eliot's heap of broken lines and littered images, and with a tinge of Coleridge, I've dubbed it Autobiographia Litter-Aria.

INGREDIENTS

You will need ten different forms of writing (suitable for youngsters) drawn from books, magazines, Google, newspapers, instruction manuals, historical documents, et cetera.

EXAMPLE

1. A paragraph from the US Constitution
2. A set of how-to instructions, such as "how to light a fire in the wilderness"
3. A page of iterations from Gertrude Stein's *Tender Buttons*
4. A paragraph from a Harry Potter book

And so forth. Write a number from 1 through 10 at the top of each, and photocopy a set for each student.

Instructions

STEP 1

Ask students to fold a sheet of paper in half and jot down the numbers 1 through 10 in the left-hand column. Then pass out the writing examples and encourage the students to peruse each one and write down the line (phrase, sentence, fragment, et cetera) that they find most compelling, interesting, curious, and/or quirky next to the number associated with that example. This will usually take fifteen or twenty minutes, depending on the size of the class. Encourage students not to think too much about it, to trust their intuition regarding which lines to select. To give your students a laugh, you might quote Marianne Moore who once wrote, "To cite passages is to pull one quill from a porcupine."

STEP 2

When students seem settled, ask them to turn their papers over and, in the right-hand column, write down ten lines that come to mind under the category "My favorite memories." (Note: The subject of this category is entirely up to you—it could be "My favorite facts and fictions" or "Interesting information about animals" or any other topic.) Tell students that these lines can include quotes from parents and friends; vignettes or anecdotes; fragmentary memories or dreams; lists of favorite foods, games, activities, family rituals; phrases from songs or movies, et cetera.

STEP 3

When they finish, students should open their papers and see what interesting conjunctions occur between the two columns. Here's an example of the first column:

1. "... in order to form a more perfect union ..." (historical document)
2. "make a fire with friction" (instruction manual)
3. "Any change was in the ends of the centre. A heap was heavy. There was no change." (Gertrude Stein excerpt)
4. "Something came whizzing down the kitchen chimney as he spoke and caught him sharply on the back of the head. Next moment, thirty or forty letters came pelting out of the fireplace like bullets." (Harry Potter excerpt)

For the next five to ten minutes, have students begin to assemble poems from these curious parts, with minor tweaks and unexpected amendments. Here's an example of what might emerge:

In order to form a more perfect union,
make a fire with friction
like playing rocks, paper, scissors was in my family
where any change was the end of a certain
centering and the beginning of a-kilter. A letter
shoots out of the fire: There is a rumbling
then zillions of letters come shooting

out of the fire. I remember the first time
I heard the word *un-*
happy, and it was not uncomfortable. The fire,
the un- that illuminates all union.

CONCLUSION

Conduct this exercise a few times throughout the term, and students will begin to notice and appreciate the kinds of lines and language—as well as tones, structures, and content—they tend to gravitate to. When young writers are given an opportunity to realize that they are unique—not simply because they create shocking syntax or dazzling enjambments but also because of the very nuanced and subtle ways in which they attend to the multiplicitous world—a new variety of writing and attentiveness and understanding become possible. Or, as Eliot would say, *Shantih shantih shantih.*

Putting Two and Two Together

Dara Wier

ABOUT

This exercise can be done in various contexts with a variety of potential creators, conspirators, collaborators, and combination pickers in an atmosphere of spirited open-heartedness. It is suitable for all ages. Its exponential potential can be explored, exploited, extrapolated, or evaporated. The main goal is to write a poem that uses words in ways you haven't used them before and to create a poem—or something that looks like a poem—with surprising combinations of words.

WHAT TO DO

First, find words. Some possible ways to do this are:

- Recall any chance encounters with objects and people.
- Rely on an abecedarian determination.
- Employ a system in which numbers of syllables, or inclusion or exclusion of individual letters, determine or help determine choice of words.
- Ask students in the room to engage in a "potluck-style"

collecting of words (e.g., some can bring verbs, nouns, articles, pronouns, adverbs, adjectives). You can limit the occasion to nouns and verbs only or, for a more challenging look at content, limit students to conjunctions and articles.

-» Someone—a teacher, guest, or designated provider—can provide all the words, either with or without a purpose.

-» As a collective (teacher and participants), devise a system by which words are collected (e.g., choose the last word in each of a selection of books, poems, or prose; use the first word in each of the past twenty-six copies of *National Geographic* or the past twenty-six posts on a certain website or anywhere else).

-» As you (and students) begin thinking, you will be making up ways to generate collections of words to use as you move along (so collection generation will possibly engender as much inventive practice as what follows).

-» Each participant can choose his or her own word or words

The next step is to spend some time with the individual words you have gathered. Here are some possible ways of spending time with your words:

-» If you have access to a letterpress, spend some time letterpressing each word. The time spent with your words, setting them and seeing them in font, will make you feel closer to them, or, in rare cases, alienate you from a word. Your choice of font will greatly affect your appreciation of any word.

-» If you are a calligrapher or like to practice elaborate handwriting techniques, you can produce individual words on paper this way. This will probably contribute a great deal to the moods and tones with which you encounter various words.

-» Type your words on a manual typewriter.

-» Type your words in a Word document.

-» Put your words on good sturdy cards (in colors dependent on word sensations), and use them as you might use blocks. Cards should be beautiful. They should have character and embody suggestions to work with or against or after or toward.

-» Paint your words on pieces of paper bags or cardboard.

-» Cut your words out of cast-off books or journals or newspapers. It will look as if you're composing a ransom note at first, so part of you will be attuned to the tone of anonymity this inevitably generates.

-» Somehow create a means by which your words have three dimensions, by which your words grow less word-like and more object-like.

-» Make a film of your words, in which one word at a time flashes on the screen. Some questions you will consider in doing this: How will you decide in what order the words will be filmed? Will you have a soundtrack? Will it be found already made or will you make it, and what will it be made from?

-» As a class, determine how your words will be composed— of what materials, what size, on what, of what shapes. Construct these materials together.

Next, spend some time putting words next to one another. Here are some ways to do this:

-» One word can be placed next to another word. This will instantly give you something to think about. It will embolden you.

-» Continue to place words next to each other for a while without a clear goal. Think of this as warming up, getting ready to do something, preparing.

-» As you continue to place words next to each other, you will change the individual words by associating them with other words. Consider how the perception of each individual word changes or how differently they are received and enjoyed. This changes, too, depending on whether you put the words side by side, on top of, underneath, or floating over each other. Every potential position will shift how each word relates to other words. Think about how the meanings of words change, depending on their position.

-» Keep combining, combining, combining, combining words.

By now you will have spent a good deal of time with the words you have chosen. The last step is to consider the meanings you are making:

-» As a class or in small groups, discuss what you have been working on. Consider together the meaning you have been making. Everyone shares and compares.

-» Spend some time talking about combining words as an act of writing. You can consider so many things: juxtaposing, blending, contrasting, paralleling, unlocking locks, combining by sound, combining by reason, combining by chance, and un-combining.

-» Now, individually write a poem with your new words. Or refuse to write one—you have possibly used up your patience with these words.

What is the point of this? It is obvious and it is also unlikely that it could possibly result in similar outcomes time after time. One hopes the randomness and lack of intention built into it will alleviate personal anxieties or concerns when one feels one is going to be judged in a situation in which lack of stress can facilitate exploration. Sometimes, stressful situations generate work that must be accomplished. If one surprises oneself and starts to see patterns of something that matters, or surprises oneself and begins to feel one is writing something that is really significant, great! It's lucky if that happens.

Dreaming in Detail

Travis Nichols

The goal of this lesson is to show students how description, rather than narrative, can drive a poem. It's a two-part assignment with (fun!) homework. If possible, give students a week to gather their dream details.

THE DREAM

Ask students to keep a notebook by their beds so that when they wake up, they can describe the things—objects, people, places, animals, et cetera—they dreamed about. Students should describe them in as much detail as possible. If they need a little extra guidance, tell them that each object (or person, place, animal, et cetera) should have at least two sensory details—what it felt like, smelled like, sounded like, tasted like, et cetera. Students should try to write down as much as possible about their dream elements, using as many (and as many weird) adjectives as they can.

THE CLASS

In class, after discussing the general goofiness of the project and dreams in general, organize students into small groups. For ten to fifteen minutes, students should share their descriptions in the groups. Ask each group to decide on the three most vivid and interesting descriptions from its members.

After they finish, ask students to come together as a whole class and share their "best" descriptions. Write them on the board, and be prepared for much giggling.

You may want to ask students some simple questions to generate discussion, for example, "What do you like about these?" or "Why are they good?"

After the discussion of what a "good" description includes, ask each student to spend five to ten minutes choosing his or her three "best" descriptions, write them down, and then pass them to a classmate.

THE ASSIGNMENT

Ask students to write ten-line poems based on the dream details they received from their classmates and bring their poems to the next class.

Be a Bunch of Yous

Laura Solomon

This lesson exercises students' capacity for imagination and memory. It may be adapted to the very young, the very old, and anyone in between. The key is simply to excite the students' capacity to see themselves in space-time, as a series of stills, a flipbook of selves.

I dreamed this lesson up, literally: I was sleeping but awoke with this dream. In it, I was teaching poetry—how to write it—to a group of children who soon turned into teenagers, although by the end of the class all of the students had grown quite ancient, as had I.

I thought, *Today we will write a poem! All of us together!*

I said, "Wake up! Look at how you've changed in just this single year!"

I said to the children, "Ah, children! Close your eyes and think back to when you were very, very tiny. What do you remember? When did you begin to change? And why did you do it? Which grew first, your fingers or your toes? What are you now, and what will you be next year? Deeply imagine yourself in the past, that stranger that you were. Now be that stranger, that tiny baby. Let the tiny baby say, 'Hello stranger!' to the stranger you are now."

THE LESSON AND THE DREAM

Re-create this imaginative space with your class by allowing students to close their eyes as you help them to visualize their past and future selves as coexisting simultaneously. Feel free to improvise upon or to recite the following things:

> Are you surprised that baby you is talking to the you you are now? I am. Babies don't usually speak! But then again, this baby is baby you, and a person can always talk to himself or herself. That is what you are doing: talking to yourself. And that is one thing a poem is—a person talking to himself or herself, who is often another person altogether.

OK, so now you are in a conversation, the two of you, baby you and the you you are now. What do you talk about? Maybe the two of you can be something other than you. That way you won't get confused. In my dream, for example, I let one me be a leaf and another me be a spider on a window.

What about a third you or a fourth or fifth? By this afternoon, you will already be much older. Perhaps you will be your older brother's or sister's age or your mother's or your father's. What will that be like?

And who is that unrecognizable person in the distance? Children, look at your wrinkles and spots and saggy skin and all that life you have lived, all of it dimly or brightly glowing from behind your baggy eyes! How did you get so old so quickly?

You are over there, that old you, and here, too, this young you. Behind you is baby you. Is baby you crying or calm when elderly you tickles you under your chin?

Now let your present you talk to all those far-off-in-the-future yous. Can those future yous talk back to you as you are now? Of course they can! You can be them now, and you can be them at the same time that you are you now and baby you then. You are all of your yous at once.

When you are a very old person, what do you want to say to yourself as a child? When you are a child, what do you want to say to your very old you? What is the you that is just being born saying to the you you are now? Or what, for example, do all your yous want to say to the you you will be on the last day of your life?

THE POEM

Have your students write poems that are bouquets of yous. Give them instructions that resemble this directive:

> Vividly picturing all your yous, now begin to write a poem. Think of it as a house where you can let all the yous sing and disagree. Let the poem be a bouquet of yous. Consider in what ways your yous are different from one another and in what ways they are alike. Remember, too, your yous don't have to be people. You can let your yous masquerade as animals and plants or embody such ordinary things as paper towels, books, computers, and drinking straws. Before you begin your poem, try to write down as many of your yous' favorite words as you can. What is your favorite word today, when you are a young fireplace? What will it be tomorrow when you are a middle-aged neighborhood? What was it yesterday when you were a baby front porch? Try to use all your yous' favorite words. Favorite words often contain sounds or images that appeal to people. Use at least one favorite word in every single line.

(Soma)tic Poetry Exercises

CAConrad

(Soma)tic poetry is a praxis I developed to engage the everyday through writing. *Soma* is an Indo-Persian word associated with the divine. *Somatic,* from the Greek for "bodily," refers to body tissue or the nervous system in English. The goal is to coalesce *soma* and *somatic* while triangulating patterns of experience with the world. Experiences that are unorthodox steps in the writing process can shift a poet's perception of the quotidian, if only for a series of moments. This offers an opportunity to see details clearly. Through music, dirt, food, scent, taste, in storms, in bed, on the subway, and at the grocery store, (Soma)tic exercises and the poems that result are just waiting to be utilized or invented, everywhere and anytime.

The last large wild beasts are being hunted, poisoned, asphyxiated in one way or another, and their wildness is dying, being tamed. A desert is rising with this falling pulse. It is the duty of poets and others who have not lost their jagged, creative edges to fill that gap and resist the urge to subdue their spirits and lose themselves in the hypnotic beep of machines, war, and the banal need for power and things. With their poems and creative core, poets must return this world to its seismic levels of wildness.

The aim of (Soma)tic poetry and poetics is to promote the realization of two basic ideas: (1) everything in the world has a creative viability with the potential to spur new modes of thought and imaginative output, and (2) the most vital ingredient to bringing sustainable, humane changes to the world is creativity. This can be enacted on a daily basis.

A Three-Part (Soma)tic for the Classroom

RESILIENT TRIANGLE

Tell students to meditate on the room, choose one person to study, and find two stationary objects off the ground: a window, clock, light fixture, et cetera. Students should mentally draw a connecting line between the person he or she studied and the other two objects. Tell students to take notes about the contents of their triangles, what exactly is inside them. Ask students to imagine the triangles in different kinds of light, at different temperatures, in different seasons. Prompt them to imagine the objects within the triangles in different colors. Each person should imagine a loved one inside the triangle, floating, sick, then dying. Each person should imagine himself or herself inside the triangle, aging, dying. Ask students to imagine random objects flying into their triangles, like cartons of milk thrown through them. Then imagine dozens of cartons of milk hovering inside their triangles and the milk slowly pouring to the ground. These images become notes of the courage to be in this world.

HUMAN HIBERNACULUM

An animal goes to a hibernaculum for safety during periods of hibernation. Tell students they are going to create a human hibernaculum with their bodies, a place of highly charged energy. Organize students into groups of five or six. In each group, all the students but one should stand in a circle with their backs to the center. The last student should sit in the middle to take notes. With the right hand, each student should find the carotid artery in the neck of the person to the left; everyone should feel a pulse and have his or her pulse being felt. Tell students to hum, deep and low, from time to time to connect with one another. This rope of blood pulsing in a circle over the seated person who is taking notes shifts every five minutes as each person takes a turn sitting in the center and writes.

"CRISTO REDENTOR"

The hibernaculum exercise is physically challenging and can even be stressful. For this part of the workshop, have students sit quietly and listen to Donald Byrd's jazz song "Cristo Redentor" at top volume. This is the only song I know in which a gospel choir is used from start to finish but sings no words. The song is five minutes and forty-two seconds long. For the first one minute and fifty-two seconds, Byrd's trumpet isn't heard at all. By the time he enters, listeners are swept through the chords with a force that is difficult to prepare for.

After students listen to the song in silence, have them listen again, this time writing nonstop for the duration of the song. Sound engages the brain differently, whether the sound is language or not. As soon as most people hear language, their brains begin to decode; different hemispheres of the brain handle the different concerns. "Cristo Redentor" offers the rare opportunity to hear the human voice for a sustained amount of time without needing to decode language; the voices are instruments diffusing the pleasure and joy of song, the redemptive quality of song. Byrd asks that listeners make the redeemer their own, in their own ways.

Tell students to keep their notes with them and look at them from time to time. Encourage them to comb, sift, and rewrite their notes into poems. The poem(s) will form; you can count on it.

Eating Couplets
and Haiku

Vickie Vértiz

NUMBER OF SESSIONS

Two, approximately two hours each

AGES

Eight to ten

BACKGROUND

This exercise connects young students to different cultures through food and short-form poetry. Food (in this case, actually tasting the food) prompts students to use descriptive and sensory detail in their poems. Students will write using the five senses as they write haiku and couplets.

Encourage students to write in the language they feel most comfortable with. If English is not their first language, using their native language as a foundation will help strengthen their English skills.

Invite parents to come during the first session. Parents often enjoy bringing food (which you may need for the lessons), and their involvement helps build community.

LEARNING OBJECTIVES

-» Students will learn what a haiku is, where it comes from, and how to write one.

-» Students will learn what a couplet is and how it was used by the Peruvian poet Blanca Varela (1926–2009). Varela composed two-line poems describing an object with as few words as possible. Students will learn a little about how to write in this style.

-» Students will become familiar with these poetic forms and the cultures in which the forms originated by associating them with their eating and writing experiences.

-» Students will use a thesaurus.

-» Students will interpret words with multiple meanings in different languages. This particularly supports fourth-grade standards in reading, research, and revision.

-» Students may practice public speaking in a supportive environment.

THINGS YOU WILL NEED

-» Sharpened pencils and paper for each child

-» Food. Be sure to mix up textures, shapes, smells, surfaces, and tastes; for example, you may want to vary from sweet to salty foods. Students love to talk about food (especially, it seems, anything with a slippery or gelatin-like texture). NOTE: Ask families about food allergies when the students sign up for the class.

-» Maps of the countries where the food comes from

-» Several thesauri in the languages students will write in, if possible

-» Plates, napkins, cups, and lots of paper or reusable towels to wipe down surfaces

-» One to two other adults or tutors to help students define

words, make use of a thesaurus, and hone word choices
-» A long piece of heavy-duty string, twine, clothes pins or
   paper clips (for exhibiting student poems)

Session 1

Welcome everyone, and describe what you will be doing. Tell the students they're going to write poems about food from two different cultures after sampling the various dishes.

ICEBREAKER

Ask the students to introduce themselves. As they say their names, ask them to name a favorite food or dish they eat at home.

In this first session, go over the basics. Make sure to ask students for definitions before you write anything down on the board. Someone might know something about couplets or haiku.

Defining the words *haiku* and *couplet* should take about ten minutes. You can project the definitions onto a screen or write them on a chalkboard as a visual aid while writing the poems. Ask students to read and write down the definitions, number of lines, and syllables. Make sure they can tell you what a syllable is; if they can't, go over it with them.

WHAT IS A HAIKU?

Put examples of haiku on a projector, or write a few on the board if a projector is not available. Some historical details might help: Haiku originated in Japan and were traditionally observations of nature imbued with metaphorical meaning. Haiku have three lines: the first has five syllables, the second seven, and the last five. Check with the students and ensure they can define the basic terms, such as *metaphor*. If they can't, offer examples.

WHAT IS A COUPLET?

In this section you'll define what a couplet is; it should take about five minutes. Remember to ask students to tell you what they know about couplets first. They might provide insight that other students would find useful.

Poet Blanca Varela uses the titles of her couplets to tell readers what the poems are about. The two lines in the poem describe the object or subject of the poem. Couplets, according to the Poetry Foundation, are "a pair of successive rhyming lines, usually of the same length" in which the meaning found in the first line continues into the second line. The lines can end with periods or other appropriate punctuation, they can rhyme, or they can run into each other and complete a whole thought. Couplets are associated with English, French, and Dutch writers; however, the couplet is used in many countries and is infused with each individual culture that does so—hence Varela's manipulation of the form in her writing.

You can put a limit on the number of syllables for each line, such as eight or ten, to keep a good rhythm.

EAT AND WRITE

Wash those hands! Set up the food so students can directly contrast different shapes and tastes (put Chinese egg rolls next to Vietnamese spring rolls, for example).

Give students about a minute or so to sample each dish and notice as much as they can: smell, color, size, resemblances to other objects, et cetera. Set a timer to ding every ninety seconds so they know when to move to another dish. Once they sit down, ask them to write down smells, the feel or texture of the food, its taste, how it looks, et cetera. You can ask them to draw pictures too.

Students can now try writing a haiku or two or more. This should take twenty to thirty minutes. You and any tutors should wander through the room offering support to students who have questions or difficulties.

Help students choose original words for their poems. Encourage them to look up synonyms and antonyms to create their own word combinations to express themselves.

Once they finish their haiku, it's time to write couplets. Have students refer to their notes about how the food tastes, smells, feels, and so on.

Session 2

Have additional food available on this day. Students were probably hooked by the snacks during the first session!

Review the definitions of haiku and couplets with students when you arrive. Recall what you worked on in session 1, and talk out any problems students encountered and how they overcame them.

For the next half hour to forty-five minutes, use a set of prompts to generate more writing. Prompts that generate good ideas or words for poems could include the following:

> This food reminded me of _____.
> The food tasted/smelled/felt like _____.
> If this food were an animal, it would be a _____.
> This food _____ in my mouth.
> I wouldn't want this food, because _____.

Write the prompts on the board or sheets of paper for tutors and students. Tell students that the prompts should not be part of their poems, because all the poems would sound the same; the prompts are just to help support brainstorming. Encourage students to use uncommon words and make up new ones—anything to avoid weak adjectives. Ask students to write down their one-to-two-word answers to the questions. At that point they should have enough unique words for their haiku and couplets.

To help students revise, talk to them after they've written the first drafts of their haiku and couplets; then ask them to read the poems aloud. You may find that different students used similar words or that students took the first words they could think of and wrote them down.

To help them write stronger poems, ask students to tell you about their poems. Repeat the words or new descriptions they give you and encourage them to rewrite the poems using those exact words. Frequently students have all the right words but need to do more digging to get to a poem. You may have to try this a few times.

This is a perfect time to mention to students that finishing a poem takes many tries. Explain that editing is a very important part of writing poetry because it helps writers refine their poems. Couplets and haiku may seem simple, but students will likely find that they need to write several drafts to create poems that hit the right notes.

Take the next half hour to rehearse the readings. Make sure to let students read for only a minute to maximize audience excitement!

If you will not be having a reading, you can still invite parents to come see the students' work during the last twenty minutes of this session. Hang students' work on a string across the room with paper clips or clothespins. Students, parents, and volunteers can walk around and practically taste the couplets and haiku.

Make sure to thank everyone for their help, and thank the students for their efforts. Encouraging young writers is what this is all about.

The Sonnet as a Silver Marrow Spoon

Adam O'Riordan

A line will take us hours maybe;
Yet if it does not seem a moment's thought,
Our stitching and unstitching has been naught.
Better go down upon your marrow-bones
And scrub a kitchen pavement, or break stones...

—William Butler Yeats, "Adam's Curse"

There is a restaurant in London that advertises "nose-to-tail eating," and it prides itself that no part of an animal is left unused. I had a friend who when eating there would invariably order the bone marrow on toast. The dish came with a small implement, no bigger than a little finger, which the diner used to extract the marrow, a silver marrow spoon, perfectly engineered to slide inside the baked bone and remove its contents.

Perhaps it was the marrow and its Yeatsian echo that pushed my mind into a literary mode, but this elegant, antiquated tool always struck me as a metaphor for the sonnet: probing, incisive, finding pleasure and insight where it lies hidden, a form that allows poets to make use of what might ordinarily be overlooked or discarded.

As an eighteen-year-old undergraduate, I struggled for a long time to write a sonnet. It seemed like the correct form, the form I should be writing in. But I would become snagged in the intricacies of the meter and struggle for rhymes only to find that they felt forced.

I was at the same time aware of poems on both sides of the Atlantic influenced by the New Formalist school of poets: each iamb weighed, each volta perfectly placed, the rhymes fulsome and plangent but the sum of the whole, on second or third reading, saying very little whatsoever.

So I would strip the sonnet down to its simplest form: an idea or a story that, somewhere around the eighth or ninth line, is nudged or diverted slightly in its path so that it turns and says something else.

The thing I would like to put to a class of seniors is the sonnet in its loosest, least restrictive form. (In fact, some of my favorite sonnets are not sonnets at all. Richard Wilbur's masterly sequence "This Pleasing Anxious Being" in *Mayflies* seems to me to do everything a sonnet should but over a more leisurely eighteen to twenty lines per section.)

Seamus Heaney's sonnets in the sequence "Clearances," from his collection *The Haw Lantern*, show how something as simple as a memory of peeling potatoes can be substance enough for a poem:

> When all the others were away at Mass
> I was all hers as we peeled potatoes.
> They broke the silence, let fall one by one
> Like solder weeping off the soldering iron:
> Cold comforts set between us, things to share
> Gleaming in a bucket of clean water.
> And again let fall. Little pleasant splashes
> From each other's work would bring us to our senses.
>
> So while the parish priest at her bedside
> Went hammer and tongs at the prayers for the dying
> And some were responding and some crying

I remembered her head bent towards my head,
Her breath in mine, our fluent dipping knives—
Never closer the whole rest of our lives.

Begin by directing students to the narratives, the secrets, the unshared, the family myths or legends. Have them think back to half-remembered episodes, stories or confidences older brothers or sisters or cousins or uncles might have shared with them, casually, unthinkingly, in passing, as such stories are often shared.

Ask them to tell a story as they remember it for the first eight or nine lines and then allow themselves to comment on it from their present vantage point. What do they know now that they did not know then? What light does the present cast back onto that particular story?

The sonnet's *volta* is its turn, the point at which it shifts. We see this vividly in Shakespeare's "Sonnet 18" with its declaration in the ninth line: "But thy eternal summer shall not fade"—the addressee of the poem has so far been compared to a summer day, but at that line things change. I've added a space here to indicate the shift:

Shall I compare thee to a summer's day?
Thou art more lovely and more temperate:
Rough winds do shake the darling buds of May,
And summer's lease hath all too short a date:
Sometime too hot the eye of heaven shines,
And often is his gold complexion dimm'd;
And every fair from fair sometime declines,
By chance or nature's changing course untrimm'd;

But thy eternal summer shall not fade
Nor lose possession of that fair thou owest;
Nor shall Death brag thou wander'st in his shade,
When in eternal lines to time thou growest:

So long as men can breathe or eyes can see,
So long lives this and this gives life to thee.

The turn in a sonnet allows the poet to interrogate and cast new light on the previous eight lines. In the case of the above exercise, in which the students are relating some sort of narrative, the turn allows reassessment; it's a chance to comment upon what came before or to include a twist.

Remind students that people carry these narratives around for a long time, and so when we gaze at them through the vehicle of the sonnet, there are things about them we will discover that we did not know we knew: twists, turns, reinterpretations of that intimate cache of stories and tales that accrue over the course of childhood. These seniors on the edge of adulthood might now want to reassess, or comment upon, these stories from childhood.

If students find the story pulling away from the truth, that's OK. You might remind them that they're serving the poem, not the story, which is simply the impetus, the fuel for the piece of art they find themselves making. You might remind them here of the old adage: "Trust the poem, not the poet."

And that's it, really. Show young writers the sonnet in its simplest, most stripped-back form. Direct them to the stories from their past. Let the sonnet, memory's own silver marrow spoon, with its turn, its *volta*, generate within them comments on the stories they are telling. The writing of the sonnet—as with any poem—should be a form of discovery, a digging down into the self, like that dish in the London restaurant that most of us might balk at if it were placed before us: intimate and strange upon the tongue.

Verse Journalism: The Poet as Witness

Quraysh Ali Lansana and Georgia A. Popoff

Pulitzer Prize–winner Gwendolyn Brooks proposed localizing the news of the day one clipping at a time. In *Report from Part One*, the first book of her two-volume autobiography, Brooks named her construct "verse journalism" and defined it as "poet as fly on the wall ... poet as all-seeing eye." As she taught, poetry encourages a more robust investigation of news and events. With the benefit of poetic license, verse journalism provides poets the opportunity to explore a topic from the inside out. But unlike traditional journalism, this construct leaves room for emotion, creative imaginings, and nuanced opinion as students witness the world.

Verse journalism melds the literary forms of journalism and poetry to create an offspring distinct from both parents. There are at least four elements that distinguish verse journalism from traditional reporting:

1. Poetic form gives students the opportunity to create an intimate relationship with a news item, to personalize it.
2. Working in verse permits students to concentrate on particular aspects of a news item that they find compelling.
3. Incorporating poetic license in a journalistic process allows

students to express opinions and beliefs as well as chronicle events. Reportage becomes personal statements.

4. The opinions function within the world of the poem, the poetic environment created, rather than simply offering a platform for dogma or mere documentation.

The potential to engage students in this mode of learning about current events, as well as history, is valuable from many standpoints and has cross-curricular applications. In the verse journalism construct, students explore how people, place, and geography inform identity and life experience. Certainly history and basic research are important aspects of verse journalism; the standard journalistic questions regarding a current event (who, what, when, where, why, and how) provide entrées into the process. Once students record responses to those questions, empathy becomes a vital element in creating the poem. Students must consider the actions and question motivation for the poem to be effective.

OBJECTIVE

To help students gain an understanding of a news story or current event and build a level of empathy; to help students create a foundation for the development of critical-thinking strategies that may be applied to persuasive essays, debate, and other elements of English/language arts curriculum while strengthening students' competency in English language arts.

AGE OR GRADE LEVEL

The target group for this exercise is high-school students, though a teacher might determine that it is appropriate for middle-school classes.

ANTICIPATED TIME

Adaptable, from a single forty-five-minute session through a five-day process.

MATERIALS AND RESOURCES NEEDED

News periodicals, writing materials (paper, pens, pencils), dictionary, thesaurus.

PROCESS OVERVIEW

The lesson plan can provide a template for a single day of poetry writing or be expanded into a more comprehensive inquiry. This exercise in verse journalism creates the opportunity for students to establish an intimate relationship with a news item, to personalize it. Working in verse permits students to concentrate on particular aspects of the current event they find compelling. Student opinions are welcomed in the verse journalism construct. The inclusion of student ideas and emotions about their chosen topics should inform word choice. A note of caution, however: advise students to avoid rant or dogma.

INITIATING THE DISCUSSION

Select a poem based on a news item (see suggestions below); discuss the event that prompted the poem and the ways in which the poem explores the event and articulates the author's opinions. After reading the poem aloud, guide students in a line-by-line discussion of it. Ask them to identify the sensory elements at work in each line. Discuss how the poet reveals his or her own impressions of the circumstance. Allow time for students to select a news item and conduct research. This could include a library visit and/or homework. Engage the class in a discussion of the events they have chosen to investigate.

MOVING INTO THE WRITING COMPONENT

Next, direct students to create "blueprints" for their poems by writing responses to the following:

1. Select a news item, either current or from your past, that made an indelible impression.

2. List the who, what, when, where, why, and how. The responses to these questions should include a one- or two-sentence explanation of each topic.

3. List all the possible emotions the people involved in your news story might feel.

4. List all of the sights, sounds, and smells associated with your chosen topic.

5. Make note of your opinions and/or feelings regarding this event.

6. Permit your opinion to guide your narrative and word choice.

DRAFTING THE POEM

After the students have compiled their responses, return to the model poem shared earlier. This time, ask students to identify descriptive adjectives that will aid in describing the circumstance they have selected.

Next, engage students in a quick review of the following poetic devices:

-» Alliteration
-» Personification
-» Onomatopoeia
-» Oxymoron
-» Metaphor
-» Simile

As students create their first drafts, ask them to include at least one example of each device listed above somewhere in their poems. They may, for example, cull a sound from the blueprint and employ onomatopoeia to bring it to life, or they may give voice to a weapon to incorporate personification, et cetera. There is no line limit, but tell students that they must write at least twelve lines.

REVISING

During the revision process, in addition to the standard tightening and tweaking, ask students to ponder other significant aspects of the news event they might have missed. Encourage them to think about sensory language, ideas, actions, setting, and points of view. Peer critique is a valuable element at this point of revision.

PUBLISHING AND PERFORMANCE

Schedule an in-class verse-journalism poetry reading, allowing time for sharing background information associated with the places and people who populate these works. These stories offer fodder for other poems and narrative writings. After the in-class reading, consider publishing the poems as a newspaper or an anthology.

ADDITIONAL IDEAS

If your instruction is part of a team-teaching effort with social studies, civics, or history teachers, this process can be adapted to any historical era. Additionally, this format can be used as a related unit of study for special celebrations or observances, such as Black History Month, Women's History Month, Hispanic Heritage Month, and other observances of cultural and historical significance.

Examples to consider as models: Gwendolyn Brooks, "The *Chicago Defender* Sends a Man to Little Rock"; Wilfred Owen, "Anthem for Doomed Youth"; Oliver Rice, "Timely Enumerations Concerning Sri Lanka;" Patricia Smith, "Up on the Roof;" Brian Turner, "Ashbah."

Persona Poetry: Donning the Masks of Knowledge

Quraysh Ali Lansana and Georgia A. Popoff

The experience of a poem, either writing it or reading it, may be like putting on a costume, a winter coat, or a suit of armor—in effect, it may be much like donning a totally different personality. This is particularly true with persona poetry, in which the poem is rooted in a point of view beyond the writer's own. The Greek and Latin roots of the word persona mean "mask." This poetic form presents the voice of another speaker—animate or inanimate, real or invented—as that speaker might respond to a specific place, time, and situation. A persona poem thus offers a way to articulate knowledge of a history, a community, or an environment different somehow from the poet's own. Empathy—the ability to see through another set of eyes, feel through a distant heart—is inherent in the process of creating persona poetry. This becomes a form of acting, of role-playing, of broadening one's perspective. The stage is a blank piece of paper.

Creating persona poetry is a highly effective tool for writing and assessment in a cross-curricular context. For example, the assignment to write a poem in the voice of Louis Pasteur upon his first successful attempt at pasteurization or to speak of Buzz Aldrin stepping back into the lunar module from the moon's surface, activates imagination in ways that lecture and rote learning cannot spark. Consider the class that has just completed a science unit on oceans: each student can select an ocean-dwelling animal for the subject of a persona poem. In order to be successful, students must think in terms of how that animal starts its day, what "family life" includes, what food it would eat, et cetera. As another example, if students from a Detroit school visited the Charles H. Wright Museum of African American History, they might write in the voices of seventeenth-century West African children torn from their village or young slaves in North America. This would provide mirrors into what the students have internalized from the museum experience and reflect the overall learning from the history unit.

Writing in a persona encourages students to view the world with a wider peripheral vision. Poetry is an art of reflection and response, often speaking on behalf of others. Intimate details enliven a persona poem, which, in turn, becomes a vehicle to transport the reader into a world in which the character exists and from which that character speaks. Persona poetry creates a stage for experimentation and compassion; it also provides opportunities to acquire new knowledge and then share that knowledge with others. Persona poems are especially useful in assessment because students must utilize specific details gathered through research and class instruction. Such poems do not simply describe a person or situation; they require the poet to step outside of him or herself and inhabit another consciousness.

Persona poetry may help students understand different cultures, previous generations, and other worldviews. A high-school student rooted in one nationality may recognize his similarities to a citizen of a nation on the other side of the globe, thus becoming perhaps a little more accepting of differences and universalities. This empathy may move young people to acts of philanthropy and activism, concrete actions for change.

Persona poetry also lends itself to performance. In reading and interpreting a persona poem, students adopt voices that permit them to travel through time and geography. A young person can stand before the class as a noted historical figure, a favorite animal, or an admired celebrity, projecting elements of self while pretending to be someone or something else. Additionally, by acting out persona poems written by themselves or others, students activate both their brains and their bodies; through acting their poems, students may also develop new realizations of self-confidence and competency. All of this experiential activity is inspired by language and syntax. Persona poetry presents an interactive mode of learning and seeing.

OBJECTIVE

Students will engage in research to create poems that reflect knowledge in other core content areas while also enhancing study skills, general literacy, writing competency, and reading comprehension.

AGE AND GRADE LEVEL

Applicable to any age group or grade level; can be modified to accommodate any level of literacy, writing, and research skills.

ANTICIPATED TIME

This lesson is best suited to a weeklong (five-day) process but is adaptable to the needs of the curriculum.

MATERIALS AND RESOURCES NEEDED

Writing materials (paper, pens, pencils), dictionary, thesaurus, access to the library and computer labs.

Process Overview

INITIATING THE DISCUSSION

Provide a general introduction and overview of persona poetry, as well as the general requirements of the process. With the students, discuss how humans have the capacity to empathize with others. Talk about why details from research will be critical in understanding and speaking in the voices of whomever their persona poems portray. Ask each student to select a character from literature studied in class or a historical figure from related studies. Each student will write a persona poem in the voice of that character. (Note: This is particularly effective in connecting history and English/language arts core content.) Encourage students to select a character to whom they have a strong connection. It is fine if two students choose the same character—different students can provide wildly diverging voices arising from the same figure.

MOVING INTO THE WRITING COMPONENT

The next step engages students in fact-finding, the first key to success in this project. Create a set of questions for students to use as they search for the details they need to imagine and conjure a character's voice. Sample questions that can generate ideas for the creative writing process include the following:

- Where and what time do you wake up on an average morning? How do you feel today?
- How would you describe the place you live?
- If you can see your reflection, what do you look like?
- Do you have a family or do you live alone? What is your family like?
- Who are other significant individuals in your life?
- What is one memorable event in your past that defines your life?

-» What does the world around you look like? What sounds
  surround you?

-» Who is the most influential person in your life, and how
  do you perceive that relationship?

This work may be done in the library, the computer lab, or the class-
room—wherever needed resources are available to students.

DRAFTING THE POEM

This step builds on the notes that students took during their research.
Ask students to respond to the prompts they've received, sharing ideas
with the whole class. Remind them to respond in the first person, as if
they have morphed into their characters. This must be reinforced a great
deal, or the writing will be too literal, too data driven. Emphasize that
there isn't really a right "voice"—there are many possibilities, and the
persona will say as much about the poet creating it as it will about the
actual historical figure. Prompting from the list of questions and follow-
ing their responses to a chosen line of inquiry with the simple question
"And then what happened?" will expand the scope of nearly every stu-
dent's response. Allow free-writing time for students to develop a draft
poem of at least a few lines.

REVISING

Next, give students time to review their first drafts and ask them to con-
sider as many craft elements as possible, including word choice, simile
and metaphor, descriptive language, active verbs, et cetera. Emphasize
the importance of verb and adjective choices. Provide at least ten to fif-
teen minutes for students to make changes. Remind students to think in
terms of figurative language. This is the time, as the chef Emeril Lagasse
says so often, to "Kick it up a notch."

   Organize students into groups of two or three or four. Ask them to
share and critique one another's drafts. Ask them to look out for typos,

spelling problems, grammatical errors, and improper punctuation, in addition to responding to the poems' content. Remind students that critique is not criticism. Encourage the "sandwich" method of critique: offer a positive comment, a suggestion for improvement, and then another positive comment.

FINALIZING THE DRAFT

The final step is to give students five to ten minutes to proofread their work one more time before preparing their final copies to hand in. This step, as well as first drafts and revisions, may be assigned as homework.

PUBLISHING AND PERFORMANCE

Encourage students to read their work aloud. Allow others to respond. If a student is reticent to share, ask if someone else may read the piece aloud for the student. It can be very affirming for a student to hear his or her work read aloud by a teacher or another student.

Examples to consider as models: Margaret Atwood, "Siren Song"; Tyehimba Jess, "martha promise receives leadbelly, 1935"; Quraysh Ali Lansana, "faithless"; Sylvia Plath, "Lady Lazarus"; Kay Ryan, "Bear Song"; Anthony Thwaite, "Monologue in the Valley of the Kings."

A Poetry of Perception: Four Studies for Young People

Rebecca Lindenberg

Introduction: "Making Sense" of It All

There are many ways of imagining what poetry gives us, as readers, as humans, to enrich our experience (as readers, as humans). For my part, I have always valued poetry's subtle, splendid way of asking us to look at things (everyday things, vast and sublime things) anew—to re-see the world, to re-see the language we use for describing the world to ourselves, to cease taking these things for granted. It is precisely this function of poetry that sometimes makes the reading and writing of it feel "hard." After all, it is unnerving to encounter the common property of language—something we live within and feel we know—used as an artistic rather than journalistic medium. It's a little like walking into the house you grew up in to find all the furniture made out of gelatin or glued to the ceiling. Or like looking in the mirror and finding you don't quite recognize yourself—you feel a little estranged, you wonder at this weirdness. That wonder makes you look closer, and in looking closer, you see things that have always been there as if for the first time. This experience of being "woken up" to the world, which poetry can give us, is very exciting indeed.

I have a few exercises I find help to cultivate this experience (and appreciation) in young people, first as readers, then as writers—I'll describe four of them in detail here. I gather these activities together in orbit around the idea of *making sense*, a notion I encountered in the work of environmental writer David Abrams, who writes, "To *make sense* is to release the body from the constraints imposed by outworn ways of speaking, and hence to renew and rejuvenate one's felt awareness of the world." By "making sense" I mean, first, to ground our attention in the real, the actual, the palpable—to pay careful and mindful attention to the things we learn at the border of the five senses where the individual meets the world that he or she is moving through. To become, as novelist Wallace Stegner once put it, "an incorrigible lover of concrete things." And then to imagine language as a sixth sense that gives us another, deeper way of accessing those things, "making sense" of them by describing them, connecting them, re-imagining them, and allowing ourselves to be tenderly (sometimes profoundly) affected by them. The writer Annie Dillard once said, "Don't write what you know. Write what only you know." She did not mean that the writer ought to be in possession of specialized knowledge; she meant that the writer should try to be faithful to her unique perception of the world. These exercises and activities will help young people to do just that.

Study 1: Ideograms, Imagery, and the Dance of the Intellect

It is often less useful to think of poetry as writing *about* something, and more helpful to imagine poems as writing *around* their subject matter. I sometimes tell my students that this is how a poem is like a doughnut—the sweet matter of it defined by the invisible center. Ezra Pound talked about *logopoeia*, what he called "the dance of the intellect among words." It is from Pound, too, that we get the first activity in this series—the ideogram.

Pound "invented" the ideogram based on a misunderstanding of Chinese characters, thanks to his reading of the critic and translator Ernest Fenollosa (who was, at any rate, more of a Japanese than a Chinese scholar). Pound read that the written signifier for autumn in Chinese comprised the character for tree crowned or topped by the character for flame. From this and other observations, Pound developed his notion of the "ideogram," which remains, however inaccurate it may be as a means of understanding character-based writing systems, a useful poetic curiosity in English because it arranges concrete, metonymic signifiers around an abstract, invisible center to create an imagistic suggestion of an unfixable concept. Famously, Pound's ideogram for red is a relatively square-shaped piece, situating in its four "corners" the words *rose, cherry, iron rust*, and *flamingo*, as follows:

ROSE CHERRY
IRON RUST FLAMINGO

As humans, our sense of sight is almost certainly the most dominant of the five at our physical disposal, and it is perhaps for this reason that imagery (mindfully written) is one of the most pleasing and evocative of poetic devices. But good imagery is not good because it is surgically precise in the accuracy of its description; it is good because at the same time that it draws us a picture, it awakens a mood or a feeling or an idea. Prose, or *journalistic* language, as the poet Stéphane Mallarmé calls it, describes; *poetic* language evokes. Considering Pound's ideogram, we have two iconic examples of a very red red—the rose and the cherry. Iron rust is a reddish-brown, and I think we often think of flamingoes (partly because of how we talk about them) as being pink more than red. Three of these things we easily associate with the natural world, whereas rust (though a perfectly natural process) often conjures images of industry. So we can gather that this little text is about more than just essentializing redness. *Red* is, in this case, not one but many. It is gathered to suggest something bigger than the sum of these parts—prosperity, maybe, or southerliness, or nostalgia. Read and discuss Pound's ideogram, and invite students to suggest the mood or idea evoked by these four words, perhaps recalling William Carlos Williams's statement on imagism: "No ideas but in things."

Next, ask students to agree on a color other than red. Begin by brainstorming a list of colors beyond the standard seven or so of the familiar rainbow. In addition to orange or green, we have a spectrum of others to choose from—chartreuse, magenta, cyan, burgundy, beige, to name but a few. Asking students to push themselves past the first three or even ten colors that immediately come to mind will help to prepare them for the rest of this exercise, as well as for the activities to come. Often the first three or even five things one thinks of are "received" ideas—shared, predictable, the kinds of things that feel obvious, almost second-nature. We aspire to traverse these, arriving at the idiosyncratic, unpredictable, even startling. Once students have brainstormed a series of possible choices, put it to a vote. The color with the most votes will form the "center" around which to build the class's ideogram.

Say the students choose, for example, yellow. It is likely they will start by suggesting, again, the usual concrete items we associate with that color—lemons, bananas, the sun, corn on the cob, sunflowers. After they've exhausted those, it's important to keep asking—what else is yellow? Taxis, rubber duckies, corn tortillas, rain slickers, caution tape, butter. Then, onion skins, sticky notes, school buses, yield signs, egg yolks, urine, grapefruit rinds, fog—and now we're getting somewhere. Now we're not talking so much about what we *think of* as yellow, we're talking about what we *actually see* as yellow.

Once the board or screen is full of things we see as yellow, it's worth pausing to remind students that we aren't just making a picture of yellow.

What the class chooses will suggest something *about* yellow—but it doesn't have to be *everything* there is to say about yellow. It doesn't have to be comprehensive, just visceral, evoking "yellow-ness" (or "teal-ness" or "tan-ness"). Then, another vote. Or rather, a few rounds, in which each student gets two votes, until you narrow it down to the final four. And *ka-pow*! You've made an ideogram. If you still have class time, or if you wish to assign homework, students might be asked to produce another ideogram—perhaps of a color, or perhaps of an abstraction like liberty or health or belonging. You can always ask the students to show their work, as they might be asked to do when solving a math problem. You might insist they brainstorm at least twenty-five things from which to cull the four comprising their ideogram, and even write a short paragraph discussing why they chose the four images they finally settled on. In this way, students engage in making sense of a color or another abstraction, connecting it to an accessible series of images they perceive as somehow connected, and using those to write around rather than about the center at hand.

Study 2: Captioning the World

Ideogram-ing attaches concrete things to abstract ideas; this next exercise inverts the activity, attaching abstract ideas and descriptors to concrete things. But we're still engaged in the unifying activity of making sense, learning to re-perceive the world and asking others to let their attention linger on something "common" for a moment longer than it usually might. For this activity, which is almost a kind of fieldwork, students will need chalk (quite a bit of it), and either the students or a designated leader (perhaps the instructor) will need a camera.

For this activity, students will go out into the world (they can stick to a campus, if necessary) and label things with adjectives that describe them. But not the first or even second adjectives that suggest themselves—no writing "hard" or "sharp" on a rock, for example. Rather, the adjective students write on an object should be both apt and at least a little bit surprising. Working in pairs or small groups, students take to the field, creatively (and temporarily) "vandalizing" the environment, documenting the effort in pictures that can be compiled for a class website or photo album. In the past, I have had students label a boulder as "ancient" or a log in a running river as "undying." I've had a student draw an arrow on a brick wall, pointing to a tree whose leaves had gone vermillion with their autumn change, and on the brick wall next to the arrow, labeled the tree as "rich." Another student drew an arrow pointing to the sky on a sheer concrete wall and wrote "unknown."

Ask students to keep their descriptions to a single adjective. The constraint of the single adjective requires a little more of the imagination, which is what we're after in the end; the imagination that reaches not for escape from the real but for more and more magical access to the real. The real is not boring or fixed, and while it may sometimes include the sad and cruel, we should not toss about the phrase *the real world* as though the real were all drudgery and misery and pain. The real is infinite, and it is everywhere, and it is waiting for us to notice.

Study 3: *Zuihitsu*

As a teacher and a writer, I don't really think of writing as a craft that one learns and then repeats in order to perfect it, like blacksmithing or bread-baking. Writing is, rather, a practice that engages the writer in her whole capacity as a human: reading, thinking, feeling, choosing, and acting. A writer from whom I learned this and whom (in turn) I like to teach to students is the great Japanese poet Sei Shōnagon. Written during the eleventh-century Heian period, *The Pillow Book of Sei Shōnagon* is arguably the first and certainly the best-known illustration of the genre called *zuihitsu*, which translates literally as "following the brush" but is perhaps best interpreted as "occasional writings": series of lists, anecdotes, and observations written by a perceptive, articulate, well-educated and highly opinionated woman.

Sei Shōnagon's *Pillow Book* includes, among others, lists of "Squalid Things," "Things Worth Seeing," "Things That Lose By Being Painted," "Hateful Things," "Splendid Things," "Rare Things," and (found below) "Elegant Things."[1]

Elegant Things

A white coat worn over a violet waistcoat.
Duck eggs.
Shaved ice mixed with liana syrup and put in a new silver bowl.
A rosary of rock crystal.
Wisteria blossoms. Plum blossoms covered with snow.
A pretty child eating strawberries.

Here the idea of "elegant" is not defined in a way that narrows and contains it; rather, by an accretion of examples, an idea of "elegant" is illustrated, opened, expounded upon. Elegance seems to arise at the place where the human-made and the natural or organic come into confluence with each other, and, in keeping with the notion, it seems to include (perhaps even require) a degree of impermanence. This is one of the consolations of writing—not capturing or fixing, but noting and appreciating the ever-momentary, always-fleeting pleasures, anguishes, longings, and curiosities of the world.

When using this in the classroom, I ask students to model (though not imitate) Sei Shōnagon; I ask them to suggest a series of possible lists based upon Shōnagon's and then to choose (usually by class vote) one of

---

1. Additional examples from *The Pillow Book of Sei Shōnagon* can be found in Ivan Morris's terrific translation, available from Columbia University Press.

the proposed lists. (In one class, for example, my students chose to write about "Annoying Things.") I then separate students into smaller groups and ask them to create lists that are more than just a litany of annoyances but really evoke "annoyingness." Each small group makes its own zuihitsu for the agreed-upon concept ("Annoying Things" or "Things Found in a Supermarket" or "Sorrowful Things"), and students almost always devise lists that imagine "annoying" (or some other feeling) differently, which subsequently makes for a terrific conversation supporting the notion that "what only you know" (to return to Annie Dillard) has as much to do with attention, perception, and sensibility as it does with knowledge and experience. Among its other virtues, this exercise in "perceptual" poetry is a good antidote to the way we often talk to young people about poetry as a way of "expressing" a self. The self is not the subject here, but it is wholly present as a conduit, a medium, a means; indeed, the finest writing often happens when (to quote William Blake) "we see with, not through, the eye."

I also find this exercise particularly friendly to young people (young women, for example) who are unfortunately accustomed to thinking about how they look (as in: *appear*) rather than how they see (as in: *perceive*). To be a teenager is to be pathologically self-conscious, but this is almost antithetical to really good writing. (Here we should not confuse self-consciousness with self-awareness.) I do not intend this as an exercise in self-erasure; rather, I intend it as an exercise that empowers the student in her perceptive capacity, cultivating her relationship to her own interiority as it is altered (and as it transforms) the exterior world of which she is a citizen. Along the same lines, Shōnagon's writing addresses itself not to a broad audience, but to an intimate confidant. In its conspiratorial attitude toward its reader, *zuihitsu* invites candor, risk taking, and sometimes startling originality—all things we still subtly and often even consciously discourage in (particularly) young women. Sei Shōnagon's engagement with her (invisible, absent, but intimate) interlocutor also asks students to engage with the question: to whom are you writing? This question is, I think, among the most important in poetry. For much contemporary poetry is imbued with anxiety about its own reception, perhaps even relevance. Poetry that addresses itself to a skeptical audience will make for itself a skeptical audience—it will (by its very attitude) invite its audience into that species of relationship. Too much of our poetry comes at its audience on the defensive, thinking of the audience as a critic rather than a comrade or confidant. Such poems can come off as aloof, standoffish, or coy, or they can be evasive, sometimes even opaque. These are coping mechanisms, but not craft. From Sei Shōnagon, we can learn a poetic that is personal without being confessional or "expressive." From her, we learn to ground the poem in the "stuff of the world," as poet Kathryn Cowles often says. There's no need to be defensive when you just call 'em how you see 'em.

Study 4: Thirteen Ways of Looking at a Blackboard

If ever anything rhymed with the idea that poems write *around* rather than about their subject matter, it's got to be Wallace Stevens's notion that "Poetry should resist the intelligence almost successfully." Stevens's "Thirteen Ways of Looking at a Blackbird" also converses (if you will) elegantly with Sei Shōnagon and the other activities mentioned above. This tremendous poem is one that rewards as much close and careful reading as one can spare for it, and it deploys its many glimpses of its elusive subject via a litany of meticulous poetic gestures worth discussing with students. Here is attention and perception; here is image and comparison; here is list and accumulation and re-presentation; here is description and evocation. After inviting students to read and discuss this poem as a group, assign them to write their own "Thirteen Ways" of looking at something—something as everyday and overlookable (and ubiquitous) as a blackbird.

Here's a tip, though. The first time I engaged teenagers in this activity, they wrote thirteen ways of looking at "my hair dryer" and "my car" and "my skateboard" and "my parents" and "my church." And that's all right, because the teaching moment (should this happen) comes in letting students know that they missed what the assignment was intended to elicit from them—namely, the same activity of perception that the previous three studies cultivated. Instead they wrote about themselves, and perhaps that's to be expected. Trying to figure out who you are is, in fairness, a pretty all-consuming task. But one thing literature can ask us to do is to let go of the idea of a fixed (or fixable) self, to surrender that notion to the activity of perception and the activity of empathy. Literature has many uses and consolations, but I do think that above all, compassion (for the world and the creatures inhabiting it) is creativity's finest enterprise. Whether students write brilliant, perceptive, poetic "themes and variations" the first go-round, or whether the teachable moment arises and they have to reconsider and rewrite, the poems that finally emerge from the process almost always represent a real range of voices and foci, an impressive imaginative scope.

And so, in each of the students' "Thirteen Ways" and among the students who produce them, we get a kind of microcosm within which we can see how and why contemporary American poetry has evolved into what it has—contemporary American poetries. We are multiple and multifaceted, and there is no reason this should not be the case. Permission is, I think, as important as instruction, exuberance as useful as rigor.

Further Studies

Henry James insisted that writers ought to be people "upon whom nothing is lost." These exercises and activities are meant to encourage young people to become exactly that, and more: to become writers who can vividly, evocatively, and personally communicate their findings as observers, attentive to the subtle movements of the world, of the world in them, of language. But before (and above) anything else, literature ought to be a pleasure. The study of literature ought to enlarge the possibilities for pleasure, not contract them. Sometimes I hear people (especially young people) say they "don't understand poetry," and I hope these studies help to dissipate that anxiety. For even if you can't say what a poem is "about," perhaps because you *can't* say what the poem is about—if it knew, it wouldn't have come to be as a poem, it would have been an aphorism or essay—you might understand the text better than you think. Is it a sunny poem or a rainy poem? A night poem or a day poem? Would it open a door for you, or would it chase you down an alley with a baseball bat? Is it wearing shiny heels or dingy sneakers? "Getting it" need not be a prerequisite for having a good time. It's not you versus the malevolent puzzle master, after all; it's a meeting of consciousnesses—two activities of perception converge, and something wonderful and alchemical takes place.

Poetry Walk

Harriet Levin

BACKGROUND

I took my first poetry walks back in high school, when I was a student in the Parkway Program in Philadelphia and constantly walked around the city. The program was influenced by A.S. Neill's Summerhill School, which was run according to his principle "freedom, not license." Students chose their own classes and made their own schedules. Truly a "school without walls," Parkway wasn't housed in a central building, so that students could take advantage of the cultural institutions in the city. Classes were held in skyscrapers and museums. For example, rug weaving—taught by Afghani weavers whom the Fels Institute brought to Philadelphia to participate in a special exhibit—was held at the University of Pennsylvania Museum of Archaeology and Anthropology. Professionals at a Center City advertising firm taught marketing. University of Pennsylvania graduate students taught Poetry Workshop at Smokey Joe's Bar on the UPenn campus. (Undoubtedly, not a place where underage students would be permitted to enter today—in any case, Smokey Joe's, an underground pub with literary ambience, served as a far better source of inspiration than a cinderblock classroom.)

Although I walked around Center City all through my teenage years and wrote poems in my head, I took my first formal poetry walks while a student in Larry Levis's seminar, The Hundred-Line Poem, at the University of Iowa. Most students in the MFA program didn't extend their writing past thirty lines. At the time, Larry was reinventing the narrative and writing the long, gorgeous poems that would become his opus. He happened to live downstairs from me, and I saw him many times composing on a yellow legal pad the poems that would become his book *The Dollmaker's Ghost*. I wrote all one hundred lines of my poem walking to his class. I lived two miles from campus, and each time I came to a corner, I stopped and wrote down another line. The poem, "Amulet," appeared in my first book. It is filled with the rhythms of my walk, and it practically wrote itself.

THE PLAN

Take a thirty- to forty-minute walk with students, and ask them to write at five-minute planned stops. Encourage them to be receptive to the world around them instead of imposing their egos on the landscape. Tell them they need to open themselves to the environment. Poets look at the world the way scientists do, observing minutiae until its patterns and habits are realized.

A problem many beginning poets have is that they don't understand that poems are visceral. They think poetry is mainly abstract ideas in abstract language. The best way to kill someone's appreciation for poetry is to talk about what a poem *represents*. The thrill of reading an Emily Dickinson poem is finding out that a poem becomes its own reality. Dickinson used the technique of thesis/antithesis, making the meaning of her poems very elusive. Dickinson herself is well known for her visceral definition of poetry in her 1870 remark to Thomas Wentworth Higginson: "If I read a book and it makes my whole body so cold no fire can ever warm me, I know that is poetry. If I feel physically as if the top of my head were taken off, I know that is poetry. These are the only ways I know it. Is there any other way?"

When I take a poetry walk with my students at Drexel University, we leave the campus and head toward Schuylkill River Park. It's a twenty-minute walk in each direction. Leaving campus, we walk down Walnut Street and over the Walnut Street Bridge. We walk a block, and then the whole class stops. During this time, the students look around and each composes a line and writes it down. Then we walk another block, stop again, and write another line. I have the students write about six or seven lines before I tell them that the next line they write should be related in some way to one of their previous lines, and the next line after that should relate to a different previous line, and so on, connecting every sixth and seventh line or so to a previous line. We strive for twenty-line poems.

For your class, have your students walk for a block or so outside your school, absorbing what they see, before they start to compose their lines. The students can write whatever they like, but they must base their work on things they can see. There's a lot to see in a busy city or town, but if your school is in a more subdued environment, it's fun to help your students focus on small oddities.

Share the poems: before my students and I go inside, they read their poems aloud, sometimes attracting the attention of passersby, which gives the reading an added thrill. The great thing about these poems is that the students think they were writing unconnected observations, but every time we do this exercise, they marvel at how well connected the final poems turn out. It may be that randomness is impossible because of the logical structure of grammar, but whatever "meaning" these finished pieces create occurs through language and as such is a worthwhile lesson. Another added benefit of this lesson is that students get to experience writing by the line. Many beginning writers do not understand the integrity of the line and write what amounts to chopped-up prose. This exercise forces students to write their poems one line at a time.

Love Is the Universe

Emilie Coulson

AGE RANGE

Ten to thirteen

TIME

Fifty minutes

OVERVIEW

Preteen students, when confronted with the opportunity to write poetry, are often more willing and eager to jump into big topics than are older poets. The magnitude of the universe, the speed of time and change, and of course encounters with love are all in the forefront of middle-school minds. With all these big ideas come big, abstract words, nestling right into the heart of the writers' bravest, barest poems. Most of the time we tell young writers to avoid abstraction. But sometimes a poet needs an abstraction as a runway—a place from which to launch toward some more specific truth.

This is what I call the "love is the universe" problem. "Love is the universe" was the first line of a poem that a sixth-grade student of mine started to write and never finished. So much was tied up in the idea behind the line, and he was really excited about it. But in using one huge idea to explain another huge idea, the student felt overwhelmed by what to do next. At that point, the poet had only a vague sense of what he wanted to convey. Eventually he chose only one of the abstract ideas (love!) and wrote a poem that connected the idea to his own experience.

This activity allows students to find concrete images that tie abstract words to real, familiar places.

PURPOSE

To add concrete images to student poems and to help students find connections between concrete images and abstract ideas

MATERIALS

Magazines with pictures, photos that students bring in (optional), glue sticks, journals or paper, pencils and pens

BEFORE CLASS STARTS

Write a list of abstract ideas, words, and emotions on the board. This might include a wide range of concepts: love, time, distance, change, hilarity, anger, home, happiness, growth, full, freedom, memory, chance, honesty, and worry.

ONCE CLASS BEGINS

Ask students for a definition of one or two of the words. They may use examples to define the concepts, such as, "Happiness is like when you're riding home from the grocery store and you can smell the rotisserie chicken your family just bought for dinner." Encourage these examples, and maybe write some of the "definitions" next to the abstract word. Explain that, in poetry, examples that writers and readers are familiar with or that are specific can be the best way to describe something complex. This portion of the lesson should take about ten minutes.

Next, ask students to look through photos from magazines or that they brought in. Each student should choose one photo that best represents one of the words on the board. Give this portion of the lesson ten minutes.

Once students find their pictures, ask them to paste the pictures in their journals or on a piece of paper. Then ask them to describe what is happening in their pictures. Ask each student to start with a word from the board. For example, if the word is *freedom*, the first line might be, "Freedom is a skateboard." The lines that follow should further define that word by continuing to describe other details of the picture, including the circumstances that may have led to that picture being taken. Allow twenty minutes.

> Freedom is a skateboard flying up in the air.
> Freedom is finding a brand-new skate park that you're
>   allowed to stay at until sunset.
> Freedom is the sun hitting your board.

TIPS

Make sure the available pictures have strong potential narratives. Even if they don't, encourage students to describe exactly what they're seeing. Some may find it helpful to make a list of everything in the picture. Then remind them to use the five senses. What does it smell like in this scene? What does it sound like?

When students finish describing their scenes, they will have the first draft of a poem full of concrete images. Then share! Allow ten minutes.

BONUS

For a next step, students can each choose another word from the board and take a "photo" in their memory of a time in their life that captures the meaning of that word. They can then start a new poem with their words and descriptions of their experiences.

Advice for Teachers

Stephen Burt

I teach at a very selective college these days, and I taught at a rather selective one before that; I've been away from K–12 education for a while, and have recently been reintroduced to its delights and rigors through my older son, now on the K end. So when the editors of *Open the Door* asked me to share, or create, a syllabus for middle- and high-school teachers who want to teach poetry—that is, poetry reading, poetry writing, the history and the appreciation of poetry, all of which go together at their best—I was first flattered, and then compliant, and then troubled by the request. This was not only because my own teaching has almost always involved college students—if you teach tenth graders or eighth graders every week, rather than visiting a high school class from time to time, then you know things about kids that age that I don't know—but also because the request and the reasons behind it say something about where poetry is, and where it has not been, in K–12 education, lo these past decades.

I had the good fortune to meet a gaggle of graduate students in education last year, most of whom would be high-school English teachers soon, and most of them told me they weren't sure how to teach poetry. They didn't "get it"; they couldn't communicate what they liked to their students. As a result, they taught it entirely as creative writing (students read all and only one another's work); or they taught it, somewhat reluctantly, as it had been taught to them, as a short set of ultra-American and multicultural "classics" (Robert Frost, Emily Dickinson, Langston Hughes, and not even the most interesting poems by those three very interesting poets); or as evidence of what people used to like; or as puzzles to be solved—intellectual games with no emotional point beyond a test.

That's not helpful. Nor, I fear, would a syllabus—my favorite poems and my favorite exercises, week by week, for you and your students—be as helpful as it could, because if you are a middle- or high-school teacher, you know your students better than I do. You also know your own evolving tastes. What should you teach when you teach poems and poetry? The answer depends on what you like and what you think they might like, and on what sort of reading you care most about. In lieu of a syllabus and a lesson plan, then, here's some advice as you make up your own.

1. TEACH WHAT YOU LIKE

If you want to get your students to read poetry, and to enjoy reading poetry, and to write intelligibly about poetry, you must read it, and enjoy reading it, yourself. This doesn't mean you have to love each poem you teach (some of you will have some poems you must teach, due to schoolwide or statewide or AP requirements), but it does mean that you should seek to discover what poems you admire, and then think about why, and teach them alongside whatever else you offer. If your favorite poet is Elizabeth Bishop, work her into your lessons. If your favorite poet is Mary Oliver or Sharon Olds or Sarah Morgan Bryan Piatt or Kathleen Fraser or Emily Dickinson or Bruce Smith or Hart Crane or Alfred, Lord Tennyson, find a way to bring that poet's poems into your course.

If you are a teacher who loves literature but does not already love poetry (there are many such teachers in America's best high schools), pick up anthologies and leaf through them until you find some work that you like. I recommend, for poetry in general, *The Norton Anthology of Poetry*, and for the early twentieth century, the first volume of *The Norton Anthology of Modern and Contemporary Poetry*. For contemporary poetry, consult more than one anthology—try to find anthologies whose editors have radically opposite tastes (say, J.D. McClatchy and Paul Hoover).

You can also ask your students to read an entire book (a single volume, not a *Collected Poems*) by an author you like, if you think the students will like her, too. I've done this repeatedly with college students, asking them to assimilate, for example, Terrance Hayes's *Lighthead*, Frank O'Hara's *Lunch Poems*, and Laura Kasischke's *Gardening in the Dark*. All three books worked well (O'Hara uses a gaggle of proper nouns, but he's so informal that most of my students don't mind; Kasischke and Hayes excel at depicting specifically teenaged experience).

For earlier periods, if you are able to explore them at length, try anthologies devoted to single centuries, such as those edited by Alastair Fowler, John Hollander, Isobel Armstrong, or Christopher Ricks.

You might also consult textbooks. They are no substitute for a syllabus that you design yourself, but they can be helpful as you design it. Helen Vendler's *Poems, Poets, Poetry* (with a useful short anthology in the back) and Mary Kinzie's *A Poet's Guide to Poetry* are two of the best.

2. DO NOT PROCEED CHRONOLOGICALLY

Some courses begin at the start of English poetry or in Shakespeare's day and just march forward toward the present.

Don't do that. It's teeth-grindingly counterproductive: students get the most alien, most obviously difficult poetry first. Worse yet, they think they must learn poetry historically—as a series of events—and that they must always work hard to understand it. They do have to work hard to understand some of it, but they will likely want to do so only if they already know the rewards of understanding poems that do not present such a high bar.

So don't start with hard things. Don't start with the remote past, or at least not with the remote past exclusively. Start instead either with a selection of more or less recent works—works that you, too, admire!—or with a selection of works from several periods. A unit of poems for eleventh or twelfth graders might begin with Shakespeare's sonnet 18 ("Shall I compare thee to a summer's day?") and sonnet 130 ("My mistress' eyes are nothing like the sun") as the oldest poems in a selection of simultaneously presented poems that includes living writers such as C.D. Wright, Kay Ryan, W.S. Merwin, and Juan Felipe Herrera.

That said, please do not confine yourself to living, or to recent, writers; make the eighteenth century, and the Renaissance, and the American Renaissance, and the classics in translation (or in the original, if you can) available to your students, too. Just don't put them first.

3. GIVE STUDENTS A SENSE OF AGENCY: LET THEM PICK POEMS (FROM AMONG THE POEMS YOU CHOOSE)

When I teach poetry in a seminar (rather than a college lecture-hall) format, I always assign more poems than we will have time to discuss. In each class, I call on a student—usually a randomly chosen student (I sometimes use a Twister spinner for this "choice")—to select a poem from among the ones we've read, and to read that poem to us.

This method means that any poem you discuss will have at least one student in the room who has committed himself or herself to that poem and who has made a tentative claim to liking it.

4. REMEMBER THAT YOUR STUDENTS' TASTES ALREADY DIFFER FROM ONE ANOTHER

Some students prefer rhyme and meter and "old" poetry as long as it's not too recherché. Others want poems to sound "modern." The taste of some students is guided by an interest in hip-hop or classical music or country music. Try to work with them; try to find things you like that they can like, too. Some students find supposedly difficult, even impenetrable, contemporary poems more fun, more accessible, and easier to discuss than older poems that seemed clear to their first readers. What's clear to you may not be clear to them.

5. DO NOT FEAR PARAPHRASE, AND DO NOT FEAR OLD POEMS (THOUGH STUDENTS DO)

Rhyme and meter can put many students off, though they attract others. Complex or archaic vocabulary and reference to alien systems of knowledge (usually religion but sometimes farming, science, English geography, et cetera) almost always put students off. That doesn't mean you should avoid poems with those references, much less that you should avoid poems with meter and rhyme. Instead, counter alienation and avoid confusion by using paraphrase, sometimes quite brutal paraphrase, to make the core of an older poem evident. Only once students know what it is saying can they describe how it says what it says or what it avoids saying (Frost: "All the fun's in how you say a thing"). If you use paraphrase well, along with enthusiasm and attention to what your students already know, you can do well with supposedly quite difficult or "advanced" texts.

Good older poets who wrote unusual numbers of relatively accessible poems (poems that I think could engage attentive ninth graders) include the Shakespeare of the sonnets, Lord Rochester (John Wilmot) if you can get away with it (almost all of his best poems are obscene), William Blake, Thomas Hardy, A.E. Housman, Walt Whitman, Emily Dickinson, Thomas Traherne, Christina Rossetti, and Robert Burns.

6. ALL POEMS RAISE QUESTIONS; ONLY SOME HAVE ANSWERS

Here are some thoughts, not about what to teach, but about how to teach what you teach. Many college students have been trained to look, in every poem, for a "message": either a moral lesson about how to live, or a thesis, a problem, and then a solution, such as the same students might put into, or take from, an argumentative essay.

Some poems work that way; many don't. All poems, even the most recherché, are about something because they are about somebody; they show how somebody feels. All poems, like all other kinds of human speech and writing, address some sort of discovery or problem—from "My love has left me, and life seems meaningless now" to "I can't find my socks." But only some poems answer all the questions they raise, just as only some problems have solutions.

It's important to me that my students see poems as versions of human emotions. It's also important to me that they see poems as worth the time it takes to investigate them, to ask why these words occur in this order, with these sounds, these overtones. And it has become increasingly important to me that students see how poetry—like life—does not always offer clear solutions to the problems it describes. Sometimes all a person can do is describe. Or howl. Or write "Howl."

7. POETRY IS AN ART FORM

To enjoy poetry, to go home thinking about it, students must see it as an artistic practice welcomed in but neither confined to, nor designed for, school.

Americans happen to live in a place and a time when the techniques and history of English-language poetry—like the techniques and history of music written for orchestras and string quartets—become available primarily through formal institutions of education. That's a contingent truth about those art forms, not a necessary one. The techniques and history of other art forms—rock music, for example, and hip-hop and dance music, and scripted television programs—become available to contemporary Americans primarily through nonacademic channels, so contemporary Americans tend to think of the latter group as artless or uncomplicated and of the former group as sophisticated or hard.

They need to think otherwise. Nonacademic art forms are not inimical to analysis: critics have written good, long academic essays about TV. Nor do academically supported art forms require analysis before we can enjoy them. Some people—many people—listened to Mozart and

Beethoven for fun before there were courses in music theory and music appreciation; otherwise there would not be courses in music theory and music appreciation. If poetry existed to be put on a test and for no other reason, nobody would ever write it.

Analogies to nonacademic art forms (art forms independent of the academy) can help you disarticulate poetry, an art form, from school, an institution. You can do that without being anti-intellectual, if you do it right. You don't need to pretend that song lyrics are "the same thing" as poetry made for the page. TV shows aren't novels, and sculptures aren't paintings, and jazz isn't baroque counterpoint, and baroque counterpoint isn't rock and roll. We learn how to appreciate, and then to describe, each form of art only by paying attention to good examples—whether in or out of school.

8. POEMS FIRST, LIVES AND CONTEXTS LATER (IF AT ALL)

We have come to care about John Keats's life because he wrote his poems. The same is true for Elizabeth Bishop, Langston Hughes, Sylvia Plath, John Ashbery, Ogden Nash, Lord Rochester, and almost every other poet whose poetry you might teach. If you want your students to care about poems as poems, rather than as evidence of an eventful life, approach them as poems first and last. Give biographies when they are needed, but give poems, as many as you can, to your students one at a time. I do not mean that you should black out the name of the author, only that you should not lead with biography or context or literary history ("this is Romantic poetry"). If they like the poem enough, students will want to learn about the author and about her milieu in good time; if they don't like the poem, why should they care about the author?

Leading with poems also counteracts the pervasive fallacy by which students think that true poems are written only by exceptional, super-special individuals—people privileged or cursed as we mortals can never be. That fallacy is the single most annoying thing about the way popular culture represents poets (or "poets"—"Jim Morrison, American

Poet"). Some poets had troubled lives, and many had privileged back-grounds (which gave them the chance to read a lot and to learn some languages), but others led outwardly uneventful lives. Lord Byron died fighting for Greek independence; Lorine Niedecker, for a while, cleaned hospital floors.

9. ENCOURAGE STUDENTS TO READ MORE THAN YOU ASSIGN

If you have enough time and space in your schedule, it can be very helpful to ask your students to bring in poems they already like. While you shouldn't let their choices take over your course, it's important to encourage them to read more widely than your syllabus dictates. For sources, you might give your students a list of online anthologies and literary magazines and ask each one to bring in a favorite poem culled from reading among them. The proliferation of online mags, which they can read without leaving school or spending money, makes this sort of assignment much easier now, especially at the high-school level.

The Poetry Foundation (www.poetryfoundation.org) has a great archive, as do the Academy of American Poets (www.poets.org) and the British Poetry Library (www.poetrylibrary.org.uk). Some helpful online or partly online US magazines for contemporary poetry include *AGNI*, *Boston Review*, *Mudlark*, *No Tell Motel*, *SHAMPOO*, *UbuWeb* for avant-garde work, *Contemporary Poetry Review* for formally conservative writing, and too many others to name here.

10. MAJOR POETS EVENTUALLY REVEAL THEMSELVES

For all the weight I am encouraging you to give to your students' expressed tastes as they come into the classroom and as they develop there, and for all the attention I am encouraging you to give to individual poems (as opposed to whole poets' careers), you will want to keep in mind that there are experiences you can only have, discoveries that you can only make, with the major figures of the art.

We go on reading Shakespeare and John Donne and Walt Whitman and Emily Dickinson and Thomas Hardy, and we will probably go on reading Elizabeth Bishop and James K. Baxter and Gertrude Stein and Langston Hughes and John Ashbery and Philip Larkin, because (a) they offer wisdom; (b) they add sounds and forms to the language; (c) they let us see reality more sharply; (d) they let us escape it more convincingly and without sacrificing our intellects; and (e) they use existing forms with exceptional gravity, power, precision, or panache. Experience suggests that people who read them attentively want to continue reading and rereading them. It's part of your job, I think, to create more of those experiences, as it is part of mine.

Afterword: A Call to Action
(or What to Do After Reading This Book)

Here you are, and here we are. The end of the book.

Chances are you picked this up in the first place because you love poetry. There are a thousand types of poetry and a thousand ways to love it. The goal of *Open the Door* was not to suggest only one way children might learn about poetry but rather to point to some of the many options for teaching poetry to children and to suggest some of the many reasons for doing so.

As you have seen from these pages, much is being done, and is being done really well. Much more, of course, is possible. The editors did lots of thinking about how people deliver poetry to children both in and out of schools, but we're wondering now what else one might do to connect poetry with other subjects and disciplines. In what ways might teachers combine poetry with painting, music, theater, or dance? What about science? Math? It's easy to ask rhetorical questions at the end of a book, but still, what would a poetry and science fair look like? What would a dance and poetry spelling bee consist of? What exactly are Poetry Pasta, Verse and Vinyasa, and the Lunar Lyric Club? We're waiting for you to let us know!

This book presents only an outline of what's possible, a series of starting points in a much broader conversation. As you begin conversations with kids in your community about poetry, as you discover what their specific needs are and what excites them most about poetry or art or literature, as you work on the rich and exciting project of sharing poems with kids, as you explore what's been done already and the promising new territory that lies ahead—keep in mind these words of Michael Dickman: *Say yes*.

Dorothea Lasky
Brooklyn, New York

Dominic Luxford
San Francisco, California

Jesse Nathan
Menlo Park, California

Contributors

Jimmy Santiago Baca has two recent books of poetry: *The Lucia Poems* and *The Esai Poems* (both from Sherman Asher Publishing).

Eric Baus is the author of three books of poetry: *Scared Text* (The Center for Literary Publishing / Colorado State University), winner of the Colorado Prize; *Tuned Droves* (Octopus Books); and *The To Sound*, winner of the Verse Prize (Wave Books). He has taught poetry to elementary school students and at several universities. He currently lives in Denver and edits Marcel Press with Andrea Rexilius.

Terry Blackhawk serves on the board of the Association of Writers and Writing Programs and is a founding board member of the Writers in the Schools (WITS) Alliance. Her poetry collections include *Body & Field* (Michigan State University), *Escape Artist* (BkMk Press), and *The Dropped Hand* (Marick). Her poems have appeared in numerous anthologies and journals, including *Marlboro Review, Michigan Quarterly Review, Florida Review, Borderlands*, and *Nimrod*. She has received widespread recognition for her teaching, including a Creative Writing Educator of the Year award from the Michigan Youth Arts Festival (2008), a Humanities Award from the Wayne County Arts, History, and Humanities Council (2008), and the 2007 Detroit Bookwoman of the Year award from the Women's National Book Association.

Elizabeth Bradfield is the author of two collections of poetry: *Approaching Ice* (Persea) and *Interpretive Work* (Arktoi Books). Her poems have appeared in *The Atlantic, Orion*, the *Believer*, and *Poetry*, and she has won the Audre Lorde Prize, a Stegner Fellowship from Stanford University, and a scholarship to the Bread Loaf Writers' Conference, among other honors. The founder and editor in chief of Broadsided Press, she lives on Cape Cod and works as a teacher and naturalist.

Stephen Burt is a professor of English at Harvard. He writes about poetry regularly for the *Believer, Nation, London Review of Books, Rain Taxi,* and other journals in Great Britain and the United States. His books include *The Art of the Sonnet*, with David Mikics (Harvard University Press), *Close Calls with Nonsense: Reading New Poetry* (Graywolf Press), and *The Forms of Youth: Twentieth-Century Poetry and Adolescence* (Columbia University Press). Graywolf Press will publish his next book of poems, *Belmont*, in 2013.

Michael Cirelli is the author of *Everyone Loves the Situation* (Penmanship), *Vacations on the Black Star Line* (Hanging Loose), and *Lobster with Ol' Dirty Bastard* (Hanging Loose). He is a Pushcart Prize winner, and his work has appeared in *Best American Poetry, World Literature Today*, and *King Magazine*, among other publications. He is the executive director of Urban Word NYC and has written two poetry curricula books, *Poetry Jam* (Recorded Books) and *Hip-Hop Poetry & the Classics* (Milk Mug). He teaches courses on hip-hop and the teaching of English at New York University, Michigan State University, and the University of Wisconsin–Madison. He has also appeared on HBO's *Def Poetry Jam* and *Brave New Voices*.

Jack Collom was born in Chicago and as a young man joined the US Air Force. He was posted in Libya and Germany before returning to the United States. He then earned a BA in forestry and English and an MA in English literature from the University of Colorado. Collom started publishing his poetry in the 1960s. His more recent publications are *Entering the City* (Backwaters Press), *Dog Sonnets* (Jensen / Daniels), the 500-plus-page collection *Red Car Goes By* (Tuumba Press), and *Situations, Sings* with Lyn Hejinian (Adventures in Poetry).

CAConrad is the author of *A Beautiful Marsupial Afternoon: New (Soma)tics* (Wave Books), *The Book of Frank* (Wave Books),

Advanced Elvis Course (Soft Skull), *Deviant Propulsion* (Soft Skull), and a collaboration with poet Frank Sherlock titled *The City Real & Imagined* (Factory School). A 2011 Pew Fellow and a 2012 Ucross Fellow, he edits the online video poetry journals *JUPITER 88* and *Paranormal Poetics*.

Emilie Coulson is the director of education at 826 Valencia, a nonprofit organization dedicated to supporting students' creative and expository writing skills. She has taught poetry workshops to writers of all ages and published poetry in various forums and publications. She is the coauthor of a new musical, *Victory Farm*, originally produced by the American Folklore Theatre in her hometown of Fish Creek, Wisconsin.

Kevin Coval is artistic director of Young Chicago Authors and cofounder of its teen poetry festival, Louder Than A Bomb. He is the author of *Slingshots (A Hip-Hop Poetica)*, which was a finalist for the American Library Association Book of the Year, and *Everyday People* (both from EM Press). He has performed in seven countries on four continents and was featured on four seasons of Russell Simmons's HBO *Def Poetry Jam*. Coval writes for the *Huffington Post* and can be heard regularly on National Public Radio in Chicago. Haymarket Books published his most recent collection, *L-vis Lives*.

Christina Davis is the author of *An Ethic* (Nightboat Books) and *Forth a Raven* (Alice James Books). Her poems have appeared in the *American Poetry Review*, *jubilat*, *Pleiades*, the *Paris Review*, and other publications. A graduate of the University of Pennsylvania and Oxford University, she is a recipient of a Witter Bynner Award from the Library of Congress (selected by Kay Ryan) and currently serves as curator of the Woodberry Poetry Room, Harvard University.

Jordan Davis writes about poetry for the *Constant Critic*, and his essays and reviews have also appeared in *Slate*, *Nation*, and the *Times Literary Supplement*.

Michael Dickman was born and raised in Portland, Oregon. He is the author of *The End of the West* and *Flies*, and the coauthor, with his brother Matthew Dickman, of *50 American Plays*, all published by Copper Canyon Press. He lives and works in Princeton, New Jersey.

Alex Dimitrov's first book of poems, *Begging for It*, is just out from Four Way Books. Dimitrov is the recipient of the Stanley Kunitz Prize for younger poets from the *American Poetry Review* and the founder of Wilde Boys, a queer poetry salon in New York City. His poems have appeared or are forthcoming from the *Kenyon Review*, *Yale Review*, *Slate*, *Tin House*, and the *Boston Review*.

Dave Eggers is the founder and editor of McSweeney's, an independent publishing house based in San Francisco, and a cofounder of 826 National, a network of nonprofit writing and tutoring centers for youth located in eight cities around the United States. He is the author of, among other books, *What Is the What*, *The Wild Things*, and *A Hologram for the King*, all published by McSweeney's. He lives in Northern California.

Andrew Ek is a writer, a teacher, and an architectural engineering student. He is currently curriculum director and board president of the Nebraska Writers Collective, which sends writers into schools to teach workshops and literary performance. He also hosts the Encyclopedia Show: Omaha, a monthly literary variety show.

Martin Jude Farawell directs the Dodge Poetry Program, which includes the biennial Dodge Poetry Festival, Dodge Poets in the Schools, and the Dodge Poetry Archive, currently being developed to make audio and video recordings from past Dodge Festivals available on the web.

He taught creative writing, literature, and composition at the secondary and undergraduate levels for ten years. A graduate of the New York University Creative Writing Program, Farawell is the author of a chapbook, *Genesis: A Sequence of Poems*. His work has appeared in the *Cortland Review*, *Poetry East*, *Southern Review*, and other journals and anthologies. His plays have been performed off-off-Broadway and by regional, college, community, and international theaters, most recently the Neo Ensemble Theatre in Los Angeles.

Katie Ford is the author of *Deposition* and *Colosseum* (both by Graywolf Press). She is the recipient of a Lannan Literary Fellowship in Poetry and a Larry Levis Reading Award. *Publishers Weekly* named *Colosseum* a Best Book of 2008, and the *Virginia Quarterly Review* included it on the Top Ten Books of Poetry of 2008 list. Ford teaches at Franklin & Marshall College and lives in Philadelphia with her husband and daughter.

Terri Glass served as program director for California Poets in the Schools from 2008 to 2011 and recently returned to school to study nonfiction in the Stonecoast MFA Program in Creative Writing. She has been teaching poetry writing to both children and adults in the Bay Area for more than twenty years via workshops in schools, colleges, hospitals, and wildlife and senior centers. She is the author of two books of poetry, *Unveiling the Mystical Light* (Fisher-Dizick Publishing) and *The Song of Yes*, and a poetry guide for classroom teachers, *Language of the Awakened Heart*.

Susan Grigsby is a freelance writer and teaching artist for institutions that include the St. Louis Poetry Center, Interchange, COCA, and the Center for the Art of Translation's Poetry Inside Out program. She has a master of arts in teaching, specializing in the integration of creative writing across the curriculum. Her poetry has been published in various journals, including *Quarterly West*, *Sycamore Review*, and *Sou'wester*. Her books for children include *In the Garden with Dr. Carver* and *First Peas to the Table*.

Matthea Harvey is the author of *Sad Little Breathing Machine* (Graywolf Press) and *Pity the Bathtub Its Forced Embrace of the Human Form* (Alice James Books). Her third book of poems, *Modern Life* (Graywolf Press) was a finalist for the National Book Critics Circle Award and a *New York Times* Notable Book. Her first children's book, *The Little General and the Giant Snowflake*, illustrated by Elizabeth Zechel, was published by Tin House Books in 2009. An illustrated erasure, titled *Of Lamb*, with images by Amy Jean Porter, was published by McSweeney's a year later. Harvey is a contributing editor to *jubilat*, *Meatpaper* and *BOMB*. She teaches poetry at Sarah Lawrence and lives in Brooklyn.

Mimi Herman established Poetry Out Loud in North Carolina in 2005 and was the North Carolina Poetry Out Loud coordinator from 2005 to 2011. She is the United Arts Council Arts Integration Institute director, a *Teaching Artist Journal* associate editor, and a teacher. She holds an MFA in creative writing from Warren Wilson College and has worked as an educational consultant since 1990, engaging more than twenty-five thousand students, teachers, and artists.

Bob Holman has taught at the New School, Columbia University, New York University, and Naropa, as well as the Stony Brook Writing Program at the Turkana Basin Institute (Kenya). He has taught in Banff, Gambia, Costa Rica, Medellin, Vilnius, London, Durban, Kathmandu, Dubai, Budapest, Addis Ababa, and elsewhere. After working at the St. Mark's Poetry Project and starting the slam at the Nuyorican Poets Cafe, he founded the Bowery Poetry Club, where he is currently artistic director. He is devoted to using poetry as an activist tool to create awareness about the endangered language crisis and is a codirector of the Endangered Language Alliance. He created a TV series on this subject with Ram Devineni and Beatriz Seigner that aired on Link TV. Holman is the host of *Word Up! Languages in Danger!*, produced by David Grubin for PBS.

Ilya Kaminsky is the director of the Harriet Monroe Poetry Institute at the Poetry Foundation. He is the author of *Dancing in Odessa* (Tupelo Press) and coeditor of *The Ecco Anthology of International Poetry*.

James Kass is a writer, an educator, and a producer. He is the founder and executive director of Youth Speaks and is widely credited with helping launch the youth spoken-word movement, working with tens of thousands of young people from across the country and helping to launch more than fifty programs nationwide to help kids find, develop, and publicly present their voices. Kass has received several awards for his writing, his work in the nonprofit sector, and his work as an educator. He recently curated the poetry for the first White House Poetry Jam, performing in front of the First Family, and was invited to be one of the first thirty-five people to meet the Obama administration's arts action team. He served on the steering committee for the Oakland International Hip Hop Museum (On Up), chaired the Community Engagement Advisory Board for the Yerba Buena Center for the Arts, and was an advisory board member for slambush.net, 826 Valencia, and the New York City Hip-Hop Theater Festival.

Jeff Kass teaches creative writing and English literature at Pioneer High School in Ann Arbor, Michigan, and at Eastern Michigan University. In addition, he is the literary arts director at the Ann Arbor Teen Center, the Neutral Zone. He is the author of the poetry chapbook *Invisible Staircase*, the essay chapbook *From the Front of the Room*, and the one-man performance poetry show *Wrestle the Great Fear*. He is also the author of the teaching guidebook *Underneath: The Archaeological Approach to Teaching Creative Writing* and the short-story collection *Knuckleheads* (Dzanc Books).

Kenneth Koch (1925–2002) was an American poet, playwright, and professor at Columbia University for almost forty years. He credits his work through the Teachers & Writers Collaborative for his popular books on teaching poetry to children, *Wishes, Lies, and Dreams: Teaching Children to Write Poetry,* 1970, and *Rose, Where Did You Get That Red,* 1973. He is the author of more than thirty volumes of poetry and plays.

Yusef Komunyakaa teaches at New York University. His thirteen books of poetry include *Taboo* (Farrar, Straus and Giroux), *Dien Cai Dau* (Wesleyan University Press), *Neon Vernacular* (Wesleyan University Press, for which he received the Pulitzer Prize), *Warhorses* (Farrar, Straus and Giroux), and most recently *The Chameleon Couch* (Farrar, Straus and Giroux). His plays, performance art, and libretti have been performed internationally and include *Saturnalia*, *Testimony*, and *Gilgamesh*.

Deborah Landau is the author of *The Last Usable Hour* (Copper Canyon Press), a Lannan Literary Selection, and *Orchidelirium* (Anhinga Press), which won the Robert Dana-Anhinga Prize for Poetry. She is a clinical professor in and director of the New York University Creative Writing Program.

Quraysh Ali Lansana is the author of five books of poetry, including *They Shall Run: Harriet Tubman Poems* (Third World) and a children's book titled *The Big World* (Addison-Wesley). He has edited eight anthologies, including *Dream of a Word: The Tia Chucha Press Poetry Anthology* (Tia Chucha). Lansana is an associate professor of English and creative writing at Chicago State University, where he served as director of the Gwendolyn Brooks Center for Black Literature and Creative Writing from 2002 to 2011. A former faculty member in the Drama Division of the Juilliard School, he earned an MFA in creative writing at New York University, where he was a departmental fellow. *Our Difficult Sunlight: A Guide to Poetry, Literacy & Social Justice in Classroom & Community* (with Georgia A. Popoff) was published in 2011 by Teachers & Writers Collaborative and was a 2012 NAACP Image Award nominee. His third book of poetry, *mystic turf,* was released in November 2012 by Willow Books.

Dorothea Lasky is the author of three poetry

collections, *AWE*, *Black Life*, and *Thunderbird*, all from Wave Books. She is also the author of nine chapbooks, including *Matter: A Picturebook* (Argos Books), *The Blue Teratorn* (YesYes Books), and *Poetry Is Not a Project* (Ugly Duckling Presse). Her poems have appeared in the *Paris Review*, *New Yorker*, *Boston Review*, and the *American Poetry Review*, among other periodicals. Lasky is a graduate of the University of Massachusetts Amherst MFA program for Poets and Writers, holds a doctorate in creativity and education from the University of Pennsylvania, and attended Harvard and Washington University. Born in St. Louis in 1978, she currently lives in New York City.

Harriet Levin is the author of *The Christmas Show* (Beacon Press) and *Girl in Cap and Gown* (Mammoth Books). She won the Barnard Women Poets Prize, the Poetry Society of America's Alice Fay di Castagnola Award, and a PEW Fellowship in the Arts Discipline Award. Her poetry and fiction have appeared in the *Kenyon Review*, the *Iowa Review*, *Harvard Review*, *Ploughshares*, and *Prairie Schooner*. A former New York State poet-in-the-schools, she teaches at Drexel University and codirects the program in writing and publishing.

Rebecca Lindenberg is the author of *Love, an Index* (McSweeney's). Her poems, essays, and criticism have appeared in the *Believer*, *Poetry*, *Iowa Review*, *Smartish Pace*, *32 Poems*, *Diagram*, *Conjunctions*, *Mid-American Review*, *Colorado Review*, *Denver Quarterly*, and elsewhere. She is the grateful recipient of a 2012 MacDowell Arts Colony residency, a 2011 NEA grant, and a 2009–2010 Provincetown Fine Arts Work Center fellowship. She lives and writes in northern Utah.

Phillip Lopate's most recent book of poetry, *At the End of the Day* (Marsh Hawk Press, 2010) brings together the majority of his poems, written over the course of his lifetime. Among his many awards are grants from the Guggenheim Foundation, the New York Public Library, the New York Foundation for the Arts, and the National Endowment for the Arts. For many years, Lopate worked as a writer-in-the-schools, and his memoir *Being With Children* (Poseidon, 1989) was a product of his association with the Teachers & Writers Collaborative.

Dominic Luxford is the editor of *The McSweeney's Book of Poets Picking Poets*, the founding poetry editor of the *Believer*, and a founding editor of the McSweeney's Poetry Series. His writing has appeared in the *Emily Dickinson Journal*, *Economist*, the *Believer*, and *McSweeney's*. For several years, Luxford was an elementary school tutor for the H.E.A.R.T. (Help Encourage a Reader Today) Program in Portland, Oregon. He now lives in San Francisco.

Matt Mason has won two Nebraska Book Awards and has organized and run poetry programming with the US Department of State in Kathmandu, Nepal, and Minsk, Belarus. He has been on five teams at the National Poetry Slam, edits the Poetry Menu, a listing of every Nebraska poetry event, and founded Morpo Press in 1997. The Backwaters Press released his first full-length collection, *Things We Don't Know We Don't Know*, in 2006. He also has nine poetry chapbooks published and is executive director of the nonprofit Nebraska Writers Collective. He runs the monthly Omaha Healing Arts Poetry Slam as well as several reading series.

Anthony McCann is the author of the poetry collections *I Heart Your Fate*, *Moongarden* (both from Wave Books), and *Father of Noise* (Fence Books). In addition to teaching courses for the School of Critical Studies at the California Institute of the Arts, he works with the Cal Arts Community Arts Partnership (CAP). For CAP, he designs and teaches an intensive writing course in a free summer arts program for high school students.

Michael McGriff was born and raised in Coos Bay, Oregon. His books include *Dismantling the Hills* (University of Pittsburgh Press), *To Build My Shadow a Fire: The Poetry and Translations of David Wevill* (Truman State University Press), and *Home Burial* (Copper Canyon Press). He cotranslated Tomas Transtromer's *The Sorrow Gondola*, and his poetry, translations, and essays have appeared in numerous publications, including the *American Poetry Review*, *Bookforum*, *Slate*, *Narrative*, the *Believer*, and the *Wall Street Journal*. He has received a Lannan Literary Fellowship, a Stegner Fellowship, and a National Endowment for the Arts Literary Fellowship. He is the founding editor of Tavern Books, a publishing house devoted to poetry in translation and the revival of out-of-print books.

Megan McNamer, executive director of the Missoula Writing Collaborative, studied music at the University of Montana and ethnomusicology at the University of Washington. In addition to her literary pursuits, she teaches occasional courses in world music and plays Balinese gamelan. Her essays have appeared in *Sports Illustrated*, *Salon*, and the *Sun*, among other publications. She has been a finalist in fiction writing contests sponsored by Glimmer Train Press and New Millennium Writings.

Pamela Michael is a writer, activist, and radio producer. She has spent decades working to integrate environmental and arts education into the lives of children and their communities. Cofounder, with Robert Hass, of the much-honored River of Words program, her Watershed Explorer Curriculum has been used to train thousands of teachers, youth leaders, and other educators to connect kids to their watersheds and their imaginations, inspiring them to create art and poetry. She has served as the organization's executive director since its founding in 1995 and was recently named director of the Center for Environmental Literacy at Saint Mary's College of California. Michael has taught writing and poetry to both children and adults throughout the United States and abroad.

Valzhyna Mort was born in Minsk, Belarus, and moved to the United States in 2005. She is the author of *Factory of Tears* and *Collected Body* (both published by Copper Canyon Press). In Slovenia she received the Crystal Vilenica poetry award, and in Germany the Hubert Burda Prize for young Eastern European poets. She won a Lannan Literary Fellowship in 2009 and the

Bess Hokin Prize from the Poetry Foundation in 2010.

Eileen Myles, born in Cambridge, Massachusetts, and educated in Catholic schools, graduated from the University of Massachusetts, Boston in 1971 and moved to New York City in 1974 to be a poet. *Snowflake/different streets*, a double volume of poems, came out in 2012 from Wave Books. John Ashbery described Myles's *Inferno (A Poet's Novel)* (OR Books), which details a female writer's coming of age, as "zingingly funny and melancholy." Alison Bechdel called *Inferno* "this shimmering document." Myles's more than twenty books include *Sorry, Tree* (Wave Books), *Cool for You* (Soft Skull), *Skies* (Black Sparrow), *Not Me* (Semiotexte), and *Chelsea Girls* (Black Sparrow). *The Importance of Being Iceland: Travel Essays in Art* (Semiotexte) received a Creative Capital/Warhol Foundation Arts Writers Grant in 2007. In 2010, Myles received the Shelley Memorial Award from the Poetry Society of America for her poetry. She has taught at Columbia University, and she writes about books, art, and culture for a wide variety of publications, including *Artforum*, *Bookforum*, and *Parkett*.

Jesse Nathan is the author of a chapbook of poems, *Dinner*. His writing has appeared in the *Oxford American*, the *Nation*, *jubilat*, *American Poetry Review*, and elsewhere. He is a founding editor of the McSweeney's Poetry Series, and he served as managing editor of the Best American Nonrequired Reading from 2009 to 2011. Nathan was born in Berkeley, grew up on a farm in Kansas, and presently lives in Menlo Park, California, where he is working on a PhD in English literature at Stanford.

Travis Nichols is the author of two poetry collections, *Iowa* (Letter Machine Editions) and *See Me Improving* (Copper Canyon Press), as well as two novels, *Off We Go Into the Wild Blue Yonder* and the forthcoming *The More You Ignore Me* (both from Coffee House Press). He is a media officer at Greenpeace USA and lives in Washington, DC.

Patrick Oliver is founder and program manager of Say It Loud! and creator and host of *Literary Nation Talk Radio*, a live weekly broadcast. He is the publisher and editor of *Essence* magazine's bestselling anthology *Turn the Page and You Don't Stop: Sharing Successful Chapters in Our Lives with Youth*. As a literary consultant, Oliver has organized and facilitated programs, panels, and workshops for individuals, educational institutions, businesses, and organizations throughout the United States. He currently lives in Los Angeles.

Adam O'Riordan was born in Manchester, England, in 1982. He was educated at Oxford University and the University of London. In 2008 he became the youngest poet-in-residence at the Wordsworth Trust, the "Centre for British Romanticism." His collection *In the Flesh* (Chatto & Windus) won a Somerset Maugham Award in 2011.

Liam O'Rourke has been an English teacher at Pierrepont School in Westport, Connecticut, since 2003.

Meghan O'Rourke is the author of *The Long Goodbye* (Riverhead Books), a memoir about the loss of her mother, and of the poetry collections *Once* and *Halflife* (both from W.W. Norton). She has taught at New York University, Princeton, and the New School.

Ron Padgett is the author of more than fourteen books, including his most recent collection of poems *How Long* (Coffee House Press). His awards include a Fulbright Fellowship, a National Endowment for the Arts Translation Fellowship, a Guggenheim Fellowship, and a Shelley Memorial Award. From 1978–1980 he served as director of the St. Mark's Poetry Project and then served as publications director of Teachers & Writers Collaborative for twenty years. In 2008 he was elected a Chancellor of the Academy of American Poets.

Georgia A. Popoff is a community poet, an educator, and managing editor of the *Comstock Review*. She provides professional development training for schools and community-based organizations and presents on these topics at conferences both nationally and abroad. Her first collection of poems is *Coaxing Nectar from Longing* (Hale Mary); her second, *The Doom Weaver*, was released by Main Street Rag. Teachers & Writers Collaborative published *Our Difficult Sunlight: A Guide to Poetry, Literacy, & Social Justice in Classroom & Community*, coauthored with Quraysh Ali Lansana. In the mid-1990s, Popoff competed in the National Poetry Slam. She has also served as central New York State program director for Partners for Arts Education and as a board member of the Association of Teaching Artists. She currently teaches at the Downtown Writer's Center in Syracuse, New York.

Robin Reagler is the executive director of Writers in the Schools (WITS) in Houston, Texas. She also leads the WITS Alliance, an international group of more than twenty similar literary education programs in the United States, Canada, and the United Kingdom. Her poems and essays have been published in a variety of books and journals. Her chapbook, *Dear Red Airplane*, was published by Seven Kitchens in 2011.

Theodore Roethke (1908–1963) took ten years to write his first book, *Open House* (Knopf), which was critically acclaimed upon its publication. He won the Pulitzer Prize for poetry in 1954 for *The Waking* (Doubleday), and he won the National Book Award for poetry twice, in 1959 for *Words for the Wind* (Indiana University Press) and posthumously in 1965 for *The Far Field* (Doubleday).

Bertha Rogers's most recent poetry collection, *Heart Turned Back*, was published by Salmon, in Ireland, in 2010. Her translation of the Anglo-Saxon riddle poems, *Uncommon Creatures, Singing Things*, is forthcoming from Birch Brook Press. With her husband, Ernest M. Fishman, she founded and directs Bright Hill Press and Literary Center in Treadwell, New York.

Laura Solomon was born in 1976 in Birmingham, Alabama. Her books include *Bivouac* (Slope Editions), *Blue and Red Things*

(Ugly Duckling Presse), and *The Hermit* (Ugly Duckling Presse). Other publications include a chapbook, *Letters by Which Sisters Will Know Brothers* (Katalanché Press) and *Haiku des Pierres/Haiku of Stones* by Jacques Poullaoueq, a translation from the French with Sika Fakambi (Editions Apogée). Her poetry has been included in the anthology *Poets on Painters* (Wichita State Press), has appeared in magazines across North America and Europe, and has been translated into ten languages.

William Stafford (1914–1993) was appointed the twentieth poet laureate in 1970. His first major collection of poetry, *Traveling Through the Dark* (Harper & Row), was published when he was forty-eight years old. It won the 1963 National Book Award for poetry.

Amy Swauger has been director of the Teachers & Writers Collaborative, a literary arts education organization in New York City, since 2005. Swauger was previously executive director of the National Academy of Education and of Washington Independent Writers. Prior to that, she held a number of positions with the American Association of University Women (AAUW), including director of the association and of the AAUW Legal Advocacy Fund. She has served on the boards of several nonprofit organizations, including the DC Rape Crisis Center and CFRE International, and she is an adviser to the Schimel Lode, a family foundation in Washington, DC. Swauger earned a degree in journalism and political science from American University.

Jim Trelease is an educator and author who promotes reading aloud to children as a way to instill in them a love of literature. He is the author of *The Read-Aloud Handbook*, which has sold over a million copies all over the world.

Vickie Vértiz was born to and raised by Mexican parents in southeast Los Angeles. Arising from her work as a student, an activist, and a cultural worker in Los Angeles and the San Francisco Bay Area, her writing explores the intersections of gender, identity, and Latino subcultures. Her writing has been widely anthologized and can be found in *In Your Ear* and *La Lunada: An Anthology of Spoken-Word Poetry Celebrating Sixty Full Moons and Community Ritual at Galería de la Raza*. She is currently the cocurator for the reading series "Cruzando Fronteras: Contemporary Poetry in Spanish in San Francisco." Vértiz has a master's degree in public affairs from the University of Texas, Austin.

Karen Volkman teaches in the MFA writing program at the University of Montana in Missoula. Her latest book of poetry is *Nomina* (BOA Editions). Her first book, *Crash's Law* (W.W. Norton), was a National Poetry Series selection. Her second book, *Spar* (University of Iowa Press), won the James Laughlin Award and the Iowa Poetry Prize. She is the recipient of awards and fellowships from the National Endowment for the Arts, the Poetry Society of America, the MacDowell Colony, Yaddo, and the Akademie Schloss Solitude.

Dara Wier teaches poetry workshops and form and theory seminars in the MFA Program for Poets and Writers at the University of Massachusetts Amherst. Her newest work, *You Good Thing* (Wave Books), is a book of grief-fueled sonnets cast as spells to bring back the dead, a fool's quintessential inevitable errand. Her most recent books, both from Wave Books, are *Selected Poems* and *Reverse Rapture*, a book-length quasi-narrative recording of the adventures in words of a band of comrades, brothers and sisters, out in a lost world, protecting one another. Along with Emily Pettit and Guy Pettit, Wier publishes books, chapbooks, broadsides, and comics via Factory Hollow Press, the publishing aspect of Flying Object, a nonprofit arts collective in Hadley, Massachusetts, founded and directed by Guy Pettit.

Matthew Zapruder's most recent poetry book is *Come on All You Ghosts* (Copper Canyon Press). He lives in San Francisco.

The Harriet Monroe Poetry Institute is an independent forum created by the Poetry Foundation to provide a space in which fresh thinking about poetry, in both its intellectual and its practical needs, can flourish free of any allegiance other than to the best ideas. The Institute convenes leading poets, scholars, publishers, educators, and other thinkers from inside and outside the poetry world to address issues of importance to the art form of poetry and to identify and champion solutions for the benefit of the art.

The Poetry Foundation, publisher of *Poetry* magazine, is an independent literary organization committed to a vigorous presence for poetry in our culture. It exists to discover and celebrate the best poetry and to place it before the largest possible audience. The Poetry Foundation seeks to be a leader in shaping a receptive climate for poetry by developing new audiences, creating new avenues for delivery, and encouraging new kinds of poetry through innovative partnerships, prizes, and programs.

The Poets in the World Series is an HMPI project that supports the research and publication of poetry and poetics from around the world and highlights the importance of creating a space for poetry in local communities in the United States.

Current Publications
Katharine Coles, HMPI inaugural director

Poetry and New Media: A Users' Guide, report of the Poetry and New Media Working Group, Harriet Monroe Poetry Institute, 2009

Blueprints: Bringing Poetry into Communities, edited by Katharine Coles (University of Utah Press, 2011)

Code of Best Practices in Fair Use for Poetry, created with American University's Center for Social Media and Washington College of Law, 2011

Forthcoming Projects
Ilya Kaminsky, 2011–2013, HMPI director

Strangest of Theatres: Poets Writing Across Borders, edited by Jared Hawkley, Susan Rich, and Brian Turner (McSweeney's, 2013)

15 Essential Poems from Latin America, edited by Raúl Zurita and Forrest Gander (Copper Canyon Press, 2013)

On the Road, edited by Eliot Weinberger (Open Letter Books, 2013)

New Cathay: Contemporary Chinese Poetry, edited by Ming Di (Tupelo Press, 2013)

An Anthology of European Poetry, edited by Valzhyna Mort (Red Hen Press, 2013)

An Anthology of Anglophone Poetry, edited by Catherine Barnett (Tupelo Press, 2013)

Fifteen Iraqi Poets, edited by Dunya Mikhail (New Directions Publishing, 2013)

An Anthology of Swedish Poetry, coedited/translated by Malena Mörling and Jonas Ellerström (Milkweed Editions, 2013)

Credits

Elizabeth Bradfield, "Attending the Living Word/World: Using Haibun to Discover Poetry." This selection includes Bashō, "Seeing Nambu Road" from *Backroads to Far Towns: Bashō's Travel Journal*, translated by Cid Corman and Susumu Kamaike. Copyright © 2004. Reprinted with the permission of The Permissions Company, Inc., on behalf of White Pine Press, www.whitepine.org. Tish Davis, "Finding Good Soil" from *Modern Haibun and Tanka Prose* (Winter 2009). Reprinted with the permission of the author. Sean Hill, "Milledgeville Haibun" from *Blood Ties & Brown Liquor*. Copyright © 2008 by Sean Hill. Reprinted with the permission of The University of Georgia Press.

Jack Collom, "The Process of Opening Gifts: How Permission Catalyzes Writing." This selection includes poems from *Moving Windows*, Copyright © 1985 by Teachers & Writers Collaborative. Reprinted with the permission of Teachers & Writers Collaborative. Poems from *Poetry Everywhere, Second Edition*, Copyright © 2005 by Teachers and Writers Collaborative. Reprinted with the permission of Teachers and Writers Collaborative. Billy Collins, "Introduction to Poetry" from *The Apple That Astonished Paris*. Copyright © 1996 by Billy Collins. Reprinted with the permission of The Permissions Company, Inc., on behalf of the University of Arkansas Press, www.uapress.com.

Jordan Davis, "Fears, Truths, and Waking Life: On the Teaching of Kenneth Koch." This selection includes excerpts from Kenneth Koch, "Some General Instructions" from *On the Great Atlantic Rainway: Selected Poems 1959-1988*. Copyright © 1994 by Kenneth Koch. Used by permission of Alfred A. Knopf, a division of Random House, Inc. For on-line information about other Random House, Inc. books and authors, see the Internet web site at http://www.randomhouse.com.

Alex Dimitrov, "Poems Are for Everybody." This selection contains Frank O'Hara, "Today" from *The Collected Poems of Frank O'Hara*. Copyright © 1971 by Maureen Granville-Smith. Used by permission of Alfred A. Knopf, a division of Random House, Inc. For on-line information about other Random House, Inc. books and authors, see the Internet web site at http://www.randomhouse.com.

Matthea Harvey, "Poetry Is an Egg with a Horse Inside." This selection includes Ogden Nash, "The Shrimp." Copyright © 1962 by Ogden Nash. Reprinted by permission of Curtis Brown, Ltd. and Carlton Publishing Group. May Swenson, "Southbound on the Freeway" from *Poems to Solve*. Copyright © 1966 by May Swenson. Reprinted with the permission of the Literary Estate of May Swenson. Issa, "Pissing in the snow" from *The Essential Haiku: Versions of Basho, Buson, and Issa*, translated by Robert Hass. Copyright © 1994 by Robert Hass. Reprinted by permission of HarperCollins Publishers. Basho, "Year after year" from *The Essential Haiku: Versions of Basho, Buson, and Issa*, translated by Robert Hass. Copyright © 1994 by Robert Hass. Reprinted by permission of HarperCollins Publishers. Richard Wright, "With indignation" from *Haiku: This Other World*. Copyright © 1998 by Richard Wright. Reprinted with the permission of Skyhorse Publishing, Inc, and John Hawkins & Associates, Inc.

Kenneth Koch, excerpts from *Wishes, Lies, and Dreams: Teaching Children to Write Poetry*. Copyright © 1999 by Kenneth Koch. Reprinted by permission of International Creative Management Inc. for the Estate of Kenneth Koch.

Rebecca Lindenberg, "A Poetry of Perception: Four Studies for Young People." This selection